Praise for *Learning TypeScript*

If you ever screamed back at red squiggly lines in your code, then go read *Learning TypeScript*. Goldberg masterfully puts everything in context while staying practical, showing us that TypeScript is never a restriction, but a valuable asset.

—*Stefan Baumgartner, senior product architect, Dynatrace;*
founder, oida.dev

Josh puts TypeScript's most important concepts front and center, and explains them with clear examples and a touch of humor. A must-read for the JavaScript author who wants to write TypeScript like a pro.

—*Andrew Branch, software engineer on TypeScript, Microsoft*

Learning TypeScript is an excellent resource for programmers who have coded at least a little before, but may have shied away from typed languages. It goes a level deeper than the TypeScript handbook to give you confidence in using TypeScript in your own projects.

—*Boris Cherny, software engineer, Meta;*
author, Programming TypeScript

We don't know what types code is but we're very proud of Josh and are sure it will be a lovely book.

—*Frances and Mark Goldberg*

Josh is that rare individual who is passionate about both acquiring a deep command of the fundamentals and explaining concepts to beginners. I think this book will quickly become a canonical resource for TypeScript novices and experts alike.

—*Beyang Liu, CTO and cofounder, Sourcegraph*

Reading *Learning TypeScript* is like spending time with a warm and smart friend who delights in telling you fascinating things. You'll walk away entertained and educated about TypeScript whether you knew a lot or a little beforehand.

—*John Reilly, group principal engineer, Investec;*
maintainer, ts-loader; Definitely Typed historian

Learning TypeScript is a comprehensive yet approachable guide to the TypeScript language and ecosystem. It covers the broad feature set of TypeScript while providing suggestions and explaining trade-offs based on broad experience.

—*Daniel Rosenwasser, program manager, TypeScript, Microsoft;*
TC39 representative

This is my favorite resource for learning TypeScript. From introductory to advanced topics, it's all clear, concise, and comprehensive. I found Josh to be an excellent—and fun—writer.

—*Loren Sands-Ramshaw, author,* The GraphQL Guide;
TypeScript SDK engineer, Temporal

If you are looking to be an effective TypeScript developer, *Learning TypeScript* has you covered all the way from beginning to advanced concepts.

—*Basarat Ali Syed, principal engineer, SEEK;*
author, Beginning NodeJS *and* TypeScript Deep Dive;
Youtuber (Basarat Codes); Microsoft MVP

This book is a great way to learn the language and a perfect complement to the TypeScript Handbook.

—*Orta Therox, ex-TypeScript compiler engineer, Puzmo*

Josh is one of the clearest and most dedicated TypeScript communicators in the world, and his knowledge is finally in book form! Beginners and experienced devs alike will love the careful curation and sequencing of topics. The tips, notes, and warnings in the classic O'Reilly style are worth their weight in gold.

—*Shawn "swyx" Wang, head of DX, Airbyte*

This book will truly help you learn TypeScript. The theory chapters together with the practice projects strike a good learning balance and cover just about every aspect of the language. Reviewing this book even taught this old dog some new tricks. I finally understand the subtleties of Declaration Files. Highly recommended.

—*Lenz Weber-Tronic, full stack developer, Mayflower Germany; maintainer, Redux*

Learning TypeScript is an accessible, engaging book that distills Josh's years of experience developing a TypeScript curriculum to teach you everything you need to know in just the right order. Whatever your programming background, you're in good hands with Josh and *Learning TypeScript*.

—*Dan Vanderkam, senior staff software engineer, Google; author,* Effective TypeScript

Learning TypeScript is the book I wish I had when I first got into TypeScript. Josh's passion for teaching new users oozes from every page. It's thoughtfully organized into easily digestible chunks, and it covers everything you need to become a TypeScript expert.

—*Brad Zacher, software engineer, Meta; core maintainer, typescript-eslint*

Learning TypeScript
Enhance Your Web Development Skills Using Type-Safe JavaScript

Josh Goldberg

Beijing · Boston · Farnham · Sebastopol · Tokyo

Learning TypeScript

by Josh Goldberg

Published by O'Reilly Media, Inc., 1005 Gravenstein Highway North, Sebastopol, CA 95472.

O'Reilly books may be purchased for educational, business, or sales promotional use. Online editions are also available for most titles (*http://oreilly.com*). For more information, contact our corporate/institutional sales department: 800-998-9938 or *corporate@oreilly.com*.

Acquisitions Editor: Amanda Quinn	**Indexer:** nSight, Inc.
Development Editor: Rita Fernando	**Interior Designer:** David Futato
Production Editor: Clare Jensen	**Cover Designer:** Karen Montgomery
Copyeditor: Piper Editorial Consulting LLC	**Illustrator:** Kate Dullea
Proofreader: nSight, Inc.	

June 2022: First Edition

Revision History for the First Edition

2022-06-03:	First Release
2022-07-01:	Second Release
2022-08-26:	Third Release
2023-05-05:	Fourth Release

See *http://oreilly.com/catalog/errata.csp?isbn=9781098110338* for release details.

978-1-098-11033-8

[LSI]

This book is dedicated to my incredible partner, Mariah, who introduced me to the joy of adopting backyard cats and has regretted it ever since. Toot.

Table of Contents

Part IV.   Extra Credit

Preface

My journey to TypeScript was not a direct or quick one. I started off in school primarily writing Java, then C++, and like many new developers raised on statically typed languages, I looked down on JavaScript as "just" the sloppy little scripting language people throw onto websites.

My first substantial project in the language was a silly remake of the original *Super Mario Bros.* video game in pure HTML5/CSS/JavaScript and, typical of many first projects, was an absolute mess. In the beginning of the project I instinctively disliked JavaScript's weird flexibility and lack of guardrails. It was only toward the end that I really began to respect JavaScript's features and quirks: its flexibility as a language, its ability to mix and match small functions, and its ability to *just work* in user browsers within seconds of page load.

By the time I finished that first project, I had fallen in love with JavaScript.

Static analysis (tools that analyze your code without running it) such as TypeScript also gave me a queasy gut feeling at first. *JavaScript is so breezy and fluid*, I thought, *why bog ourselves down with rigid structures and types?* Were we reverting back to the worlds of Java and C++ that I had left behind?

Coming back to my old projects, it took me all of 10 minutes of struggling to read through my old, convoluted JavaScript code to understand how messy things could get without static analysis. The act of cleaning that code up showed me all the places I would have benefited from some structure. From that point on, I was hooked onto adding as much static analysis to my projects as I could.

It's been nearly a decade since I first tinkered with TypeScript, and I enjoy it as much as ever. The language is still evolving with new features and is more useful than ever in providing *safety* and *structure* to JavaScript.

I hope that by reading *Learning TypeScript* you can learn to appreciate TypeScript the way I do: not just as a means to find bugs and typos—and certainly not a substantial change to JavaScript code patterns—but as JavaScript *with types*: a beautiful system for declaring the way our JavaScript should work, and helping us stick to it.

Who Should Read This Book

If you have an understanding of writing JavaScript code, can run basic commands in a terminal, and are interested in learning about TypeScript, this book is for you.

Maybe you've heard TypeScript can help you write a lot of JavaScript with fewer bugs *(true!)* or document your code well for other people to read *(also true!)*. Maybe you've seen TypeScript show up in a lot of job postings, or in a new role you're starting.

Whatever your reason, as long as you come in knowing the fundamentals of JavaScript—variables, functions, closures/scope, and classes—this book will take you from no TypeScript knowledge to mastering the fundamentals and most important features of the language. By the end of this book, you will understand:

- The history and context for why TypeScript is useful on top of "vanilla" JavaScript
- How a type system models code
- How a type checker analyzes code
- How to use development-only type annotations to inform the type system
- How TypeScript works with IDEs (Integrated Development Environments) to provide code exploration and refactoring tools

And you will be able to:

- Articulate the benefits of TypeScript and general characteristics of its type system.
- Add type annotations where useful in your code.
- Represent moderately complex types using TypeScript's built-in inferences and new syntax.
- Use TypeScript to assist local development in refactoring code.

Why I Wrote This Book

TypeScript is a wildly popular language in both industry and open source:

- GitHub's 2021 and 2020 State of the Octoverses have it at the platform's fourth top language, up from seventh in 2019 and 2018 and tenth in 2017.
- StackOverflow's 2021 Developer Survey has it at the world's third most loved language (72.73% of users).

- The 2020 State of JS Survey shows TypeScript has consistently high satisfaction and usage amounts as both a build tool and variant of JavaScript.

For frontend developers, TypeScript is well supported in all major UI libraries and frameworks, including Angular, which strongly recommends TypeScript, as well as Gatsby, Next.js, React, Svelte, and Vue. For backend developers, TypeScript generates JavaScript that runs natively in Node.js; Deno, a similar runtime by Node's creator, emphasizes directly supporting TypeScript files.

However, despite this plethora of popular project support, I was rather disappointed by the lack of good introductory content online when I first learned the language. Many of the online documentation sources didn't do a great job of explaining what a "type system" is or how to use it. They often assumed a great deal of prior knowledge in both JavaScript and strongly typed languages, or were written with only cursory code examples.

Not seeing an O'Reilly book with a cute animal cover introducing TypeScript years ago was a disappointment. While other books on TypeScript from publishers including O'Reilly now exist prior to this one, I couldn't find a book that focuses on the foundations of the language quite the way I wanted: why it works the way it does and how its core features work together. A book that starts with a foundational explanation of the language before adding on features one-by-one. I'm thrilled to be able to make a clear, comprehensive introduction to TypeScript language fundamentals for readers who aren't already familiar with its principles.

Navigating This Book

Learning TypeScript has two purposes:

- You can read through it once to understand TypeScript as a whole.
- Later, you can refer back to it as a practical introductory TypeScript language reference.

This book ramps up from concepts to practical use across three general sections:

- Part I, "Concepts": How JavaScript came to be, what TypeScript adds to it, and the foundations of a *type system* as TypeScript creates it.
- Part II, "Features": Fleshing out how the type system interacts with the major parts of JavaScript you'd work with when writing TypeScript code.
- Part III, "Usage": Now that you understand the features that make up the TypeScript language, how to use them in real-world situations to improve your code reading and editing experience.

I've thrown in a Part IV, "Extra Credit" section at the end to cover lesser-used but still occasionally useful TypeScript features. You won't need to deeply know them to consider yourself a TypeScript developer. But they're all useful concepts that will likely come up as you use TypeScript for real-world projects. Once you've finished understanding the first three sections, I highly recommend studying up on the extra credit section.

Each chapter starts with a haiku to get into the spirit of its contents and ends with a pun. The web development community as a whole and TypeScript's community within it are known for being jovial and welcoming of newcomers. I tried to make this book pleasant to read for learners like me who don't appreciate long, dry writings.

Examples and Projects

Unlike many other resources that introduce TypeScript, this book intentionally focuses on introducing language features with standalone examples showing just the new information rather than delving into medium- or large-sized projects. I prefer this method of teaching because it puts a spotlight on the TypeScript language first and foremost. TypeScript is useful across so many frameworks and platforms—many of which undergo API updates regularly—that I didn't want to keep anything framework- or platform-specific in this book.

That being said, it is supremely useful when learning a programming language to exercise concepts immediately after they're introduced. I highly recommend taking a break after each chapter to rehearse that chapter's contents. Each chapter ends with a suggestion to visit its section on *https://learningtypescript.com* and work through the examples and projects listed there.

Conventions Used in This Book

The following typographical conventions are used in this book:

Italic
> Indicates new terms, URLs, email addresses, filenames, and file extensions.

`Constant width`
> Used for program listings, as well as within paragraphs to refer to program elements such as variable or function names, data types, statements, and keywords.

 This element signifies a tip or suggestion.

This element signifies a general note.

This element indicates a warning or caution.

Using Code Examples

Supplemental material (code examples, exercises, etc.) is available for download at *https://learningtypescript.com*.

If you have a technical question or a problem using the code examples, please send email to *bookquestions@oreilly.com*.

This book is here to help you get your job done. In general, if example code is offered with this book, you may use it in your programs and documentation. You do not need to contact us for permission unless you're reproducing a significant portion of the code. For example, writing a program that uses several chunks of code from this book does not require permission. Selling or distributing examples from O'Reilly books does require permission. Answering a question by citing this book and quoting example code does not require permission. Incorporating a significant amount of example code from this book into your product's documentation does require permission.

We appreciate, but generally do not require, attribution. An attribution usually includes the title, author, publisher, and ISBN. For example: *"Learning Typescript* by Josh Goldberg (O'Reilly). Copyright 2022 Josh Goldberg, 978-1-098-11033-8."

If you feel your use of code examples falls outside fair use or the permission given above, feel free to contact us at *permissions@oreilly.com*.

O'Reilly Online Learning

 For more than 40 years, *O'Reilly Media* has provided technology and business training, knowledge, and insight to help companies succeed.

Our unique network of experts and innovators share their knowledge and expertise through books, articles, and our online learning platform. O'Reilly's online learning platform gives you on-demand access to live training courses, in-depth learning paths, interactive coding environments, and a vast collection of text and video from O'Reilly and 200+ other publishers. For more information, visit *http://oreilly.com*.

How to Contact Us

Please address comments and questions concerning this book to the publisher:

O'Reilly Media, Inc.
1005 Gravenstein Highway North
Sebastopol, CA 95472
800-889-8969 (in the United States or Canada)
707-829-7019 (international or local)
707-829-0104 (fax)
support@oreilly.com
https://www.oreilly.com/about/contact.html

We have a web page for this book, where we list errata, examples, and any additional information. You can access this page at *https://oreil.ly/learning-typescript*.

For news and information about our books and courses, visit *https://oreilly.com*.

Find us on LinkedIn: *https://linkedin.com/company/oreilly-media*.

Follow us on Twitter: *https://twitter.com/oreillymedia*.

Watch us on YouTube: *https://www.youtube.com/oreillymedia*.

Acknowledgments

This book was a team effort, and I'd like to sincerely thank everybody who made it possible. First and foremost my superhuman editor-in-chief, Rita Fernando, for an incredible amount of patience and excellent guidance throughout the authoring journey. Additional shoutout to the rest of the O'Reilly crew: Kristen Brown, Suzanne Huston, Clare Jensen, Carol Keller, Elizabeth Kelly, Cheryl Lenser, Elizabeth Oliver, and Amanda Quinn. You all rock!

Many deep thanks to the tech reviewers for their consistently top-notch pedagogical insights and TypeScript expertise: Mike Boyle, Ryan Cavanaugh, Sara Gallagher, Michael Hoffman, Adam Reineke, and Dan Vanderkam. This book wouldn't be the same without you, and I hope I successfully captured the intent of all your great suggestions!

Further thanks to the assorted peers and praise quoters who gave spot reviews on the book that helped me improve technical accuracy and writing quality: Robert Blake, Andrew Branch, James Henry, Adam Kaczmarek, Loren Sands-Ramshaw, Nik Stern, and Lenz Weber-Tronic. Every suggestion helps!

Lastly, I'd like to thank my family for their love and support over the years. My parents, Frances and Mark, and brother, Danny—thanks for letting me spend time with Legos and books and video games. To my spouse Mariah Goldberg for her patience during my long bouts of editing and writing, and our cats Luci, Tiny, and Jerry for distinguished fluffiness and keeping me company.

PART I

Concepts

CHAPTER 1

From JavaScript to TypeScript

JavaScript today
Supports browsers decades past
Beauty of the web

Before talking about TypeScript, we need to first understand where it came from: JavaScript!

History of JavaScript

JavaScript was designed in 10 days by Brendan Eich at Netscape in 1995 to be approachable and easy to use for websites. Developers have been poking fun at its quirks and perceived shortcomings ever since. I'll cover some of them in the next section.

JavaScript has evolved tremendously since 1995, though! Its steering committee, TC39, has released new versions of ECMAScript—the language specification that JavaScript is based on—yearly since 2015 with new features that bring it in line with other modern languages. Impressively, even with regular new language versions, JavaScript has managed to maintain backward compatibility for decades in varying environments, including browsers, embedded applications, and server runtimes.

Today, JavaScript is a wonderfully flexible language with a lot of strengths. One should appreciate that while JavaScript has its quirks, it's also helped enable the incredible growth of web applications and the internet.

> Show me the perfect programming language and I'll show you a language with no users.
>
> —Anders Hejlsberg, TSConf 2019

Vanilla JavaScript's Pitfalls

Developers often refer to using JavaScript without any significant language extensions or frameworks as "vanilla": referring to it being the familiar, original flavor. I'll soon go over why TypeScript adds just the right flavor to overcome these particular major pitfalls, but it's useful to understand just why they can be painful. All these weaknesses become more pronounced the larger and longer-lived a project gets.

Costly Freedom

Many developers' biggest gripe with JavaScript is unfortunately one of its key features: JavaScript provides virtually no restrictions in how you structure your code. That freedom makes it a ton of fun to start a project in JavaScript!

As you get to have more and more files, though, it becomes apparent how that freedom can be damaging. Take the following snippet, presented out of context from some fictional painting application:

```
function paintPainting(painter, painting) {
  return painter
    .prepare()
    .paint(painting, painter.ownMaterials)
    .finish();
}
```

Reading that code without any context, you can only have vague ideas on how to call the `paintPainting` function. Perhaps if you've worked in the surrounding codebase you may recall that `painter` should be what's returned by some `getPainter` function. You might even make a lucky guess that `painting` is a string.

Even if those assumptions are correct, though, later changes to the code may invalidate them. Perhaps `painting` is changed from a string to some other data type, or maybe one or more of the painter's methods are renamed.

Other languages might refuse to let you run code if their compiler determines it would likely crash. Not so with dynamically typed languages—those that run code without checking if it will likely crash first—such as JavaScript.

The freedom of code that makes JavaScript so fun becomes a real pain when you want safety in running your code.

Loose Documentation

Nothing exists in the JavaScript language specification to formalize describing what function parameters, function returns, variables, or other constructs in code are meant to be. Many developers have adopted a standard called JSDoc to describe functions and variables using block comments. The JSDoc standard describes how you might write documentation comments placed directly above constructs such as functions and variables, formatted in a standard way. Here's an example, again taken out of context:

```
/**
 * Performs a painter painting a particular painting.
 *
 * @param {Painting} painter
 * @param {string} painting
 * @returns [boolean] Whether the painter painted the painting.
 */
function paintPainting(painter, painting) { /* ... */ }
```

JSDoc has key issues that often make it unpleasant to use in a large codebase:

- Nothing stops JSDoc descriptions from being wrong about code.
- Even if your JSDoc descriptions were previously correct, during code refactors it can be difficult to find all the now-invalid JSDoc comments related to your changes.
- Describing complex objects is unwieldy and verbose, requiring multiple stand-alone comments to define types and their relationships.

Maintaining JSDoc comments across a dozen files doesn't take up too much time, but across hundreds or even thousands of constantly updating files can be a real chore.

Weaker Developer Tooling

Because JavaScript doesn't provide built-in ways to identify types, and code easily diverges from JSDoc comments, it can be difficult to automate large changes to or gain insights about a codebase. JavaScript developers are often surprised to see features in typed languages such as C# and Java that allow developers to perform class member renamings or jump to the place an argument's type was declared.

You may protest that modern IDEs such as VS Code do provide some development tools such as automated refactors to JavaScript. True, but: they use TypeScript or an equivalent under the hood for many of their JavaScript features, and those development tools are not as reliable or as powerful in most JavaScript code as they are in well-defined TypeScript code.

TypeScript!

TypeScript was created internally at Microsoft in the early 2010s then released and open sourced in 2012. The head of its development is Anders Hejlsberg, notable for also having lead the development of the popular C# and Turbo Pascal languages. TypeScript is often described as a "superset of JavaScript" or "JavaScript with types." But what *is* TypeScript?

TypeScript is four things:

Programming language
    A language that includes all the existing JavaScript syntax, plus new TypeScript-specific syntax for defining and using types

Type checker
    A program that takes in a set of files written in JavaScript and/or TypeScript, develops an understanding of all the constructs (variables, functions...) created, and lets you know if it thinks anything is set up incorrectly

Compiler
    A program that runs the type checker, reports any issues, then outputs the equivalent JavaScript code

Language service
    A program that uses the type checker to tell editors such as VS Code how to provide helpful utilities to developers

Getting Started in the TypeScript Playground

You've read a good amount about TypeScript by now. Let's get you writing it!

The main TypeScript website includes a "Playground" editor at *https://www.typescript lang.org/play*. You can type code into the main editor and see many of the same editor suggestions you would see when working with TypeScript locally in a full IDE (Integrated Development Environment).

Most of the snippets in this book are intentionally small and self-contained enough that you could type them out in the Playground and tinker with them for fun.

TypeScript in Action

Take a look at this code snippet:

```
const firstName = "Georgia";
const nameLength = firstName.length();
//                          ~~~~~~
// This expression is not callable.
```

The code is written in normal JavaScript syntax—I haven't introduced TypeScript-specific syntax yet. If you were to run the TypeScript type checker on this code, it would use its knowledge that the length property of a string is a number—not a function—to give you the complaint shown in the comment.

If you were to paste that code into the playground or an editor, it would be told by the language service to give you a little red squiggly under length indicating TypeScript's displeasure with your code. Hovering over the squigglied code would give you the text of the complaint (Figure 1-1).

```
const firstName = "Lizzo";
const nameLength = firstName.length();

              (property) String.length: number

              Returns the length of a String object.

              This expression is not callable.
              Type 'Number' has no call signatures. ts(2349)

              View Problem    No quick fixes available
```

Figure 1-1. TypeScript reporting an error on string length not being callable

Being told of these simple errors in your editor as you type them is a lot more pleasant than waiting until a particular line of code happens to be run and throw an error. If you tried to run that code in JavaScript, it would crash!

Freedom Through Restriction

TypeScript allows us to specify what types of values may be provided for parameters and variables. Some developers find having to explicitly write out in your code how particular areas are supposed to work to be restrictive at first.

But! I would argue that being "restricted" in this way is actually a good thing! By restricting our code to only being able to be used in the ways you specify, TypeScript can give you confidence that changes in one area of code won't break other areas of code that use it.

If, say, you change the number of required parameters for a function, TypeScript will let you know if you forget to update a place that calls the function.

In the following example, sayMyName was changed from taking in two parameters to taking one parameter, but the call to it with two strings wasn't updated and so is triggering a TypeScript complaint:

```
// Previously: sayMyName(firstName, lastName) { ...
function sayMyName(fullName) {
  console.log(`You acting kind of shady, ain't callin' me ${fullName}`);
}

sayMyName("Beyoncé", "Knowles");
//                    ~~~~~~~~~
// Expected 1 argument, but got 2.
```

That code would run without crashing in JavaScript, but its output would be different from expected (it wouldn't include "Knowles"):

```
You acting kind of shady, ain't callin' me Beyoncé
```

Calling functions with the wrong number of arguments is exactly the sort of short-sighted JavaScript freedom that TypeScript restricts.

Precise Documentation

Let's look at a TypeScript-ified version of the `paintPainting` function from earlier. Although I haven't yet gone over the specifics of TypeScript syntax for documenting types, the following snippet still hints at the great precision with which TypeScript can document code:

```
interface Painter {
  finish(): boolean;
  ownMaterials: Material[];
  paint(painting: string, materials: Material[]): boolean;
}

function paintPainting(painter: Painter, painting: string): boolean { /* ... */ }
```

A TypeScript developer reading this code for the first time could understand that `painter` has at least three properties, two of which are methods. By baking in syntax to describe the "shapes" of objects, TypeScript provides an excellent, enforced system for describing how objects look.

Stronger Developer Tooling

TypeScript's typings allow editors such as VS Code to gain much deeper insights into your code. They can then use those insights to surface intelligent suggestions as you type. These suggestions can be incredibly useful for development.

If you've used VS Code to write JavaScript before, you might have noticed that it suggests "autocompletions" as you write code with built-in types of objects like strings. If, say, you start typing the member of something known to be a string, TypeScript can suggest all the members of the strings (Figure 1-2).

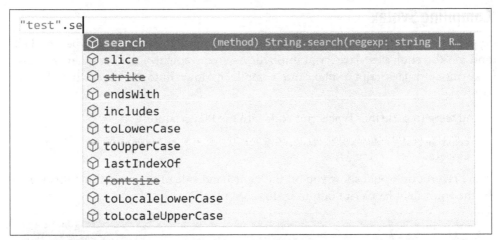

```
"test".se
    search              (method) String.search(regexp: string | R...
    slice
    strike
    endsWith
    includes
    toLowerCase
    toUpperCase
    lastIndexOf
    fontsize
    toLocaleLowerCase
    toLocaleUpperCase
```

Figure 1-2. TypeScript providing autocompletion suggestions in JavaScript for a string

When you add TypeScript's type checker for understanding code, it can give you these useful suggestions even for code you've written. Upon typing `painter.` in the `paintPainting` function, TypeScript would take its knowledge that the `painter` parameter is of type `Painter` and the `Painter` type has the following members (Figure 1-3).

```
interface Painter {
  finish(): boolean;
  ownMaterials: Material[];
  paint(painting: string, materials: Material[]): boolean;
}

function paintPainting(painter: Painter, painting: string): boolean
  painter.
       finish              (method) Painter.finish(): boolean
       ownMaterials
       paint
```

Figure 1-3. TypeScript providing autocompletion suggestions in JavaScript for a string

Snazzy! I'll cover a plethora of other useful editor features in Chapter 12, "Using IDE Features".

Compiling Syntax

TypeScript's compiler allows us to input TypeScript syntax, have it type checked, and get the equivalent JavaScript emitted. As a convenience, the compiler may also take modern JavaScript syntax and compile it down into its older ECMAScript equivalents.

If you were to paste this TypeScript code into the Playground:

```
const artist = "Augusta Savage";
console.log({ artist });
```

The Playground would show you on the right-hand side of the screen that this would be the equivalent JavaScript output by the compiler (Figure 1-4).

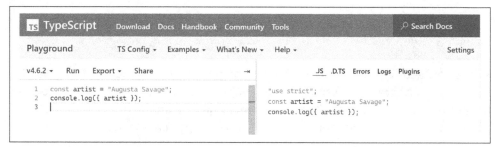

Figure 1-4. TypeScript Playground compiling TypeScript code into equivalent JavaScript

The TypeScript Playground is a great tool for showing how source TypeScript becomes output JavaScript.

 Many JavaScript projects use dedicated transpilers such as Babel (*https://babeljs.io*) instead of TypeScript's own to transpile source code into runnable JavaScript. You can find a list of common project starters on *https://learningtypescript.com/starters*.

Getting Started Locally

You can run TypeScript on your computer as long as you have Node.js installed. To install the latest version of TypeScript globally, run the following command:

```
npm i -g typescript
```

Now, you'll be able to run TypeScript on the command line with the `tsc` (**TypeScript Compiler**) command. Try it with the `--version` flag to make sure it's set up properly:

```
tsc --version
```

It should print out something like Version X.Y.Z—whichever version is current as of you installing TypeScript:

```
$ tsc --version
Version 4.7.2
```

Running Locally

Now that TypeScript is installed, let's have you set up a folder locally to run Type-Script on code. Create a folder somewhere on your computer and run this command to create a new *tsconfig.json* configuration file:

```
tsc --init
```

A *tsconfig.json* file declares the settings that TypeScript uses when analyzing your code. Most of the options in that file aren't going to be relevant to you in this book (there are a lot of uncommon edge cases in programming that the language needs to account for!). I'll cover them in Chapter 13, "Configuration Options". The important feature is that now you can run tsc to tell TypeScript to compile all the files in that folder and TypeScript will refer to that *tsconfig.json* for any configuration options.

Try adding a file named *index.ts* with the following contents:

```
console.blub("Nothing is worth more than laughter.");
```

Then, run tsc and provide it the name of that *index.ts* file:

```
tsc index.ts
```

You should get an error that looks roughly like:

```
index.ts:1:9 - error TS2339: Property 'blub' does not exist on type 'Console'.

1 console.blub("Nothing is worth more than laughter.");
          ~~~~

Found 1 error.
```

Indeed, blub does not exist on the console. What was I thinking?

Before you fix the code to appease TypeScript, note that tsc created an *index.js* for you with contents including the console.blub.

 This is an important concept: even though there was a *type error* in our code, the *syntax* was still completely valid. The TypeScript compiler will still produce JavaScript from an input file regardless of any type errors.

Correct the code in *index.ts* to call `console.log` and run `tsc` again. There should be no complaints in your terminal, and the *index.js* file should now contain updated output code:

```
console.log("Nothing is worth more than laughter.");
```

I highly recommend playing with the book's snippets as you read through them, either in the playground or in an editor with Type-Script support, meaning it runs the TypeScript language service for you. Small self-contained exercises, as well as larger projects, are also available to help you practice what you've learned on *https://learningtypescript.com*.

Editor Features

Another benefit of creating a *tsconfig.json* file is that when editors are opened to a particular folder, they will now recognize that folder as a TypeScript project. For example, if you open VS Code in a folder, the settings it uses to analyze your TypeScript code will respect whatever's in that folder's *tsconfig.json*.

As an exercise, go back through the code snippets in this chapter and type them in your editor. You should see drop-downs suggesting completions for names as you type them, especially for members such as the `log` on `console`.

Very exciting: you're using the TypeScript language service to help yourself write code! You're on your way to being a TypeScript developer!

VS Code comes with great TypeScript support and is itself built in TypeScript. You don't *have* to use it for TypeScript—virtually all modern editors have excellent TypeScript support either built-in or available via plugins—but I do recommend it for at least trying out TypeScript while reading through this book. If you do use a different editor, I also recommend enabling its TypeScript support. I'll cover editor features more deeply in Chapter 12, "Using IDE Features".

What TypeScript Is Not

Now that you've seen how wonderful TypeScript is, I have to warn you about some limitations. Every tool excels at some areas and has limitations in others.

A Remedy for Bad Code

TypeScript helps you structure your JavaScript, but other than enforcing type safety, it doesn't enforce any opinions on what that structure should look like.

Good!

TypeScript is a language that everyone is meant to be able to use, not an opinionated framework with a target audience. You can write code using whatever architectural patterns you're used to from JavaScript, and TypeScript will support them.

If anybody tries to tell you that TypeScript forces you to use classes, or makes it hard to write good code, or whatever code style complaints are out there, give them a stern look and tell them to pick up a copy of *Learning TypeScript*. TypeScript does not enforce code style opinions such as whether to use classes or functions, nor is it associated with any particular application framework—Angular, React, etc.—over others.

Extensions to JavaScript (Mostly)

TypeScript's design goals explicitly state that it should:

- Align with current and future ECMAScript proposals
- Preserve runtime behavior of all JavaScript code

TypeScript does not try to change how JavaScript works at all. Its creators have tried very hard to avoid adding new code features that would add to or conflict with JavaScript. Such a task is the domain of TC39, the technical committee that works on ECMAScript itself.

There are a few older features in TypeScript that were added many years ago to reflect common use cases in JavaScript code. Most of those features are either relatively uncommon or have fallen out of favor, and are only covered briefly in Chapter 14, "Syntax Extensions". I recommend staying away from them in most cases.

 As of 2022, TC39 is investigating adding a syntax for type annotations to JavaScript. The latest proposals have them acting as a form of comments that do not impact code at runtime and are used only for development-time systems such as TypeScript. It will be many years until type comments or some equivalent are added to JavaScript, so they won't be mentioned elsewhere in this book.

Slower Than JavaScript

Sometimes on the internet, you might hear some opinionated developers complain that TypeScript is slower than JavaScript at runtime. That claim is generally inaccurate and misleading. The only changes TypeScript makes to code are if you ask it to compile your code down to earlier versions of JavaScript to support older runtime environments such as Internet Explorer 11. Many production frameworks don't use TypeScript's compiler at all, instead using a separate tool for transpilation (the part of compiling that converts source code from one programming language into another) and TypeScript only for type checking.

TypeScript does, however, add some time to building your code. TypeScript code must be compiled down to JavaScript before most environments, such as browsers and Node.js, will run it. Most build pipelines are generally set up so that the performance hit is negligible, and slower TypeScript features such as analyzing code for likely mistakes are done separately from generating runnable application code files.

 Even projects that seemingly allow running TypeScript code directly, such as ts-node and Deno, themselves internally convert TypeScript code to JavaScript before running it.

Finished Evolving

The web is nowhere near finished evolving, and thus neither is TypeScript. The TypeScript language is constantly receiving bug fixes and feature additions to match the ever-shifting needs of the web community. The basic tenets of TypeScript you'll learn in this book will remain about the same, but error messages, fancier features, and editor integrations will improve over time.

In fact, while this edition of the book was published with TypeScript version 4.7.2 as the latest, by the time you started reading it, we can be certain a newer version has been released. Some of the TypeScript error messages in this book might even already be out of date!

Summary

In this chapter, you read up on the context for some of JavaScript's main weaknesses, where TypeScript comes into play, and how to get started with TypeScript:

- A brief history of JavaScript
- JavaScript's pitfalls: costly freedom, loose documentation, and weaker developer tooling
- What TypeScript is: a programming language, a type checker, a compiler, and a language service
- TypeScript's advantages: freedom through restriction, precise documentation, and stronger developer tooling

- Getting started writing TypeScript code on the TypeScript Playground and locally on your computer
- What TypeScript is not: a remedy for bad code, extensions to JavaScript (mostly), slower than JavaScript, or finished evolving

 Now that you've finished reading this chapter, practice what you've learned on *https://learningtypescript.com/from-javascript-to-typescript*.

What happens if you spot errors running the TypeScript compiler?
You'd better go catch them!

CHAPTER 2

The Type System

JavaScript's power
Comes from flexibility
Be careful with that!

I talked briefly in Chapter 1, "From JavaScript to TypeScript" about the existence of a "type checker" in TypeScript that looks at your code, understands how it's meant to work, and lets you know where you might have messed up. But how does a type checker work, really?

What's in a Type?

A "type" is a description of what a JavaScript value *shape* might be. By "shape" I mean which properties and methods exist on a value, and what the built-in `typeof` operator would describe it as.

For example, when you create a variable with the initial value `"Aretha"`:

```
let singer = "Aretha";
```

TypeScript can infer, or figure out, that the `singer` variable is of *type* string.

The most basic types in TypeScript correspond to the seven basic kinds of primitives in JavaScript:

- `null`
- `undefined`
- `boolean` // `true` or `false`
- `string` // `""`, `"Hi!"`, `"abc123"`, ...
- `number` // `0`, `2.1`, `-4`, ...
- `bigint` // `0n`, `2n`, `-4n`, ...
- `symbol` // `Symbol()`, `Symbol("hi")`, ...

For each of these values, TypeScript understands the type of the value to be one of the seven basic primitives:

- `null; // null`
- `undefined; // undefined`
- `true; // boolean`
- `"Louise"; // string`
- `1337; // number`
- `1337n; // bigint`
- `Symbol("Franklin"); // symbol`

If you ever forget the name of a primitive, you can type a `let` variable with a primitive value into the TypeScript Playground (*https://typescriptlang.org/play*) or an IDE and hover your mouse over the variable's name. The resultant popover will include the name of the primitive, such as this screenshot showing hovering over a string variable (Figure 2-1).

```
2
3
4        let singer: string
5   let singer = "Ella Fitzgerald";
6
```

Figure 2-1. TypeScript showing a string variable's type in its hover information

TypeScript is also smart enough to be able to infer the type of a variable whose starting value is computed. In this example, TypeScript knows that the ternary expression always results in a string, so the `bestSong` variable is a `string`:

```
// Inferred type: string
let bestSong = Math.random() > 0.5
    ? "Chain of Fools"
    : "Respect";
```

Back in the TypeScript Playground (*https://typescriptlang.org/play*) or your IDE, try hovering your cursor on that `bestSong` variable. You should see some info box or message telling you that TypeScript has inferred the `bestSong` variable to be type `string` (Figure 2-2).

```
    let bestSong: string
let bestSong = Math.random() > 0.5
    ? "Chain of Fools"
    : "Respect";
```

Figure 2-2. TypeScript reporting a let *variable as being its* string *literal type from its ternary expression*

 Recall the differences between objects and primitives in JavaScript: classes such as Boolean and Number wrap around their primitive equivalents. TypeScript best practice is generally to refer to the lower-case names, such as boolean and number, respectively.

Type Systems

A *type system* is the set of rules for how a programming language understands what types the constructs in a program may have.

At its core, TypeScript's type system works by:

- Reading in your code and understanding all the types and values in existence
- For each value, seeing what type its initial declaration indicates it may contain
- For each value, seeing all the ways it's used later on in code
- Complaining to the user if a value's usage doesn't match with its type

Let's walk through this type inference process in detail.

Take the following snippet, in which TypeScript is emitting a type error about a member property being erroneously called as a function:

```
let firstName = "Whitney";
firstName.length();
//        ~~~~~~
// This expression is not callable.
//   Type 'Number' has no call signatures.
```

TypeScript came to that complaint by, in order:

1. Reading in the code and understanding there to be a variable named firstName
2. Concluding that firstName is of type string because its initial value is a string, "Whitney"
3. Seeing that the code is trying to access a .length member of firstName and call it like a function

4. Complaining that the `.length` member of a string is a number, not a function (*it can't be called like a function*)

Understanding TypeScript's type system is an important skill for understanding Type-Script code. Code snippets in this chapter and throughout the rest of this book will display more and more complex types that TypeScript will be able to infer from code.

Kinds of Errors

While writing TypeScript, the two kinds of "errors" you'll come across most frequently are:

Syntax
Blocking TypeScript from being converted to JavaScript

Type
Something mismatched has been detected by the type checker

The differences between the two are important.

Syntax errors

Syntax errors are when TypeScript detects incorrect syntax that it cannot understand as code. These block TypeScript from being able to properly generate output Java-Script from your file. Depending on the tooling and settings you're using to convert your TypeScript code to JavaScript, you might still get some kind of JavaScript output (in default `tsc` settings, you will). But if you do, it likely won't look like what you expect.

This input TypeScript has a syntax error for an unexpected `let`:

```
let let wat;
//      ~~~
// Error: ',' expected.
```

Its compiled JavaScript output, depending on the TypeScript compiler version, may look something like:

```
let let, wat;
```

 Although TypeScript will do its best to output JavaScript code regardless of syntax errors, the output code will likely not be what you wanted. It's best to fix syntax errors before attempting to run the output JavaScript.

Type errors

Type errors occur when your syntax is valid but the TypeScript type checker has detected an error with the program's types. These do not block TypeScript syntax from being converted to JavaScript. They do, however, often indicate something will crash or behave unexpectedly if your code is allowed to run.

You saw this in Chapter 1, "From JavaScript to TypeScript" with the `console.blub` example, where the code was syntactically valid but TypeScript could detect it would likely crash when run:

```
console.blub("Nothing is worth more than laughter.");
//      ~~~~
// Error: Property 'blub' does not exist on type 'Console'.
```

Even though TypeScript may output JavaScript code despite the presence of type errors, type errors are generally a sign that the output JavaScript likely won't run the way you wanted. It's best to read them and consider fixing any reported issues before running JavaScript.

 Some projects are configured to block running code during development until all TypeScript type errors—not just syntax—are fixed. Many developers, myself included, generally find this to be annoying and unnecessary. Most projects have a way to not be blocked, such as with the *tsconfig.json* file and configuration options covered in Chapter 13, "Configuration Options".

Assignability

TypeScript reads variables' initial values to determine what type those variables are allowed to be. If it later sees an assignment of a new value to that variable, it will check if that new value's type is the same as the variable's.

TypeScript is fine with later assigning a different value of the same type to a variable. If a variable is, say, initially a `string` value, later assigning it another `string` would be fine:

```
let firstName = "Carole";
firstName = "Joan";
```

If TypeScript sees an assignment of a different type, it will give us a type error. We couldn't, say, initially declare a variable with a `string` value and then later on put in a `boolean`:

```
let lastName = "King";
lastName = true;
// Error: Type 'boolean' is not assignable to type 'string'.
```

TypeScript's checking of whether a value is allowed to be provided to a function call or variable is called *assignability*: whether that value is *assignable* to the expected type it's passed to. This will be an important term in later chapters as we compare more complex objects.

Understanding Assignability Errors

Errors in the format "Type...is not assignable to type..." will be some of the most common types of errors you'll see when writing TypeScript code.

The first type mentioned in that error message is the value the code is attempting to assign to a recipient. The second type mentioned is the recipient being assigned the first type. For example, when we wrote lastName = true in the previous snippet, we were trying to *assign* the value of true—type boolean—to the recipient variable lastName—type string.

You'll see more and more complex assignability issues as you progress through this book. Remember to read them carefully to understand reported differences between actual and expected types. Doing so will make it much easier to work with TypeScript when it's giving you grief over type errors.

Type Annotations

Sometimes a variable doesn't have an initial value for TypeScript to read. TypeScript won't attempt to figure out the initial type of the variable from later uses. It'll consider the variable by default to be implicitly the any type: indicating that it could be anything in the world.

Variables that can't have their initial type inferred go through what's called an *evolving any*: rather than enforce any particular type, TypeScript will evolve its understanding of the variable's type each time a new value is assigned.

Here, assigning the evolving any variable rocker is first assigned a string, which means it has string methods such as toUpperCase, but then is evolved into a number:

```
let rocker; // Type: any

rocker = "Joan Jett"; // Type: string
rocker.toUpperCase(); // Ok

rocker = 19.58; // Type: number
rocker.toPrecision(1); // Ok

rocker.toUpperCase();
//     ~~~~~~~~~~~
// Error: 'toUpperCase' does not exist on type 'number'.
```

TypeScript was able to catch that we were calling the toUpperCase() method on a variable evolved to type number. However, it wasn't able to tell us earlier whether it was intentional that we were evolving the variable from string to number in the first place.

Allowing variables to be evolving any typed—and using the any type in general—partially defeats the purpose of TypeScript's type checking! TypeScript works best when it knows what types your values are meant to be. Much of TypeScript's type checking can't be applied to any typed values because they don't have known types to be checked. Chapter 13, "Configuration Options" will cover how to configure TypeScript's implicit any complaints.

TypeScript provides a syntax for declaring the type of a variable without having to assign it an initial value, called a *type annotation*. A type annotation is placed after the name of a variable and includes a colon followed by the name of a type.

This type annotation indicates the rocker variable is meant to be type string:

```
let rocker: string;
rocker = "Joan Jett";
```

These type annotations exist only for TypeScript—they don't affect the runtime code and are not valid JavaScript syntax. If you run tsc to compile TypeScript source code to JavaScript, they'll be erased. For example, the previous example would be compiled to roughly the following JavaScript:

```
// output .js file
let rocker;
rocker = "Joan Jett";
```

Assigning a value whose type is not assignable to the variable's annotated type will cause a type error.

This snippet assigns a number to a rocker variable previously declared as type string, causing a type error:

```
let rocker: string;
rocker = 19.58;
// Error: Type 'number' is not assignable to type 'string'.
```

You'll see through the next few chapters how type annotations allow you to augment TypeScript's insights into your code, allowing it to give you better features during development. TypeScript contains an assortment of new pieces of syntax, such as these type annotations that exist only in the type system.

Nothing that exists only in the type system gets copied over into emitted JavaScript. TypeScript types don't affect emitted JavaScript.

Unnecessary Type Annotations

Type annotations allow us to provide information to TypeScript that it wouldn't have been able to glean on its own. You could also use them on variables that have immediately inferable types, but you wouldn't be telling TypeScript anything it doesn't already know.

The following `: string` type annotation is redundant because TypeScript could already infer that `firstName` be of type `string`:

```
let firstName: string = "Tina";
//            ~~~~~~~~ Does not change the type system...
```

If you do add a type annotation to a variable with an initial value, TypeScript will check that it matches the type of the variable's value.

The following `firstName` is declared to be of type `string`, but its initializer is the `number` 42, which TypeScript sees as an incompatibility:

```
let firstName: string = 42;
//  ~~~~~~~~~
// Error: Type 'number' is not assignable to type 'string'.
```

Many developers—myself included—generally prefer not to add type annotations on variables where the type annotations wouldn't change anything. Having to manually write out type annotations can be cumbersome—especially when they change, and for the complex types I'll show you later in this book.

It can sometimes be useful to include explicit type annotations on variables to clearly document the code and/or to make TypeScript protected against accidental changes to the variable's type. We'll see in later chapters how explicit type annotations can sometimes explicitly tell TypeScript information it wouldn't have inferred normally.

Type Shapes

TypeScript does more than check that the values assigned to variables match their original types. TypeScript also knows what member properties should exist on objects. If you attempt to access a property of a variable, TypeScript will make sure that property is known to exist on that variable's type.

Suppose we declare a `rapper` variable of type `string`. Later on, when we use that `rapper` variable, operations that TypeScript knows work on strings are allowed:

```
let rapper = "Queen Latifah";
rapper.length; // ok
```

Operations that TypeScript doesn't know to work on strings will not be allowed:

```
rapper.push('!');
//     ~~~~
// Property 'push' does not exist on type 'string'.
```

Types can also be more complex shapes, most notably objects. In the following snippet, TypeScript knows the `cher` object doesn't have a `middleName` key and complains:

```
let cher = {
  firstName: "Cherilyn",
  lastName: "Sarkisian",
};

cher.middleName;
//   ~~~~~~~~~~
//   Property 'middleName' does not exist on type
//   '{ firstName: string; lastName: string; }'.
```

TypeScript's understanding of object shapes allows it to report issues with the usage of objects, not just assignability. Chapter 4, "Objects" will describe more of TypeScript's powerful features around objects and object types.

Modules

The JavaScript programming language did not include a specification for how files can share code between each other until relatively recently in its history. ECMAScript 2015 added "ECMAScript modules," or ESM, to standardize `import` and `export` syntax between files.

For reference, this module file imports a `value` from a sibling `./values` file and exports a `doubled` variable:

```
import { value } from "./values";

export const doubled = value * 2;
```

To match with the ECMAScript specification, in this book I'll use the following nomenclature:

Module
    A file with a top-level `export` or `import`

Script
    Any file that is not a module

TypeScript is able to work with those modern module files as well as older files. Anything declared in a module file will be available only in that file unless an explicit `export` statement in that file exports it. A variable declared in one module with the same name as a variable declared in another file won't be considered a naming conflict (unless one file imports the other file's variable).

The following `a.ts` and `b.ts` files are both modules that export a similarly named `shared` variable without issue. `c.ts` causes a type error because it has a naming conflict between an imported `shared` and its own value:

```
// a.ts
export const shared = "Cher";

// b.ts
export const shared = "Cher";

// c.ts
import { shared } from "./a";
//       ~~~~~~
// Error: Import declaration conflicts with local declaration of 'shared'.

export const shared = "Cher";
//           ~~~~~~
// Error: Individual declarations in merged declaration
// 'shared' must be all exported or all local.
```

If a file is a script, though, TypeScript will consider it to be globally scoped, meaning all scripts have access to its contents. That means variables declared in a script file cannot have the same name as variables declared in other script files.

The following `a.ts` and `b.ts` files are considered scripts because they do not have module-style `export` or `import` statements. That means their variables of the same name conflict with each other as if they were declared in the same file:

```
// a.ts
const shared = "Cher";
//    ~~~~~~
// Cannot redeclare block-scoped variable 'shared'.

// b.ts
const shared = "Cher";
//    ~~~~~~
// Cannot redeclare block-scoped variable 'shared'.
```

If you see these "Cannot redeclare…" errors in a TypeScript file, it may be because you have yet to add an `export` or `import` statement to the file. Per the ECMAScript specification, if you need a file to be a module without an `export` or `import` statement, you can add an `export {};` somewhere in the file to force it to be a module:

```
// a.ts and b.ts
const shared = "Cher"; // Ok

export {};
```

 TypeScript will not recognize the types of imports and exports in TypeScript files written using older module systems such as CommonJS. TypeScript will generally see values returned from CommonJS style require functions to be typed as any.

Summary

In this chapter, you saw how TypeScript's type system works at its core:

- What a "type" is and the primitive types recognized by TypeScript
- What a "type system" is and how TypeScript's type system understands code
- How type errors compare to syntax errors
- Inferred variable types and variable assignability
- Type annotations to explicitly declare variable types and avoid evolving **any** types
- Object member checking on type shapes
- ECMAScript module files' declaration scoping compared to script files

 Now that you've finished reading this chapter, practice what you've learned on *https://learningtypescript.com/the-type-system*.

Why did the number and string break up?
They weren't each other's types.

CHAPTER 3

Unions and Literals

Nothing is constant
Values may change over time
(well, except constants)

Chapter 2, "The Type System" covered the concept of the "type system" and how it can read values to understand the types of variables. Now I'd like to introduce two key concepts that TypeScript works with to make inferences on top of those values:

Unions
> Expanding a value's allowed type to be two or more possible types

Narrowing
> Reducing a value's allowed type to *not* be one or more possible types

Put together, unions and narrowing are powerful concepts that allow TypeScript to make informed inferences on your code many other mainstream languages cannot.

Union Types

Take this `mathematician` variable:

```
let mathematician = Math.random() > 0.5
    ? undefined
    : "Mark Goldberg";
```

What type is `mathematician`?

It's neither only `undefined` nor only `string`, even though those are both potential types. `mathematician` can be *either* `undefined` or `string`. This kind of "either or" type is called a *union*. Union types are a wonderful concept that let us handle code cases where we don't know exactly which type a value is, but do know it's one of two or more options.

TypeScript represents union types using the | (pipe) operator between the possible values, or *constituents*. The previous mathematician type is thought of as string | undefined. Hovering over the mathematician variable would show its type as string | undefined (Figure 3-1).

```
                let mathematician: string | undefined
        let mathematician = Math.random() > 0.5
            ? undefined
            : "Mark Goldberg";
```

Figure 3-1. TypeScript reporting the mathematician variable as being type string | undefined

Declaring Union Types

Union types are an example of a situation when it might be useful to give an explicit type annotation for a variable even though it has an initial value. In this example, thinker starts off null but is known to potentially contain a string instead. Giving it an explicit string | null type annotation means TypeScript will allow it to be assigned values of type string:

```
let thinker: string | null = null;

if (Math.random() > 0.5) {
    thinker = "Susanne Langer"; // Ok
}
```

Union type declarations can be placed anywhere you might declare a type with a type annotation.

The order of a union type declaration does not matter. You can write boolean | number or number | boolean and TypeScript will treat both the exact same.

Union Properties

When a value is known to be a union type, TypeScript will only allow you to access member properties that exist on all possible types in the union. It will give you a type-checking error if you try to access a member property that doesn't exist on all possible types.

In the following snippet, `physicist` is of type `number | string`. While `.toString()` exists in both types and is allowed to be used, `.toUpperCase()` and `.toFixed()` are not because `.toUpperCase()` is missing on the `number` type and `.toFixed()` is missing on the `string` type:

```
let physicist = Math.random() > 0.5
    ? "Marie Curie"
    : 84;

physicist.toString(); // Ok

physicist.toUpperCase();
//        ~~~~~~~~~~~
// Error: Property 'toUpperCase' does not exist on type 'string | number'.
//   Property 'toUpperCase' does not exist on type 'number'.

physicist.toFixed();
//        ~~~~~~~
// Error: Property 'toFixed' does not exist on type 'string | number'.
//   Property 'toFixed' does not exist on type 'string'.
```

Blocking access to properties that don't exist on all union types is a safety measure. If an object is not known to definitely be a type that contains a property, TypeScript will believe it unsafe to try to use that property. The property might not exist!

To use a property of a union typed value that only exists on a subset of the potential types, your code will need to indicate to TypeScript that the value at that location in code is one of those more specific types: a process called *narrowing*.

Narrowing

Narrowing is when TypeScript infers from your code that a value is of a more specific type than what it was defined, declared, or previously inferred as. Once TypeScript knows that a value's type is more narrow than previously known, it will allow you to treat the value like that more specific type. A logical check that can be used to narrow types is called a *type guard*.

Let's cover two of the common type guards TypeScript can use to deduce type narrowing from your code.

Assignment Narrowing

If you directly assign a value to a variable, TypeScript will narrow the variable's type to that value's type.

Here, the `admiral` variable is declared initially as a `number | string`, but after being assigned the value `"Grace Hopper"`, TypeScript knows it must be a `string`:

```
let admiral: number | string;

admiral = "Grace Hopper";

admiral.toUpperCase(); // Ok: string

admiral.toFixed();
//       ~~~~~~~
// Error: Property 'toFixed' does not exist on type 'string'.
```

Assignment narrowing comes into play when a variable is given an explicit union type annotation and an initial value too. TypeScript will understand that while the variable may later receive a value of any of the union typed values, it starts off as only the type of its initial value.

In the following snippet, `inventor` is declared as type `number | string`, but TypeScript knows it's immediately narrowed to a `string` from its initial value:

```
let inventor: number | string = "Hedy Lamarr";

inventor.toUpperCase(); // Ok: string

inventor.toFixed();
//       ~~~~~~~
// Error: Property 'toFixed' does not exist on type 'string'.
```

Conditional Checks

A common way to get TypeScript to narrow a variable's value is to write an `if` statement checking the variable for being equal to a known value. TypeScript is smart enough to understand that inside the body of that `if` statement, the variable must be the same type as the known value:

```
// Type of scientist: number | string
let scientist = Math.random() > 0.5
    ? "Rosalind Franklin"
    : 51;

if (scientist === "Rosalind Franklin") {
    // Type of scientist: string
    scientist.toUpperCase(); // Ok
}

// Type of scientist: number | string
scientist.toUpperCase();
//        ~~~~~~~~~~~
// Error: Property 'toUpperCase' does not exist on type 'string | number'.
//    Property 'toUpperCase' does not exist on type 'number'.
```

Narrowing with conditional logic shows TypeScript's type-checking logic mirroring good JavaScript coding patterns. If a variable might be one of several types, you'll generally want to check its type for being what you need. TypeScript is forcing us to play it safe with our code. Thanks, TypeScript!

Typeof Checks

In addition to direct value checking, TypeScript also recognizes the `typeof` operator in narrowing down variable types.

Similar to the `scientist` example, checking if `typeof researcher` is `"string"` indicates to TypeScript that the type of `researcher` must be `string`:

```
let researcher = Math.random() > 0.5
    ? "Rosalind Franklin"
    : 51;

if (typeof researcher === "string") {
    researcher.toUpperCase(); // Ok: string
}
```

Logical negations from ! and `else` statements work as well:

```
if (!(typeof researcher === "string")) {
    researcher.toFixed(); // Ok: number
} else {
    researcher.toUpperCase(); // Ok: string
}
```

Those code snippets can be rewritten with a ternary statement, which is also supported for type narrowing:

```
typeof researcher === "string"
    ? researcher.toUpperCase() // Ok: string
    : researcher.toFixed(); // Ok: number
```

Whichever way you write them, `typeof` checks are a practical and often used way to narrow types.

TypeScript's type checker recognizes several more forms of narrowing that we'll see in later chapters.

Literal Types

Now that I've shown union types and narrowing for working with values that may be two or more potential types, I'd like to go in the opposite direction by introducing *literal types*: more specific versions of primitive types.

Take this `philosopher` variable:

```
const philosopher = "Hypatia";
```

What type is `philosopher`?

At first glance, you might say `string`—and you'd be correct. `philosopher` is indeed a `string`.

But! `philosopher` is not just any old `string`. It's specifically the value `"Hypatia"`. Therefore, the `philosopher` variable's type is technically the more specific `"Hypatia"`.

Such is the concept of a *literal type*: the type of a value that is known to be a specific value of a primitive, rather than any of those primitive's values at all. The primitive type `string` represents the set of all possible strings that could ever exist; the literal type `"Hypatia"` represents just that one string.

If you declare a variable as `const` and directly give it a literal value, TypeScript will infer the variable to be that literal value as a type. This is why, when you hover a mouse over a `const` variable with an initial literal value in an IDE such as VS Code, it will show you the variable's type as that literal (Figure 3-2) instead of the more general primitive (Figure 3-3).

```
const mathematician: "Mark Goldberg"
const mathematician = "Mark Goldberg";
```

Figure 3-2. TypeScript reporting a `const` variable as being specifically its literal type

```
let mathematician: string
let mathematician = "Mark Goldberg";
```

Figure 3-3. TypeScript reporting a `let` variable as being generally its primitive type

You can think of each *primitive* type as a *union* of every possible matching *literal* value. In other words, a primitive type is the set of all possible literal values of that type.

Other than the `boolean`, `null`, and `undefined` types, all other primitives such as `number` and `string` have a infinite number of literal types. The common types you'll find in typical TypeScript code are just those:

- `boolean`: just `true | false`
- `null` and `undefined`: both just have one literal value, themselves

- number: 0 | 1 | 2 | ... | 0.1 | 0.2 | ...
- string: "" | "a" | "b" | "c" | ... | "aa" | "ab" | "ac" | ...

Union type annotations can mix and match between literals and primitives. A representation of a lifespan, for example, might be represented by any `number` *or* one of a couple known edge cases:

```
let lifespan: number | "ongoing" | "uncertain";

lifespan = 89; // Ok
lifespan = "ongoing"; // Ok

lifespan = true;
// Error: Type 'true' is not assignable to
// type 'number | "ongoing" | "uncertain"'
```

Literal Assignability

You've seen how different primitive types such as `number` and `string` are not assignable to each other. Similarly, different literal types within the same primitive type—e.g., `0` and `1`—are not assignable to each other.

In this example, `specificallyAda` is declared as being of the literal type `"Ada"`, so while the value `"Ada"` may be given to it, the types `"Byron"` and `string` are not assignable to it:

```
let specificallyAda: "Ada";

specificallyAda = "Ada"; // Ok

specificallyAda = "Byron";
// Error: Type '"Byron"' is not assignable to type '"Ada"'.

let someString = ""; // Type: string

specificallyAda = someString;
// Error: Type 'string' is not assignable to type '"Ada"'.
```

Literal types are, however, allowed to be assigned to their corresponding primitive types. Any specific literal string is still a `string`.

In this code example, the value `":)"`, which is of type `":)"`, is being assigned to the `someString` variable previously inferred to be of type `string`:

```
someString = ":)";
```

Who would have thought a simple variable assignment would be so theoretically intense?

Strict Null Checking

The power of narrowed unions with literals is particularly visible when working with potentially undefined values, an area of type systems TypeScript refers to as *strict null checking*. TypeScript is part of a surge of modern programming languages that utilize strict null checking to fix the dreaded "billion-dollar mistake."

The Billion-Dollar Mistake

> I call it my billion-dollar mistake. It was the invention of the null reference in 1965… This has led to innumerable errors, vulnerabilities, and system crashes, which have probably caused a billion dollars of pain and damage in the last 40 years.
>
> —Tony Hoare, 2009

The "billion-dollar mistake" is a catchy industry term for many type systems allowing null values to be used in places that require a different type. In languages without strict null checking, code like this example that assign `null` to a `string` is allowed:

```
const firstName: string = null;
```

If you've previously worked in a typed language such as C++ or Java that suffers from the billion-dollar mistake, it may be surprising to you that some languages don't allow such a thing. If you've never worked in a language without strict null checking before, it may be surprising that some languages allowed the billion-dollar mistake in the first place!

The TypeScript compiler contains a multitude of options that allow changing how it runs. Chapter 13, "Configuration Options" will cover TypeScript compiler options in depth. One of the most useful opt-in options, `strictNullChecks`, toggles whether strict null checking is enabled. Roughly speaking, disabling `strictNullChecks` adds `| null | undefined` to every type in your code, thereby allowing any variable to receive `null` or `undefined`.

With the `strictNullChecks` option set to `false`, the following code is considered totally type safe. That's wrong, though; `nameMaybe` might be `undefined` when `.toLowerCase` is accessed from it:

```
let nameMaybe = Math.random() > 0.5
    ? "Tony Hoare"
    : undefined;

nameMaybe.toLowerCase();
// Potential runtime error: Cannot read property 'toLowerCase' of undefined.
```

With strict null checking enabled, TypeScript sees the potential crash in the code snippet:

```
let nameMaybe = Math.random() > 0.5
    ? "Tony Hoare"
    : undefined;

nameMaybe.toLowerCase();
// Error: Object is possibly 'undefined'.
```

Without strict null checking enabled, it's much harder to know whether your code is safe from errors due to accidentally null or undefined values.

TypeScript best practice is generally to enable strict null checking. Doing so helps prevent crashes and eliminates the billion-dollar mistake.

Truthiness Narrowing

Recall from JavaScript that *truthiness*, or being *truthy*, is whether a value would be considered true when evaluated in a Boolean context, such as an && operator or if statement. All values in JavaScript are truthy except for those defined as *falsy*: false, 0, -0, 0n, "", null, undefined, and NaN.[1]

TypeScript can also narrow a variable's type from a truthiness check if only some of its potential values may be truthy. In the following snippet, geneticist is of type string | undefined, and because undefined is always falsy, TypeScript can deduce that it must be of type string within the if statement's body:

```
let geneticist = Math.random() > 0.5
    ? "Barbara McClintock"
    : undefined;

if (geneticist) {
    geneticist.toUpperCase(); // Ok: string
}

geneticist.toUpperCase();
// Error: Object is possibly 'undefined'.
```

Logical operators that perform truthiness checking work as well, namely && and ?.:

```
geneticist && geneticist.toUpperCase(); // Ok: string | undefined
geneticist?.toUpperCase(); // Ok: string | undefined
```

---

1 The deprecated document.all object in browsers is also defined as falsy in an old quirk of legacy browser compatibility. For the purposes of this book—and your own happiness as a developer—don't worry about document.all.

Unfortunately, truthiness checking doesn't go the other way. If all we know about a string | undefined value is that it's falsy, that doesn't tell us whether it's an empty string or undefined.

Here, biologist is of type false | string, and while it can be narrowed down to just string in the if statement body, the else statement body knows it can still be a string if it's "":

```
let biologist = Math.random() > 0.5 && "Rachel Carson";

if (biologist) {
    biologist; // Type: string
} else {
    biologist; // Type: false | string
}
```

Variables Without Initial Values

Variables declared without an initial value default to undefined in JavaScript. That presents an edge case in the type system: what if you declare a variable to be a type that doesn't include undefined, then try to use it before assigning a value?

TypeScript is smart enough to understand that the variable is undefined until a value is assigned. It will report a specialized error message if you try to use that variable, such as by accessing one of its properties, before assigning a value:

```
let mathematician: string;

mathematician?.length;
// Error: Variable 'mathematician' is used before being assigned.

mathematician = "Mark Goldberg";
mathematician.length; // Ok
```

Note that this reporting doesn't apply if the variable's type includes undefined. Adding | undefined to a variable's type indicates to TypeScript that it doesn't need to be defined before use, as undefined is a valid type for its value.

The previous code snippet wouldn't emit any errors if the type of mathematician is string | undefined:

```
let mathematician: string | undefined;

mathematician?.length; // Ok

mathematician = "Mark Goldberg";
mathematician.length; // Ok
```

Type Aliases

Most union types you'll see in code will generally only have two or three constituents. However, you may sometimes find a use for longer union types that are inconvenient to type out repeatedly.

Each of these variables can be one of five possible types:

```
let rawDataFirst: boolean | number | string | null | undefined;
let rawDataSecond: boolean | number | string | null | undefined;
let rawDataThird: boolean | number | string | null | undefined;
```

TypeScript includes *type aliases* for assigning easier names to reused types. A type alias starts with the `type` keyword, a new name, =, and then any type. By convention, type aliases are given names in PascalCase:

```
type MyName = ...;
```

Type aliases act as a copy-and-paste in the type system. When TypeScript sees a type alias, it acts as if you'd typed out the actual type the alias was referring to. The previous variables' type annotations could be rewritten to use a type alias for the long union type:

```
type RawData = boolean | number | string | null | undefined;

let rawDataFirst: RawData;
let rawDataSecond: RawData;
let rawDataThird: RawData;
```

That's a lot easier to read!

Type aliases are a handy feature to use in TypeScript whenever your types start getting complex. For now, that just includes long union types; later on it will include array, function, and object types.

Type Aliases Are Not JavaScript

Type aliases, like type annotations, are not compiled to the output JavaScript. They exist purely in the TypeScript type system.

The previous code snippet would compile to roughly this JavaScript:

```
let rawDataFirst;
let rawDataSecond;
let rawDataThird;
```

Because type aliases are purely in the type system, you cannot reference them in runtime code. TypeScript will let you know with a type error if you are trying to access something that won't exist at runtime:

```
type SomeType = string | undefined;

console.log(SomeType);
//          ~~~~~~~~
// Error: 'SomeType' only refers to a type, but is being used as a value here.
```

Type aliases exist purely as a development-time construct.

Combining Type Aliases

Type aliases may reference other type aliases. It can sometimes be useful to have type aliases refer to each other, such as when one type alias is a union of types that includes (is a superset of) the union types within another type alias.

This `IdMaybe` type is a union of the types within `Id` as well as `undefined` and `null`:

```
type Id = number | string;

// Equivalent to: number | string | undefined | null
type IdMaybe = Id | undefined | null;
```

Type aliases don't have to be declared in order of usage. You can have a type alias declared earlier in a file reference an alias declared later in the file.

The previous code snippet could be rewritten to have `IdMaybe` come before `Id`:

```
type IdMaybe = Id | undefined | null; // Ok
type Id = number | string;
```

Summary

In this chapter, you went over union and literal types in TypeScript, along with how its type system can deduce more specific (narrower) types from how our code is structured:

- How union types represent values that could be one of two or more types
- Explicitly indicating union types with type annotations
- How type narrowing reduces the possible types of a value
- The difference between `const` variables with literal types and `let` variables with primitive types
- The "billion-dollar mistake" and how TypeScript handles strict null checking
- Using explicit | `undefined` to represent values that might not exist
- Implicit | `undefined` for unassigned variables
- Using type aliases to save typing long type unions repeatedly

Now that you've finished reading this chapter, practice what you've learned on *https://learningtypescript.com/unions-and-literals*.

Why are const variables so serious?
They take themselves too literally.

CHAPTER 4

Objects

Object literals
A set of keys and values
Each with their own type

Chapter 3, "Unions and Literals" fleshed out union and literal types: working with primitives such as `boolean` and literal values of them such as `true`. Those primitives only scratch the surface of the complex object shapes JavaScript code commonly uses. TypeScript would be pretty unusable if it weren't able to represent those objects. This chapter will cover how to describe complex object shapes and how TypeScript checks their assignability.

Object Types

When you create an object literal with `{...}` syntax, TypeScript will consider it to be a new object type, or type shape, based on its properties. That object type will have the same property names and primitive types as the object's values. Accessing properties of the value can be done with either `value.member` or the equivalent `value['member']` syntax.

TypeScript understands that the following `poet` variable's type is that of an object with two properties: `born`, of type `number`, and `name`, of type `string`. Accessing those members would be allowed, but attempting to access any other member name would cause a type error for that name not existing:

```
const poet = {
    born: 1935,
    name: "Mary Oliver",
};

poet['born']; // Type: number
poet.name; // Type: string

poet.end;
//    ~~~
// Error: Property 'end' does not exist on
// type '{ born: number; name: string; }'.
```

Object types are a core concept for how TypeScript understands JavaScript code. Every value other than null and undefined has a set of members in its backing type shape, and so TypeScript must understand the object type for every value in order to type check it.

Declaring Object Types

Inferring types directly from existing objects is all fine and good, but eventually you'll want to be able to declare the type of an object explicitly. You'll need a way to describe an object shape separately from objects that satisfy it.

Object types may be described using a syntax that looks similar to object literals but with types instead of values for fields. It's the same syntax that TypeScript shows in error messages about type assignability.

This poetLater variable is the same type from before with name: string and born: number:

```
let poetLater: {
    born: number;
    name: string;
};

// Ok
poetLater = {
    born: 1935,
    name: "Mary Oliver",
};

poetLater = "Sappho";
// Error: Type 'string' is not assignable to
// type '{ born: number; name: string; }'
```

Aliased Object Types

Constantly writing out object types like { born: number; name: string; } would get tiresome rather quickly. It's more common to use type aliases to assign each type shape a name.

The previous code snippet could be rewritten with a type Poet, which comes with the added benefit of making TypeScript's assignability error message a little more direct and readable:

```
type Poet = {
    born: number;
    name: string;
};

let poetLater: Poet;

// Ok
poetLater = {
    born: 1935,
    name: "Sara Teasdale",
};

poetLater = "Emily Dickinson";
// Error: Type 'string' is not assignable to type 'Poet'.
```

Most TypeScript projects prefer using the interface keyword to describe object types, which is a feature I won't cover until Chapter 7, "Interfaces". Aliased object types and interfaces are almost identical: everything in this chapter applies to interfaces as well.

I bring these object types up now because understanding how TypeScript interprets object literals is an important part of learning about TypeScript's type system. These concepts will continue to be important once we switch over to features in the next section of this book.

Structural Typing

TypeScript's type system is *structurally typed*: meaning any value that happens to satisfy a type is allowed to be used as a value of that type. In other words, when you declare that a parameter or variable is of a particular object type, you're telling TypeScript that whatever object(s) you use, they need to have those properties.

The following `WithFirstName` and `WithLastName` aliased object types both only declare a single member of type `string`. The `hasBoth` variable just so happens to have both of them—even though it wasn't declared as such explicitly—so it can be provided to variables that are declared as either of the two aliased object types:

```
type WithFirstName = {
  firstName: string;
};

type WithLastName = {
  lastName: string;
};

const hasBoth = {
  firstName: "Lucille",
  lastName: "Clifton",
};

// Ok: `hasBoth` contains a `firstName` property of type `string`
let withFirstName: WithFirstName = hasBoth;

// Ok: `hasBoth` contains a `lastName` property of type `string`
let withLastName: WithLastName = hasBoth;
```

Structural typing is not the same as *duck typing*, which comes from the phrase "If it looks like a duck and quacks like a duck, it's probably a duck."

- Structural typing is when there is a static system checking the type—in Type-Script's case, the type checker.
- Duck typing is when nothing checks object types until they're used at runtime.

In summary: *JavaScript* is *duck typed* whereas *TypeScript* is *structurally typed*.

Usage Checking

When providing a value to a location annotated with an object type, TypeScript will check that the value is assignable to that object type. To start, the value must have the object type's required properties. If any member required on the object type is missing in the object, TypeScript will issue a type error.

The following `FirstAndLastNames` aliased object type requires that both the `first` and `last` properties exist. An object containing both of those is allowed to be used in a variable declared to be of type `FirstAndLastNames`, but an object without them is not:

```
type FirstAndLastNames = {
  first: string;
  last: string;
};
```

```
// Ok
const hasBoth: FirstAndLastNames = {
  first: "Sarojini",
  last: "Naidu",
};

const hasOnlyOne: FirstAndLastNames = {
  first: "Sappho"
};
// Property 'last' is missing in type '{ first: string; }'
// but required in type 'FirstAndLastNames'.
```

Mismatched types between the two are not allowed either. Object types specify both the names of required properties and the types those properties are expected to be. If an object's property doesn't match, TypeScript will report a type error.

The following `TimeRange` type expects the `start` member to be of type `Date`. The `hasStartString` object is causing a type error because its `start` is type `string` instead:

```
type TimeRange = {
  start: Date;
};

const hasStartString: TimeRange = {
  start: "1879-02-13",
  // Error: Type 'string' is not assignable to type 'Date'.
};
```

Excess Property Checking

TypeScript will report a type error if a variable is declared with an object type and its initial value has more fields than its type describes. Therefore, declaring a variable to be of an object type is a way of getting the type checker to make sure it has only the expected fields on that type.

The following `poetMatch` variable has exactly the fields described in the object type aliased by `Poet`, while `extraProperty` causes a type error for having an extra property:

```
type Poet = {
    born: number;
    name: string;
}

// Ok: all fields match what's expected in Poet
const poetMatch: Poet = {
  born: 1928,
  name: "Maya Angelou"
};
```

```
const extraProperty: Poet = {
    activity: "walking",
    born: 1935,
    name: "Mary Oliver",
};
// Error: Type '{ activity: string; born: number; name: string; }'
// is not assignable to type 'Poet'.
//   Object literal may only specify known properties,
//   and 'activity' does not exist in type 'Poet'.
```

Note that excess property checks only trigger for object literals being created in locations that are declared to be an object type. Providing an existing object literal bypasses excess property checks.

This `extraPropertyButOk` variable does not trigger a type error with the previous example's `Poet` type because its initial value happens to structurally match `Poet`:

```
const existingObject = {
    activity: "walking",
    born: 1935,
    name: "Mary Oliver",
};

const extraPropertyButOk: Poet = existingObject; // Ok
```

Excess property checks will trigger anywhere a new object is being created in a location that expects it to match an object type—which as you'll see in later chapters includes array members, class fields, and function parameters. Banning excess properties is another way TypeScript helps make sure your code is clean and does what you expect. Excess properties not declared in their object types are often either mistyped property names or unused code.

Nested Object Types

As JavaScript objects can be nested as members of other objects, TypeScript's object types must be able to represent nested object types in the type system. The syntax to do so is the same as before but with a { ... } object type instead of a primitive name.

`Poem` type is declared to be an object whose `author` property has `firstName: string` and `lastName: string`. The `poemMatch` variable is assignable to `Poem` because it matches that structure, while `poemMismatch` is not because its `author` property includes `name` instead of `firstName` and `lastName`:

```
type Poem = {
    author: {
        firstName: string;
        lastName: string;
    };
```

```
    name: string;
};

// Ok
const poemMatch: Poem = {
    author: {
        firstName: "Sylvia",
        lastName: "Plath",
    },
    name: "Lady Lazarus",
};

const poemMismatch: Poem = {
    author: {
        name: "Sylvia Plath",
    },
    // Error: Type '{ name: string; }' is not assignable
    // to type '{ firstName: string; lastName: string; }'.
    //   Object literal may only specify known properties, and 'name'
    //   does not exist in type '{ firstName: string; lastName: string; }'.
    name: "Tulips",
};
```

Another way of writing the type Poem would be to extract out the author property's shape into its own aliased object type, Author. Extracting out nested types into their own type aliases also helps TypeScript give more informative type error messages. In this case, it can say 'Author' instead of '{ firstName: string; lastName: string; }':

```
type Author = {
    firstName: string;
    lastName: string;
};

type Poem = {
    author: Author;
    name: string;
};

const poemMismatch: Poem = {
    author: {
        name: "Sylvia Plath",
    },
    // Error: Type '{ name: string; }' is not assignable to type 'Author'.
    //     Object literal may only specify known properties,
    //     and 'name' does not exist in type 'Author'.
    name: "Tulips",
};
```

It is generally a good idea to move nested object types into their own type name like this, both for more readable code and for more readable TypeScript error messages.

You'll see in later chapters how object type members can be other types such as arrays and functions.

Optional Properties

Object type properties don't all have to be required in the object. You can include a ? before the : in a type property's type annotation to indicate that it's an optional property.

This Book type requires only a pages property and optionally allows an author. Objects adhering to it may provide author or leave it out as long as they provide pages:

```
type Book = {
  author?: string;
  pages: number;
};

// Ok
const ok: Book = {
    author: "Rita Dove",
    pages: 80,
};

const missing: Book = {
    author: "Rita Dove",
};
// Error: Property 'pages' is missing in type
// '{ author: string; }' but required in type 'Book'.
```

Keep in mind there is a difference between optional properties and properties whose type happens to include undefined in a type union. A property declared as optional with ? is allowed to not exist. A property declared as required and | undefined must exist, even if the value is undefined.

The editor property in the following Writers type may be skipped in declaring variables because it has a ? in its declaration. The author property does not have a ?, so it must exist, even if its value is just undefined:

```
type Writers = {
  author: string | undefined;
  editor?: string;
};
```

```
// Ok: author is provided as undefined
const hasRequired: Writers = {
  author: undefined,
};

const missingRequired: Writers = {};
//    ~~~~~~~~~~~~~~~~
// Error: Property 'author' is missing in type
// '{}' but required in type 'Writers'.
```

Chapter 7, "Interfaces" will cover more on other kinds of properties, while Chapter 13, "Configuration Options" will describe TypeScript's strictness settings around optional properties.

Unions of Object Types

It is reasonable in TypeScript code to want to be able to describe a type that can be one or more different object types that have slightly different properties. Furthermore, your code might want to be able to type narrow between those object types based on the value of a property.

Inferred Object-Type Unions

If a variable is given an initial value that could be one of multiple object types, TypeScript will infer its type to be a union of object types. That union type will have a constituent for each of the possible object shapes. Each of the possible properties on the type will be present in each of those constituents, though they'll be ? optional types on any type that doesn't have an initial value for them.

This poem value always has a name property of type string, and may or may not have pages and rhymes properties:

```
const poem = Math.random() > 0.5
  ? { name: "The Double Image", pages: 7 }
  : { name: "Her Kind", rhymes: true };
// Type:
// {
//    name: string;
//    pages: number;
//    rhymes?: undefined;
// }
// |
// {
//    name: string;
//    pages?: undefined;
//    rhymes: boolean;
// }

poem.name; // string
```

```
poem.pages; // number | undefined
poem.rhymes; // boolean | undefined
```

Explicit Object-Type Unions

Alternately, you can be more explicit about your object types by being explicit with your own union of object types. Doing so requires writing a bit more code but comes with the advantage of giving you more control over your object types. Most notably, if a value's type is a union of object types, TypeScript's type system will only allow access to properties that exist on all of those union types.

This version of the previous poem variable is explicitly typed to be a union type that always has the name property along with either pages or rhymes. Accessing name is allowed because it always exists, but pages and rhymes aren't guaranteed to exist:

```
type PoemWithPages = {
    name: string;
    pages: number;
};

type PoemWithRhymes = {
    name: string;
    rhymes: boolean;
};

type Poem = PoemWithPages | PoemWithRhymes;

const poem: Poem = Math.random() > 0.5
  ? { name: "The Double Image", pages: 7 }
  : { name: "Her Kind", rhymes: true };

poem.name; // Ok

poem.pages;
//    ~~~~~
// Property 'pages' does not exist on type 'Poem'.
//    Property 'pages' does not exist on type 'PoemWithRhymes'.

poem.rhymes;
//    ~~~~~~
// Property 'rhymes' does not exist on type 'Poem'.
//    Property 'rhymes' does not exist on type 'PoemWithPages'.
```

Restricting access to potentially nonexistent members of objects can be a good thing for code safety. If a value might be one of multiple types, properties that don't exist on all of those types aren't guaranteed to exist on the object.

Just as how unions of literal and/or primitive types must be type narrowed to access properties that don't exist on all type constituents, you'll need to narrow those object type unions.

Narrowing Object Types

If the type checker sees that an area of code can only be run if a union typed value contains a certain property, it will narrow the value's type to only the constituents that contain that property. In other words, TypeScript's type narrowing will apply to objects if you check their shape in code.

Continuing the explicitly typed `poem` example, check whether `"pages" in poem` acts as a type guard for TypeScript to indicate that it is a `PoemWithPages`. If `poem` is not a `PoemWithPages`, then it must be a `PoemWithRhymes`:

```
if ("pages" in poem) {
    poem.pages; // Ok: poem is narrowed to PoemWithPages
} else {
    poem.rhymes; // Ok: poem is narrowed to PoemWithRhymes
}
```

Note that TypeScript won't allow truthiness existence checks like `if (poem.pages)`. Attempting to access a property of an object that might not exist is considered a type error, even if used in a way that seems to behave like a type guard:

```
if (poem.pages) { /* ... */ }
//       ~~~~~
// Property 'pages' does not exist on type 'Poem'.
//   Property 'pages' does not exist on type 'PoemWithRhymes'.
```

Discriminated Unions

Another popular form of union typed objects in JavaScript and TypeScript is to have a property on the object indicate what shape the object is. This kind of type shape is called a *discriminated union*, and the property whose value indicates the object's type is a *discriminant*. TypeScript is able to perform type narrowing for code that type guards on discriminant properties.

For example, this `Poem` type describes an object that can be either a new `PoemWithPages` type or a new `PoemWithRhymes` type, and the `type` property indicates which one. If `poem.type` is `"pages"`, then TypeScript is able to infer that the type of `poem` must be `PoemWithPages`. Without that type narrowing, neither property is guaranteed to exist on the value:

```
type PoemWithPages = {
    name: string;
    pages: number;
    type: 'pages';
};

type PoemWithRhymes = {
    name: string;
    rhymes: boolean;
    type: 'rhymes';
};

type Poem = PoemWithPages | PoemWithRhymes;

const poem: Poem = Math.random() > 0.5
  ? { name: "The Double Image", pages: 7, type: "pages" }
  : { name: "Her Kind", rhymes: true, type: "rhymes" };

if (poem.type === "pages") {
    console.log(`It's got pages: ${poem.pages}`); // Ok
} else {
    console.log(`It rhymes: ${poem.rhymes}`);
}

poem.type; // Type: 'pages' | 'rhymes'

poem.pages;
//   ~~~~~
// Error: Property 'pages' does not exist on type 'Poem'.
//   Property 'pages' does not exist on type 'PoemWithRhymes'.
```

Discriminated unions are my favorite feature in TypeScript because they beautifully combine a common elegant JavaScript pattern with TypeScript's type narrowing. Chapter 10, "Generics" and its associated projects will show more around using discriminated unions for generic data operations.

Intersection Types

TypeScript's | union types represent the type of a value that could be one of two or more different types. Just as JavaScript's runtime | operator acts as a counterpart to its & operator, TypeScript allows representing a type that is multiple types at the same time: an & *intersection type*. Intersection types are typically used with aliased object types to create a new type that combines multiple existing object types.

The following Artwork and Writing types are used to form a combined WrittenArt type that has the properties genre, name, and pages:

```
type Artwork = {
    genre: string;
    name: string;
};

type Writing = {
    pages: number;
    name: string;
};

type WrittenArt = Artwork & Writing;
// Equivalent to:
// {
//   genre: string;
//   name: string;
//   pages: number;
// }
```

Intersection types can be combined with union types, which is sometimes useful to describe discriminated unions in one type.

This `ShortPoem` type always has an `author` property, then is also a discriminated union on a `type` property:

```
type ShortPoem = { author: string } & (
    | { kigo: string; type: "haiku"; }
    | { meter: number; type: "villanelle"; }
);

// Ok
const morningGlory: ShortPoem = {
    author: "Fukuda Chiyo-ni",
    kigo: "Morning Glory",
    type: "haiku",
};

const oneArt: ShortPoem = {
    author: "Elizabeth Bishop",
    type: "villanelle",
};
// Error: Type '{ author: string; type: "villanelle"; }'
// is not assignable to type 'ShortPoem'.
//   Type '{ author: string; type: "villanelle"; }' is not assignable to
//   type '{ author: string; } & { meter: number; type: "villanelle"; }'.
//     Property 'meter' is missing in type '{ author: string; type: "villanelle"; }'
//     but required in type '{ meter: number; type: "villanelle"; }'.
```

Dangers of Intersection Types

Intersection types are a useful concept, but it's easy to use them in ways that confuse either yourself or the TypeScript compiler. I recommend trying to keep code as simple as possible when using them.

Long assignability errors

Assignability error messages from TypeScript get much harder to read when you create complex intersection types, such as one combined with a union type. This will be a common theme with TypeScript's type system (and typed programming languages in general): the more complex you get, the harder it will be to understand messages from the type checker.

In the case of the previous code snippet's `ShortPoem`, it would be much more readable to split the type into a series of aliased object types to allow TypeScript to print those names:

```
type ShortPoemBase = { author: string };
type Haiku = ShortPoemBase & { kigo: string; type: "haiku" };
type Villanelle = ShortPoemBase & { meter: number; type: "villanelle" };
type ShortPoem = Haiku | Villanelle;

const oneArt: ShortPoem = {
    author: "Elizabeth Bishop",
    type: "villanelle",
};
// Type '{ author: string; type: "villanelle"; }'
// is not assignable to type 'ShortPoem'.
//   Type '{ author: string; type: "villanelle"; }'
//   is not assignable to type 'Villanelle'.
//     Property 'meter' is missing in type
//     '{ author: string; type: "villanelle"; }'
//     but required in type '{ meter: number; type: "villanelle"; }'.
```

never

Intersection types are also easy to misuse and create an impossible type with. Primitive types cannot be joined together as constituents in an intersection type because it's impossible for a value to be multiple primitives at the same time. Trying to & two primitive types together will result in the *never* type, represented by the keyword `never`:

```
type NotPossible = number & string;
// Type: never
```

The never keyword and type is what programming languages refer to as a *bottom type*, or empty type. A bottom type is one that can have no possible values and can't be reached. No types can be provided to a location whose type is a bottom type:

```
let notNumber: NotPossible = 0;
//  ~~~~~~~~~
// Error: Type 'number' is not assignable to type 'never'.

let notString: never = "";
//  ~~~~~~~~~
// Error: Type 'string' is not assignable to type 'never'.
```

Most TypeScript projects rarely—if ever—use the never type. It comes up once in a while to represent impossible states in code. Most of the time, though, it's likely to be a mistake from misusing intersection types. I'll cover it more in Chapter 15, "Type Operations".

Summary

In this chapter, you expanded your grasp of the TypeScript type system to be able to work with objects:

- How TypeScript interprets types from object type literals
- Describing object literal types, including nested and optional properties
- Declaring, inferring, and type narrowing with unions of object literal types
- Discriminated unions and discriminants
- Combining object types together with intersection types

 Now that you've finished reading this chapter, practice what you've learned on *https://learningtypescript.com/objects*.

How does a lawyer declare their TypeScript type?
"I object!"

PART II

Features

CHAPTER 5

Functions

Function arguments
In one end, out the other
As a return type

In Chapter 2, "The Type System", you saw how to use type annotations to annotate values of variables. Now, you'll see how to do the same with function parameters and return types—and why that can be useful.

Function Parameters

Take the following `sing` function that takes in a `song` parameter and logs it:

```
function sing(song) {
  console.log(`Singing: ${song}!`);
}
```

What value type did the developer who wrote the `sing` function intend for the `song` parameter to be provided with?

Is it a `string`? Is it an object with an overridden `toString()` method? Is this code buggy? *Who knows?!*

Without explicit type information declared, we may never know—TypeScript will consider it to be the `any` type, meaning the parameter's type could be anything.

As with variables, TypeScript allows you to declare the type of function parameters with a type annotation. Now we can use a `: string` to tell TypeScript that the `song` parameter is of type `string`:

```
function sing(song: string) {
  console.log(`Singing: ${song}!`);
}
```

Much better: now we know what type `song` is meant to be!

Note that you don't need to add proper type annotations to function parameters for your code to be valid TypeScript syntax. TypeScript might yell at you with type errors, but the emitted JavaScript will still run. The previous code snippet missing a type declaration on the song parameter will still convert from TypeScript to JavaScript. Chapter 13, "Configuration Options" will cover how to configure TypeScript's complaints about parameters that are implicitly of type any the way song is.

Required Parameters

Unlike JavaScript, which allows functions to be called with any number of arguments, TypeScript assumes that all parameters declared on a function are required. If a function is called with a wrong number of arguments, TypeScript will protest in the form of a type error. TypeScript's argument counting will come into play if a function is called with either too few or too many arguments.

This singTwo function requires two parameters, so passing one argument and passing three arguments are both not allowed:

```
function singTwo(first: string, second: string) {
  console.log(`${first} / ${second}`);
}

// Logs: "Ball and Chain / undefined"
singTwo("Ball and Chain");
//       ~~~~~~~~~~~~~~~~
// Error: Expected 2 arguments, but got 1.

// Logs: "I Will Survive / Higher Love"
singTwo("I Will Survive", "Higher Love"); // Ok

// Logs: "Go Your Own Way / The Chain"
singTwo("Go Your Own Way", "The Chain", "Dreams");
//                                       ~~~~~~~~
// Error: Expected 2 arguments, but got 3.
```

Enforcing that required parameters be provided to a function helps enforce type safety by making sure all expected argument values exist inside the function. Failing to ensure those values exist could result in unexpected behavior in code, such as the previous singTwo function logging undefined or ignoring an argument.

Parameter refers to a function's declaration of what it expects to receive as an argument. *Argument* refers to a value provided to a parameter in a function call. In the previous example, first and second are parameters, while strings such as "Dreams" are arguments.

Optional Parameters

Recall that in JavaScript, if a function parameter is not provided, its argument value inside the function defaults to `undefined`. Sometimes function parameters are not necessary to provide, and the intended use of the function is for that `undefined` value. We wouldn't want TypeScript to report type errors for failing to provide arguments to those optional parameters. TypeScript allows annotating a parameter as optional by adding a ? before the : in its type annotation—similar to optional object type properties.

Optional parameters don't need to be provided to function calls. Their types therefore always have | `undefined` added as a union type.

In the following `announceSong` function, the `singer` parameter is marked optional. Its type is `string | undefined`, and it doesn't need to be provided by callers of the function. If `singer` is provided, it may be a `string` value or `undefined`:

```
function announceSong(song: string, singer?: string) {
  console.log(`Song: ${song}`);

  if (singer) {
    console.log(`Singer: ${singer}`);
  }
}

announceSong("Greensleeves"); // Ok
announceSong("Greensleeves", undefined); // Ok
announceSong("Chandelier", "Sia"); // Ok
```

These optional parameters are always implicitly able to be `undefined`. In the previous code, `singer` starts off as being of type `string | undefined`, then is narrowed to just `string` by the `if` statement.

Optional parameters are not the same as parameters with union types that happen to include | `undefined`. Parameters that aren't marked as optional with a ? must always be provided, even if the value is explicitly `undefined`.

The `singer` parameter in this `announceSongBy` function must be provided explicitly. It may be a `string` value or `undefined`:

```
function announceSongBy(song: string, singer: string | undefined) { /* ... */ }

announceSongBy("Greensleeves");
// Error: Expected 2 arguments, but got 1.

announceSongBy("Greensleeves", undefined); // Ok
announceSongBy("Chandelier", "Sia"); // Ok
```

Any optional parameters for a function must be the last parameters. Placing an optional parameter before a required parameter would trigger a TypeScript syntax error:

```
function announceSinger(singer?: string, song: string) {}
//                                       ~~~~
// Error: A required parameter cannot follow an optional parameter.
```

Default Parameters

Optional parameters in JavaScript may be given a default value with an = and a value in their declaration. For these optional parameters, because a value is provided by default, their TypeScript type does not implicitly have the | `undefined` union added on inside the function. TypeScript will still allow the function to be called with missing or `undefined` arguments for those parameters.

TypeScript's type inference works similarly for default function parameter values as it does for initial variable values. If a parameter has a default value and doesn't have a type annotation, TypeScript will infer the parameter's type based on that default value.

In the following `rateSong` function, `rating` is inferred to be of type `number`, but is an optional `number` | `undefined` in the code that calls the function:

```
function rateSong(song: string, rating = 0) {
  console.log(`${song} gets ${rating}/5 stars!`);
}

rateSong("Photograph"); // Ok
rateSong("Set Fire to the Rain", 5); // Ok
rateSong("Set Fire to the Rain", undefined); // Ok

rateSong("At Last!", "100");
//                    ~~~~~
// Error: Argument of type '"100"' is not assignable
// to parameter of type 'number | undefined'.
```

Rest Parameters

Some functions in JavaScript are made to be called with any number of arguments. The ... spread operator may be placed on the last parameter in a function declaration to indicate any "rest" arguments passed to the function starting at that parameter should all be stored in a single array.

TypeScript allows declaring the types of these rest parameters similarly to regular parameters, except with a [] syntax added at the end to indicate it's an array of arguments.

Here, `singAllTheSongs` is allowed to take zero or more arguments of type `string` for its `songs` rest parameter:

```
function singAllTheSongs(singer: string, ...songs: string[]) {
  for (const song of songs) {
    console.log(`${song}, by ${singer}`);
  }
}

singAllTheSongs("Alicia Keys"); // Ok
singAllTheSongs("Lady Gaga", "Bad Romance", "Just Dance", "Poker Face"); // Ok

singAllTheSongs("Ella Fitzgerald", 2000);
//                                 ~~~~
// Error: Argument of type 'number' is not
// assignable to parameter of type 'string'.
```

I'll cover working with arrays in TypeScript in Chapter 6, "Arrays".

Return Types

TypeScript is perceptive: if it understands all the possible values returned by a function, it'll know what type the function returns. In this example, `singSongs` is understood by TypeScript to return a `number`:

```
// Type: (songs: string[]) => number
function singSongs(songs: string[]) {
  for (const song of songs) {
    console.log(`${song}`);
  }

  return songs.length;
}
```

If a function contains multiple `return` statements with different values, TypeScript will infer the return type to be a union of all the possible returned types.

This `getSongAt` function would be inferred to return `string | undefined` because its two possible returned values are typed `string` and `undefined`, respectively:

```
// Type: (songs: string[], index: number) => string | undefined
function getSongAt(songs: string[], index: number) {
  return index < songs.length
    ? songs[index]
    : undefined;
}
```

Explicit Return Types

As with variables, I generally recommend not bothering to explicitly declare the return types of functions with type annotations. However, there are a few cases where it can be useful specifically for functions:

- You might want to enforce functions with many possible returned values always return the same type of value.
- TypeScript will refuse to try to reason through return types of recursive function.
- It can speed up TypeScript type checking in very large projects—i.e., those with hundreds of TypeScript files or more.

Function declaration return type annotations are placed after the) following the list of parameters.

For a function declaration, that falls just before the {:

```
function singSongsRecursive(songs: string[], count = 0): number {
  return songs.length ? singSongsRecursive(songs.slice(1), count + 1) : count;
}
```

For arrow functions (also known as lambdas), that falls just before the =>:

```
const singSongsRecursive = (songs: string[], count = 0): number =>
  songs.length ? singSongsRecursive(songs.slice(1), count + 1) : count;
```

If a `return` statement in a function returns a value not assignable to the function's return type, TypeScript will give an assignability complaint.

Here, the `getSongRecordingDate` function is explicitly declared as returning `Date | undefined`, but one of its return statements incorrectly provides a `string`:

```
function getSongRecordingDate(song: string): Date | undefined {
  switch (song) {
    case "Strange Fruit":
      return new Date('April 20, 1939'); // Ok

    case "Greensleeves":
      return "unknown";
      // Error: Type 'string' is not assignable to type 'Date'.

    default:
      return undefined; // Ok
  }
}
```

Function Types

JavaScript allows us to pass functions around as values. That means we need a way to declare the type of a parameter or variable meant to hold a function.

Function type syntax looks similar to an arrow function, but with a type instead of the body.

This `nothingInGivesString` variable's type describes a function with no parameters and a returned `string` value:

```
let nothingInGivesString: () => string;
```

This `inputAndOutput` variable's type describes a function with a `string[]` parameter, an optional `count` parameter, and a returned `number` value:

```
let inputAndOutput: (songs: string[], count?: number) => number;
```

Function types are frequently used to describe callback parameters (parameters meant to be called as functions).

For example, the following `runOnSongs` snippet declares the type of its `getSongAt` parameter to be a function that takes in an `index: number` and returns a `string`. Passing `getSongAt` matches that type, but `logSong` fails for taking in a `string` as its parameter instead of a `number`:

```
const songs = ["Juice", "Shake It Off", "What's Up"];

function runOnSongs(getSongAt: (index: number) => string) {
  for (let i = 0; i < songs.length; i += 1) {
    console.log(getSongAt(i));
  }
}

function getSongAt(index: number) {
  return `${songs[index]}`;
}

runOnSongs(getSongAt); // Ok

function logSong(song: string) {
  return `${song}`;
}

runOnSongs(logSong);
//         ~~~~~~~
// Error: Argument of type '(song: string) => string' is not
// assignable to parameter of type '(index: number) => string'.
//    Types of parameters 'song' and 'index' are incompatible.
//      Type 'number' is not assignable to type 'string'.
```

The error message for `runOnSongs(logSong)` is an example of an assignability error that includes a few levels of details. When complaining that two function types aren't assignable to each other, TypeScript will typically give three levels of detail, with increasing levels of specificity:

1. The first indentation level prints out the two function types.
2. The next indentation level specifies which part is mismatched.
3. The last indentation level is the precise assignability complaint of the mismatched part.

In the previous code snippet, those levels are:

1. `logSong: (song: string) => string` is the provided type being assigned to the `getSongAt: (index: number) => string` recipient
2. The `song` parameter of `logSong` being assigned to the `index` parameter of `getSongAt`
3. `song`'s `string` type is not assignable to `index`'s `number` type

 TypeScript's multiline errors can seem daunting at first. Reading through them line-by-line and understanding what each part is conveying goes a long way to comprehending the error.

Function Type Parentheses

Function types may be placed anywhere that another type would be used. That includes union types.

In union types, parentheses may be used to indicate which part of an annotation is the function return or the surrounding union type:

```
// Type is a function that returns a union: string | undefined
let returnsStringOrUndefined: () => string | undefined;

// Type is either undefined or a function that returns a string
let maybeReturnsString: (() => string) | undefined;
```

Later chapters that introduce more type syntaxes will show other places where function types must be wrapped with parentheses.

Parameter Type Inferences

It would be cumbersome if we had to declare parameter types for every function we write, including inline functions used as parameters. Fortunately, TypeScript can infer the types of parameters in a function provided to a location with a declared type.

This `singer` variable is known to be a function that takes in a parameter of type `string`, so the `song` parameter in the function later assigned to `singer` is known to be a `string`:

```
let singer: (song: string) => string;

singer = function (song) {
  // Type of song: string
  return `Singing: ${song.toUpperCase()}!`; // Ok
};
```

Functions passed as arguments to parameters with function parameter types will have their parameter types inferred as well.

For example, the `song` and `index` parameters here are inferred by TypeScript to be `string` and `number`, respectively:

```
const songs = ["Call Me", "Jolene", "The Chain"];

// song: string
// index: number
songs.forEach((song, index) => {
  console.log(`${song} is at index ${index}`);
});
```

Function Type Aliases

Remember type aliases from Chapter 3, "Unions and Literals"? They can be used for function types as well.

This `StringToNumber` type aliases a function that takes in a `string` and returns a `number`, which means it can be used later to describe the types of variables:

```
type StringToNumber = (input: string) => number;

let stringToNumber: StringToNumber;

stringToNumber = (input) => input.length; // Ok

stringToNumber = (input) => input.toUpperCase();
//                          ~~~~~~~~~~~~~~~~~~~
// Error: Type 'string' is not assignable to type 'number'.
```

Similarly, function parameters can themselves be typed with aliases that happen to refer to a function type.

This `usesNumberToString` function has a single parameter which is itself the `Number ToString` aliased function type:

```
type NumberToString = (input: number) => string;

function usesNumberToString(numberToString: NumberToString) {
  console.log(`The string is: ${numberToString(1234)}`);
}

usesNumberToString((input) => `${input}! Hooray!`); // Ok

usesNumberToString((input) => input * 2);
//                            ~~~~~~~~~
// Error: Type 'number' is not assignable to type 'string'.
```

Type aliases are particularly useful for function types. They can save a lot of horizontal space in having to repeatedly write out parameters and/or return types.

More Return Types

Now, let's look at two more return types: `void` and `never`.

Void Returns

Some functions aren't meant to return any value. They either have no `return` statements or only have `return` statements that don't return a value. TypeScript allows using a `void` keyword to refer to the return type of such a function that returns nothing.

Functions whose return type is `void` may not return a value. This `logSong` function is declared as returning `void`, so it's not allowed to return a value:

```
function logSong(song: string | undefined): void {
  if (!song) {
    return; // Ok
  }

  console.log(`${song}`);

  return true;
  // Error: Type 'boolean' is not assignable to type 'void'.
}
```

`void` can be useful as the return type in a function type declaration. When used in a function type declaration, `void` indicates that any returned value from the function would be ignored.

For example, this `songLogger` variable represents a function that takes in a `song: string` and doesn't return a value:

```
let songLogger: (song: string) => void;

songLogger = (song) => {
  console.log(`${song}`);
};

songLogger("Heart of Glass"); // Ok
```

Note that although JavaScript functions all return `undefined` by default if no real value is returned, `void` is not the same as `undefined`. `void` means the return type of a function will be ignored, while `undefined` is a literal value to be returned. Trying to assign a value of type `void` to a value whose type instead includes `undefined` is a type error:

```
function returnsVoid() {
  return;
}

let lazyValue: string | undefined;

lazyValue = returnsVoid();
// Error: Type 'void' is not assignable to type 'string | undefined'.
```

The distinction between `undefined` and `void` returns is particularly useful for ignoring any returned value from a function passed to a location whose type is declared as returning `void`. For example, the built-in `forEach` method on arrays takes in a callback that returns `void`. Functions provided to `forEach` can return any value they want. `records.push(record)` in the following `saveRecords` function returns a number (the returned value from an array's `.push()`), yet is still allowed to be the returned value for the arrow function passed to `newRecords.forEach`:

```
const records: string[] = [];

function saveRecords(newRecords: string[]) {
  newRecords.forEach(record => records.push(record));
}

saveRecords(['21', 'Come On Over', 'The Bodyguard'])
```

The `void` type is not JavaScript. It's a TypeScript keyword used to declare return types of functions. Remember, it's an indication that a function's returned value isn't meant to be used, not a value that can itself be returned.

Never Returns

Some functions not only don't return a value, but aren't meant to return at all. Never-returning functions are those that always throw an error or run an infinite loop (hopefully intentionally!).

If a function is meant to never return, adding an explicit : `never` type annotation indicates that any code after a call to that function won't run. This `fail` function only ever throws an error, so it can help TypeScript's control flow analysis with type narrowing `param` to `string`:

```
function fail(message: string): never {
    throw new Error(`Invariant failure: ${message}.`);
}

function workWithUnsafeParam(param: unknown) {
    if (typeof param !== "string") {
        fail(`param should be a string, not ${typeof param}`);
    }

    // Here, param is known to be type string
    param.toUpperCase(); // Ok
}
```

> `never` is not the same as `void`. `void` is for a function that returns nothing. `never` is for a function that never returns.

Function Overloads

Some JavaScript functions are able to be called with drastically different sets of parameters that can't be represented just by optional and/or rest parameters. These functions can be described with a TypeScript syntax called *overload signatures*: declaring different versions of the function's name, parameters, and return types multiple times before one final *implementation signature* and the body of the function.

When determining whether to emit a syntax error for a call to an overloaded function, TypeScript will only look at the function's overload signatures. The implementation signature is only used by the function's internal logic.

This `createDate` function is meant to be called either with one `timestamp` parameter or with three parameters—`month`, `day`, and `year`. Calling with either of those numbers of arguments is allowed, but calling with two arguments would cause a type error because no overload signature allows for two arguments. In this example, the first two lines are the overload signatures, and the third line is the implementation signature:

```typescript
function createDate(timestamp: number): Date;
function createDate(month: number, day: number, year: number): Date;
function createDate(monthOrTimestamp: number, day?: number, year?: number) {
  return day === undefined || year === undefined
    ? new Date(monthOrTimestamp)
    : new Date(year, monthOrTimestamp, day);
}

createDate(554356800); // Ok
createDate(7, 27, 1987); // Ok

createDate(4, 1);
// Error: No overload expects 2 arguments, but overloads
// do exist that expect either 1 or 3 arguments.
```

Overload signatures, as with other type system syntaxes, are erased when compiling TypeScript to output JavaScript.

The previous code snippet's function would compile to roughly the following JavaScript:

```javascript
function createDate(monthOrTimestamp, day, year) {
  return day === undefined || year === undefined
    ? new Date(monthOrTimestamp)
    : new Date(year, monthOrTimestamp, day);
}
```

 Function overloads are generally used as a last resort for complex, difficult-to-describe function types. It's generally better to keep functions simple and avoid using function overloads when possible.

Call-Signature Compatibility

The implementation signature used for an overloaded function's implementation is what the function's implementation uses for parameter types and return type. Thus, each parameter in a function's overload signatures must be assignable to the parameter at the same index in its implementation signature. The overload signature's return type must also be assignable to the implementation signature's return type. In other words, the implementation signature has to be compatible with all of the overload signatures.

This `format` function's implementation signature declares its first parameter to be a `string`. While the first two overload signatures are compatible for also being type `string`, the third overload signature's `() => string` type is not compatible:

```
function format(data: string): string; // Ok
function format(data: string, needle: string, haystack: string): string; // Ok

function format(getData: () => string): string;
//              ~~~~~~~
// This overload signature is not compatible with its implementation signature.

function format(data: string, needle?: string, haystack?: string) {
  return needle && haystack ? data.replace(needle, haystack) : data;
}
```

Summary

In this chapter, you saw how a function's parameters and return types can be inferred or explicitly declared in TypeScript:

- Declaring function parameter types with type annotations
- Declaring optional parameters, default values, and rest parameters to change type system behavior
- Declaring function return types with type annotations
- Describing functions that don't return a usable value with the void type
- Describing functions that don't return at all with the never type
- Declaring function types in type annotations
- Using function overloads to describe varying function call signatures

 Now that you've finished reading this chapter, practice what you've learned on *https://learningtypescript.com/functions*.

What makes a TypeScript project good?
It functions well.

CHAPTER 6

Arrays

Arrays and tuples
One flexible and one fixed
Choose your adventure

JavaScript arrays are wildly flexible and can hold any mixture of values inside:

```
const elements = [true, null, undefined, 42];

elements.push("even", ["more"]);
// Value of elements: [true, null, undefined, 42, "even", ["more"]]
```

In most cases, though, individual JavaScript arrays are intended to hold only one specific type of value. Adding values of a different type may be confusing to readers, or worse, the result of an error that could cause problems in the program.

TypeScript respects the best practice of keeping to one data type per array by remembering what type of data is initially inside an array, and only allowing the array to operate on that kind of data.

In this example, TypeScript knows the `warriors` array initially contains `string` typed values, so while adding more `string` typed values is allowed, adding any other type of data is not:

```
const warriors = ["Artemisia", "Boudica"];

// Ok: "Zenobia" is a string
warriors.push("Zenobia");

warriors.push(true);
//            ~~~~
// Argument of type 'boolean' is not assignable to parameter of type 'string'.
```

You can think of TypeScript's inference of an array's type from its initial members as similar to how it understands variable types from their initial values. TypeScript generally tries to understand the intended types of your code from how values are assigned, and arrays are no exception.

Array Types

As with other variable declarations, variables meant to store arrays don't need to have an initial value. The variables can start off `undefined` and receive an array value later.

TypeScript will want you to let it know what types of values are meant to go in the array by giving the variable a type annotation. The type annotation for an array requires the type of elements in the array followed by a [ ]:

```
let arrayOfNumbers: number[];

arrayOfNumbers = [4, 8, 15, 16, 23, 42];
```

 Array types can also be written in a syntax like `Array<number>` called *class generics*. Most developers prefer the simpler `number[]`. Classes are covered in Chapter 8, "Classes", and generics are covered in Chapter 10, "Generics".

Array and Function Types

Array types are an example of a syntax container where function types may need parentheses to distinguish what's in the function type or not. Parentheses may be used to indicate which part of an annotation is the function return or the surrounding array type.

The `createStrings` type here, which is a function type, is not the same as `stringCreators`, which is an array type:

```
// Type is a function that returns an array of strings
let createStrings: () => string[];

// Type is an array of functions that each return a string
let stringCreators: (() => string)[];
```

Union-Type Arrays

You can use a union type to indicate that each element of an array can be one of multiple select types.

When using array types with unions, parentheses may need to be used to indicate which part of an annotation is the contents of the array or the surrounding union type. Using parentheses in array union types is important—the following two types are not the same:

```
// Type is either a string or an array of numbers
let stringOrArrayOfNumbers: string | number[];

// Type is an array of elements that are each either a number or a string
let arrayOfStringOrNumbers: (string | number)[];
```

TypeScript will understand from an array's declaration that it is a union-type array if it contains more than one type of element. In other words, the type of an array's elements is the union of all possible types for elements in the array.

Here, namesMaybe is (string | undefined)[] because it has both string values and an undefined value:

```
// Type is (string | undefined)[]
const namesMaybe = [
  "Aqualtune",
  "Blenda",
  undefined,
];
```

Evolving Any Arrays

If you don't include a type annotation on a variable initially set to an empty array, TypeScript will treat the array as evolving any[], meaning it can receive any content. As with evolving any variables, we don't like evolving any[] arrays. They partially negate the benefits of TypeScript's type checker by allowing you to add potentially incorrect values.

This values array starts off containing any elements, evolves to contain string elements, then again evolves to include number | string elements:

```
// Type: any[]
let values = [];

// Type: string[]
values.push('');

// Type: (number | string)[]
values[0] = 0;
```

As with variables, allowing arrays to be evolving any typed—and using the any type in general—partially defeats the purpose of TypeScript's type checking. TypeScript works best when it knows what types your values are meant to be.

Multidimensional Arrays

A 2D array, or an array of arrays, will have two "[]"s:

```
let arrayOfArraysOfNumbers: number[][];

arrayOfArraysOfNumbers = [
  [1, 2, 3],
  [2, 4, 6],
  [3, 6, 9],
];
```

A 3D array, or an array of arrays of arrays, will have three "[]"s. 4D arrays have four "[]"s. 5D arrays have five "[]"s. You can guess where this is going for 6D arrays and beyond.

These multidimensional array types don't introduce any new concepts to array types. Think of a 2D array as taking in the original type, which just so happens to have [ ] at the end, and adding a [ ] after it.

This `arrayOfArraysOfNumbers` array is of type `number[][]`, which is also representable by `(number[])[]`:

```
// Type: number[][]
let arrayOfArraysOfNumbers: (number[])[];
```

Array Members

TypeScript understands typical index-based access for retrieving members of an array to give back an element of that array's type.

This `defenders` array is of type `string[]`, so `defender` is a `string`:

```
const defenders = ["Clarenza", "Dina"];

// Type: string
const defender = defenders[0];
```

Members of union typed arrays are themselves that same union type.

Here, `soldiersOrDates` is of type `(string | Date)[]`, so the `soldierOrDate` variable is of type `string | Date`:

```
const soldiersOrDates = ["Deborah Sampson", new Date(1782, 6, 3)];

// Type: Date | string
const soldierOrDate = soldiersOrDates[0];
```

Caveat: Unsound Members

The TypeScript type system is known to be technically *unsound*: it can get types mostly right, but sometimes its understanding about the types of values may be incorrect. Arrays in particular are a source of unsoundness in the type system. By default, TypeScript assumes all array member accesses return a member of that array, even though in JavaScript, accessing an array element with an index greater than the array's length gives `undefined`.

This code gives no complaints with the default TypeScript compiler settings:

```
function withElements(elements: string[]) {
  console.log(elements[9001].length); // No type error
}

withElements(["It's", "over"]);
```

We as readers can deduce that it'll crash at runtime with "`Cannot read property 'length' of undefined`", but TypeScript intentionally does not make sure retrieved array members exist. It sees `elements[9001]` in the code snippet as being type `string`, not `undefined`.

 TypeScript does have a `--noUncheckedIndexedAccess` flag that makes array lookups more restricted and type safe, but it's quite strict and most projects don't use it. I don't cover it in this book. Chapter 13, "Configuration Options", links to resources that explain all of TypeScript's configuration options in depth.

Spreads and Rests

Remember `...` rest parameters for functions from Chapter 5, "Functions"? Rest parameters and array spreading, both with the `...` operator, are key ways to interact with arrays in JavaScript. TypeScript understands both of them.

Spreads

Arrays can be joined together using the `...` spread operator. TypeScript understands the result array will contain values that can be from either of the input arrays.

If the input arrays are the same type, the output array will be that same type. If two arrays of different types are spread together to create a new array, the new array will be understood to be a union type array of elements that are either of the two original types.

Here, the `conjoined` array is known to contain both values that are type `string` and values that are type `number`, so its type is inferred to be (`string | number`)`[]`:

```
// Type: string[]
const soldiers = ["Harriet Tubman", "Joan of Arc", "Khutulun"];

// Type: number[]
const soldierAges = [90, 19, 45];

// Type: (string | number)[]
const conjoined = [...soldiers, ...soldierAges];
```

Spreading Rest Parameters

TypeScript recognizes and will perform type checking on the JavaScript practice of `...` spreading an array as a rest parameter. Arrays used as arguments for rest parameters must have the same array type as the rest parameter.

The `logWarriors` function below takes in only `string` values for its `...names` rest parameter. Spreading an array of type `string[]` is allowed, but a `number[]` is not:

```
function logWarriors(greeting: string, ...names: string[]) {
  for (const name of names) {
    console.log(`${greeting}, ${name}!`);
  }
}

const warriors = ["Cathay Williams", "Lozen", "Nzinga"];

logWarriors("Hello", ...warriors);

const birthYears = [1844, 1840, 1583];

logWarriors("Born in", ...birthYears);
//                      ~~~~~~~~~~~~
// Error: Argument of type 'number' is not
// assignable to parameter of type 'string'.
```

Tuples

Although JavaScript arrays may be any size in theory, it is sometimes useful to use an array of a fixed size—also known as a *tuple*. Tuple arrays have a specific known type at each index that may be more specific than a union type of all possible members of the array. The syntax to declare a tuple type looks like an array literal, but with types in place of element values.

Here, the array `yearAndWarrior` is declared as being a tuple type with a `number` at index 0 and a `string` at index 1:

```
let yearAndWarrior: [number, string];

yearAndWarrior = [530, "Tomyris"]; // Ok
```

```
yearAndWarrior = [false, "Tomyris"];
//               ~~~~~
// Error: Type 'boolean' is not assignable to type 'number'.

yearAndWarrior = [530];
// Error: Type '[number]' is not assignable to type '[number, string]'.
//   Source has 1 element(s) but target requires 2.
```

Tuples are often used in JavaScript alongside array destructuring to be able to assign multiple values at once, such as setting two variables to initial values based on a single condition.

For example, TypeScript recognizes here that `year` is always going to be a `number` and `warrior` is always going to be a `string`:

```
// year type: number
// warrior type: string
let [year, warrior] = Math.random() > 0.5
  ? [340, "Archidamia"]
  : [1828, "Rani of Jhansi"];
```

Tuple Assignability

Tuple types are treated by TypeScript as more specific than variable length array types. That means variable length array types aren't assignable to tuple types.

Here, although we as humans may see `pairLoose` as having [boolean, number] inside, TypeScript infers it to be the more general (boolean | number)[] type:

```
// Type: (boolean | number)[]
const pairLoose = [false, 123];

const pairTupleLoose: [boolean, number] = pairLoose;
//    ~~~~~~~~~~~~~~
// Error: Type '(number | boolean)[]' is not
// assignable to type '[boolean, number]'.
//   Target requires 2 element(s) but source may have fewer.
```

If `pairLoose` had been declared as a [boolean, number] itself, the assignment of its value to `pairTuple` would have been permitted.

Tuples of different lengths are also not assignable to each other, as TypeScript includes knowing how many members are in the tuple in tuple types.

Here, `tupleTwoExtra` must have exactly two members, so although `tupleThree` starts with the correct members, its third member prevents it from being assignable to `tupleTwoExtra`:

```
const tupleThree: [boolean, number, string] = [false, 1583, "Nzinga"];

const tupleTwoExact: [boolean, number] = [tupleThree[0], tupleThree[1]];
```

```
const tupleTwoExtra: [boolean, number] = tupleThree;
//      ~~~~~~~~~~~~~
// Error: Type '[boolean, number, string]' is
// not assignable to type '[boolean, number]'.
//   Source has 3 element(s) but target allows only 2.
```

Tuples as rest parameters

Because tuples are seen as arrays with more specific type information on length and element types, they can be particularly useful for storing arguments to be passed to a function. TypeScript is able to provide accurate type checking for tuples passed as ... rest parameters.

Here, the logPair function's parameters are typed string and number. Trying to pass in a value of type (string | number)[] as arguments wouldn't be type safe as the contents might not match up: they could both be the same type, or one of each type in the wrong order. However, if TypeScript knows the value to be a [string, number] tuple, it understands the values match up:

```
function logPair(name: string, value: number) {
  console.log(`${name} has ${value}`);
}

const pairArray = ["Amage", 1];

logPair(...pairArray);
// Error: A spread argument must either have a
// tuple type or be passed to a rest parameter.

const pairTupleIncorrect: [number, string] = [1, "Amage"];

logPair(...pairTupleIncorrect);
// Error: Argument of type 'number' is not
// assignable to parameter of type 'string'.

const pairTupleCorrect: [string, number] = ["Amage", 1];

logPair(...pairTupleCorrect); // Ok
```

If you really want to go wild with your rest parameters tuples, you can mix them with arrays to store a list of arguments for multiple function calls. Here, trios is an array of tuples, where each tuple also has a tuple for its second member. trios.forEach(trio => logTrio(...trio)) is known to be safe because each ...trio happens to match the parameter types of logTrio. trios.forEach(logTrio), however, is not assignable because that is attempting to pass the entire [string, [number, boolean]] as the first parameter, which is type string:

```
function logTrio(name: string, value: [number, boolean]) {
  console.log(`${name} has ${value[0]} (${value[1]})`);
}

const trios: [string, [number, boolean]][] = [
  ["Amanitore", [1, true]],
  ["Æthelflæd", [2, false]],
  ["Ann E. Dunwoody", [3, false]]
];

trios.forEach(trio => logTrio(...trio)); // Ok

trios.forEach(logTrio);
//             ~~~~~~~
// Argument of type '(name: string, value: [number, boolean]) => void'
// is not assignable to parameter of type
// '(value: [string, [number, boolean]], ...) => void'.
//   Types of parameters 'name' and 'value' are incompatible.
//     Type '[string, [number, boolean]]' is not assignable to type 'string'.
```

Tuple Inferences

TypeScript generally treats created arrays as variable length arrays, not tuples. If it sees an array being used as a variable's initial value or the returned value for a function, then it will assume a flexible size array rather than a fixed size tuple.

The following `firstCharAndSize` function is inferred as returning (string | number)[], not [string, number], because that's the type inferred for its returned array literal:

```
// Return type: (string | number)[]
function firstCharAndSize(input: string) {
  return [input[0], input.length];
}

// firstChar type: string | number
// size type: string | number
const [firstChar, size] = firstCharAndSize("Gudit");
```

There are two common ways in TypeScript to indicate that a value should be a more specific tuple type instead of a general array type: explicit tuple types and `const` assertions.

Explicit tuple types

Tuple types may be used in type annotations, such as the return type annotation for a function. If the function is declared as returning a tuple type and returns an array literal, that array literal will be inferred to be a tuple instead of a more general variable-length array.

This `firstCharAndSizeExplicit` function version explicitly states that it returns a tuple of a `string` and `number`:

```
// Return type: [string, number]
function firstCharAndSizeExplicit(input: string): [string, number] {
  return [input[0], input.length];
}

// firstChar type: string
// size type: number
const [firstChar, size] = firstCharAndSizeExplicit("Cathay Williams");
```

Const asserted tuples

Typing out tuple types in explicit type annotations can be a pain for the same reasons as typing out any explicit type annotations. It's extra syntax for you to write and update as code changes.

As an alternative, TypeScript provides an `as const` operator known as a *const assertion* that can be placed after a value. Const assertions tell TypeScript to use the most literal, read-only possible form of the value when inferring its type. If one is placed after an array literal, it will indicate that the array should be treated as a tuple:

```
// Type: (string | number)[]
const unionArray = [1157, "Tomoe"];

// Type: readonly [1157, "Tomoe"]
const readonlyTuple = [1157, "Tomoe"] as const;
```

Note that `as const` assertions go beyond switching from flexible sized arrays to fixed size tuples: they also indicate to TypeScript that the tuple is read-only and cannot be used in a place that expects it should be allowed to modify the value.

In this example, `pairMutable` is allowed to be modified because it has a traditional explicit tuple type. However, the `as const` makes the value not assignable to the mutable `pairAlsoMutable`, and members of the constant `pairConst` are not allowed to be modified:

```
const pairMutable: [number, string] = [1157, "Tomoe"];
pairMutable[0] = 1247; // Ok

const pairAlsoMutable: [number, string] = [1157, "Tomoe"] as const;
//      ~~~~~~~~~~~~~~~
// Error: The type 'readonly [1157, "Tomoe"]' is 'readonly'
// and cannot be assigned to the mutable type '[number, string]'.

const pairConst = [1157, "Tomoe"] as const;
pairConst[0] = 1247;
//        ~
// Error: Cannot assign to '0' because it is a read-only property.
```

In practice, read-only tuples are convenient for function returns. Returned values from functions that return a tuple are often destructured immediately anyway, so the tuple being read-only does not get in the way of using the function.

This `firstCharAndSizeAsConst` returns a `readonly [string, number]`, but the consuming code only cares about retrieving the values from that tuple:

```
// Return type: readonly [string, number]
function firstCharAndSizeAsConst(input: string) {
  return [input[0], input.length] as const;
}

// firstChar type: string
// size type: number
const [firstChar, size] = firstCharAndSizeAsConst("Ching Shih");
```

 Read-only objects and `as const` assertions are covered more deeply in Chapter 9, "Type Modifiers".

Summary

In this chapter, you worked with declaring arrays and retrieving their members:

- Declaring array types with [ ]
- Using parentheses to declare arrays of functions or union types
- How TypeScript understands array elements as the type of the array
- Working with ... spreads and rests
- Declaring tuple types to represent fixed-size arrays
- Using type annotations or `as const` assertions to create tuples

 Now that you've finished reading this chapter, practice what you've learned on *https://learningtypescript.com/arrays*.

What's a pirate's favorite data structure?
Arrrrr-ays!

Interfaces

Why only use the
Boring built-in type shapes when
We can make our own!

I mentioned back in Chapter 4, "Objects" that although type aliases for { ... } object types are a way to describe object shapes, TypeScript also includes an "interface" feature many developers prefer. Interfaces are another way to declare an object shape with an associated name. Interfaces are in many ways similar to aliased object types but are generally preferred for their more readable error messages, speedier compiler performance, and better interoperability with classes.

Type Aliases Versus Interfaces

Here is a quick recap of the syntax for how an aliased object type would describe an object with a born: number and name: string:

```
type Poet = {
  born: number;
  name: string;
};
```

Here is the equivalent syntax for an interface:

```
interface Poet {
  born: number;
  name: string;
}
```

The two syntaxes are almost identical.

> TypeScript developers who prefer semicolons generally put them after type aliases and not after interfaces. This preference mirrors the difference between declaring a variable with a ; versus declaring a class or function without.

TypeScript's assignability checking and error messages for interfaces also work and look just about the same as they do for object types. The following assignability errors for assigning to the `valueLater` variable would be roughly the same if `Poet` was an interface or type alias:

```
let valueLater: Poet;

// Ok
valueLater = {
  born: 1935,
  name: 'Sara Teasdale',
};

valueLater = "Emily Dickinson";
// Error: Type 'string' is not assignable to 'Poet'.

valueLater = {
  born: true,
  // Error: Type 'boolean' is not assignable to type 'number'.
  name: 'Sappho'
};
```

However, there are a few key differences between interfaces and type aliases:

- As you'll see later in this chapter, interfaces can "merge" together to be augmented—a feature particularly useful when working with third-party code such as built-in globals or npm packages.

- As you'll see in the next chapter, Chapter 8, "Classes", interfaces can be used to type check the structure of class declarations while type aliases cannot.

- Interfaces are generally speedier for the TypeScript type checker to work with: they declare a named type that can be cached more easily internally, rather than a dynamic copy-and-paste of a new object literal the way type aliases do.

- Because interfaces are considered named objects rather than an alias for an unnamed object literal, their error messages are more likely to be readable in hard edge cases.

For the latter two reasons and to maintain consistency, the rest of this book and its associated projects default to using interfaces over aliased object shapes. I generally recommend using interfaces whenever possible (i.e., until you need features such as union types from type aliases).

Types of Properties

JavaScript objects can be wild and wacky in real-world usage, including getters and setters, properties that only sometimes exist, or accepting any arbitrary property names. TypeScript provides a set of type system tools for interfaces to help us model that wackiness.

 Because interfaces and type aliases behave so similarly, the following types of properties introduced in this chapter are all also usable with aliased object types.

Optional Properties

As with object types, interface properties don't all have to be required in the object. You can indicate an interface's property is optional by including a ? before the : in its type annotation.

This `Book` interface requires only a `pages` property and optionally allows an `author`. Objects adhering to it may provide `author` or leave it out as long as they provide `pages`:

```
interface Book {
  author?: string;
  pages: number;
};

// Ok
const ok: Book = {
    author: "Rita Dove",
    pages: 80,
};

const missing: Book = {
    author: "Rita Dove"
};
// Error: Property 'pages' is missing in type
// '{ author: string; }' but required in type 'Book'.
```

The same caveats around the difference between optional properties and properties whose type happens to include `undefined` in a type union apply to interfaces as well as object types. Chapter 13, "Configuration Options" will describe TypeScript's strictness settings around optional properties.

Read-Only Properties

You may sometimes wish to block users of your interface from reassigning properties of objects adhering to that interface. TypeScript allows you to add a `readonly` modifier before a property name to indicate that once set, that property should not be set to a different value. These `readonly` properties can be read from normally, but not reassigned to anything new.

For example, the `text` property in the below `Page` interface gives back a `string` when accessed, but causes a type error if assigned a new value:

```
interface Page {
    readonly text: string;
}

function read(page: Page) {
    // Ok: reading the text property doesn't attempt to modify it
    console.log(page.text);

    page.text += "!";
    //    ~~~~
    // Error: Cannot assign to 'text'
    // because it is a read-only property.
}
```

Note that `readonly` modifiers exist only in the type system, and only apply to the usage of that interface. It won't apply to an object unless that object is used in a location that declares it to be of that interface.

In this continuation of the `read` example, the `text` property is allowed to be modified outside of the `read` function because its parent object isn't explicitly described as a `Text` until inside the function. `pageIsh` is allowed to be used as a `Page` because a writable property is assignable to a `readonly` property (mutable properties can be read from, which is all a `readonly` property needs):

```
const pageIsh = {
  text: "Hello, world!",
};

// Ok: pageIsh is an inferred object type with text, not a Page
page.text += "!";

// Ok: read takes in Page, which happens to
// be a more specific version of pageIsh's type
read(pageIsh);
```

Declaring the variable `pageIsh` with the explicit type annotation : `Page` would have indicated to TypeScript that its `text` property was `readonly`. Its inferred type, however, was not `readonly`.

Read-only interface members are a handy way to make sure areas of code don't unexpectedly modify objects they're not meant to. However, remember that they're a type system construct only and don't exist in the compiled JavaScript output code. They only protect from modification during development with the TypeScript type checker.

Functions and Methods

It's very common in JavaScript for object members to be functions. TypeScript therefore allows declaring interface members as being the function types previously covered in Chapter 5, "Functions".

TypeScript provides two ways of declaring interface members as functions:

- *Method* syntax: declaring that a member of the interface is a function intended to be called as a member of the object, like `member(): void`

- *Property* syntax: declaring that a member of the interface is equal to a standalone function, like `member: () => void`

The two declaration forms are an analog for the two ways you can declare a JavaScript object as having a function.

Both `method` and `property` members shown here are functions that may be called with no parameters and return a `string`:

```
interface HasBothFunctionTypes {
  property: () => string;
  method(): string;
}

const hasBoth: HasBothFunctionTypes = {
  property: () => "",
  method() {
    return "";
  }
};

hasBoth.property(); // Ok
hasBoth.method(); // Ok
```

Both forms can receive the `?` optional modifier to indicate they don't need to be provided:

```
interface OptionalReadonlyFunctions {
  optionalProperty?: () => string;
  optionalMethod?(): string;
}
```

Method and property declarations can mostly be used interchangeably. The main differences between them that I'll cover in this book are:

- Methods cannot be declared as readonly; properties can.
- Interface merging (covered later in this chapter) treats them differently.
- Some of the operations performed on types covered in Chapter 15, "Type Operations" treat them differently.

Future versions of TypeScript may add the option to be more strict about the differences between methods and property functions.

For now, the general style guide I recommend is:

- Use a method function if you know the underlying function may refer to this, most commonly for instances of classes (covered in Chapter 8, "Classes").
- Use a property function otherwise.

Don't sweat it if you mix up these two, or don't understand the difference. It'll rarely impact your code unless you're being intentional about this scoping and which form you choose.

Call Signatures

Interfaces and object types can declare *call signatures*, which is a type system description of how a value may be called like a function. Only values that may be called in the way the call signature declares will be assignable to the interface—i.e., a function with assignable parameters and return type. A call signature looks similar to a function type, but with a : colon instead of an => arrow.

The following FunctionAlias and CallSignature types both describe the same function parameters and return type:

```
type FunctionAlias = (input: string) => number;

interface CallSignature {
  (input: string): number;
}

// Type: (input: string) => number
const typedFunctionAlias: FunctionAlias = (input) => input.length; // Ok

// Type: (input: string) => number
const typedCallSignature: CallSignature = (input) => input.length; // Ok
```

Call signatures can be used to describe functions that additionally have some user-defined property on them. TypeScript will recognize a property added to a function declaration as adding to that function declaration's type.

The following `keepsTrackOfCalls` function declaration is given a `count` property of type `number`, making it assignable to the `FunctionWithCount` interface. It can therefore be assigned to the `hasCallCount` argument of type `FunctionWithCount`. The function at the end of the snippet was not given a `count`:

```
interface FunctionWithCount {
  count: number;
  (): void;
}

let hasCallCount: FunctionWithCount;

function keepsTrackOfCalls() {
  keepsTrackOfCalls.count += 1;
  console.log(`I've been called ${keepsTrackOfCalls.count} times!`);
}

keepsTrackOfCalls.count = 0;

hasCallCount = keepsTrackOfCalls; // Ok

function doesNotHaveCount() {
  console.log("No idea!");
}

hasCallCount = doesNotHaveCount;
// Error: Property 'count' is missing in type
// '() => void' but required in type 'FunctionWithCalls'
```

Index Signatures

Some JavaScript projects create objects meant to store values under any arbitrary `string` key. For these "container" objects, declaring an interface with a field for every possible key would be impractical or impossible.

TypeScript provides a syntax called an *index signature* to indicate that an interface's objects are allowed to take in any key and give back a certain type under that key. They're most commonly used with string keys because JavaScript object property lookups convert keys to strings implicitly. An index signature looks like a regular property definition but with a type after the key, and array brackets surrounding them, like `{ [i: string]: ... }`.

This `WordCounts` interface is declared as allowing any `string` key with a `number` value. Objects of that type aren't bound to receiving any particular key—as long as the value is a `number`:

```
interface WordCounts {
  [i: string]: number;
}

const counts: WordCounts = {};

counts.apple = 0; // Ok
counts.banana = 1; // Ok

counts.cherry = false;
// Error: Type 'boolean' is not assignable to type 'number'.
```

Index signatures are convenient for assigning values to an object but aren't completely type safe. They indicate that an object should give back a value no matter what property is being accessed.

This publishDates value safely gives back Frankenstein as a Date but tricks TypeScript into thinking its Beloved is defined even though it's undefined:

```
interface DatesByName {
  [i: string]: Date;
}

const publishDates: DatesByName = {
  Frankenstein: new Date("1 January 1818"),
};

publishDates.Frankenstein; // Type: Date
console.log(publishDates.Frankenstein.toString()); // Ok

publishDates.Beloved; // Type: Date, but runtime value of undefined!
console.log(publishDates.Beloved.toString()); // Ok in the type system, but...
// Runtime error: Cannot read property 'toString'
// of undefined (reading publishDates.Beloved)
```

When possible, if you're looking to store key-value pairs and the keys aren't known ahead of time, it is generally safer to use a Map. Its .get method always returns a type with | undefined to indicate that the key might not exist. Chapter 9, "Type Modifiers" will discuss working with generic container classes such as Map and Set.

Mixing properties and index signatures

Interfaces are able to include explicitly named properties and catchall string index signatures, with one catch: each named property's type must be assignable to its catchall index signature's type. You can think of mixing them as telling TypeScript that named properties give a more specific type, and any other property falls back to the index signature's type.

Here, HistoricalNovels declares that all properties are type number, and additionally the Oroonoko property must exist to begin with:

```
interface HistoricalNovels {
  Oroonoko: number;
  [i: string]: number;
}

// Ok
const novels: HistoricalNovels = {
  Outlander: 1991,
  Oroonoko: 1688,
};

const missingOroonoko: HistoricalNovels = {
  Outlander: 1991,
};
// Error: Property 'Oroonoko' is missing in type
// '{ Outlander: number; }' but required in type 'HistoricalNovels'.
```

One common type system trick with mixed properties and index signatures is to use a more specific property type literal for the named property than an index signature's primitive. As long as the named property's type is assignable to the index signature's—which is true for a literal and a primitive, respectively—TypeScript will allow it.

Here, `ChapterStarts` declares that a property under `preface` must be 0 and all other properties have the more general `number`. That means any object adhering to `ChapterStarts` must have a `preface` property equal to 0:

```
interface ChapterStarts {
  preface: 0;
  [i: string]: number;
}

const correctPreface: ChapterStarts = {
  preface: 0,
  night: 1,
  shopping: 5
};

const wrongPreface: ChapterStarts = {
  preface: 1,
  // Error: Type '1' is not assignable to type '0'.
};
```

Numeric index signatures

Although JavaScript implicitly converts object property lookup keys to strings, it is sometimes desirable to only allow numbers as keys for an object. TypeScript index signatures can use a `number` type instead of `string` but with the same catch as named properties that their types must be assignable to the catchall `string` index signature's.

The following `MoreNarrowNumbers` interface would be allowed because `string` is assignable to `string | undefined`, but `MoreNarrowStrings` would not because `string | undefined` is not assignable to `string`:

```
// Ok
interface MoreNarrowNumbers {
  [i: number]: string;
  [i: string]: string | undefined;
}

// Ok
const mixesNumbersAndStrings: MoreNarrowNumbers = {
  0: '',
  key1: '',
  key2: undefined,
}

interface MoreNarrowStrings {
  [i: number]: string | undefined;
  // Error: 'number' index type 'string | undefined'
  // is not assignable to 'string' index type 'string'.
  [i: string]: string;
}
```

Nested Interfaces

Just like object types can be nested as properties of other object types, interface types can also have properties that are themselves interface types (or object types).

This `Novel` interface contains an `author` property that must satisfy an inline object type and a `setting` property that must satisfy the `Setting` interface:

```
interface Novel {
    author: {
        name: string;
    };
    setting: Setting;
}

interface Setting {
    place: string;
    year: number;
}

let myNovel: Novel;

// Ok
myNovel = {
    author: {
        name: 'Jane Austen',
    },
```

```
    setting: {
        place: 'England',
        year: 1812,
    }
};

myNovel = {
    author: {
        name: 'Emily Brontë',
    },
    setting: {
        place: 'West Yorkshire',
    },
    // Error: Property 'year' is missing in type
    // '{ place: string; }' but required in type 'Setting'.
};
```

Interface Extensions

Sometimes you may end up with multiple interfaces that look similar to each other. One interface may contain all the same members of another interface, with a few extras added on.

TypeScript allows an interface to *extend* another interface, which declares it as copying all the members of another. An interface may be marked as extending another interface by adding the extends keyword after its name (the "derived" interface), followed by the name of the interface to extend (the "base" interface). Doing so indicates to TypeScript that all objects adhering to the derived interface must also have all the members of the base interface.

In the following example, the Novella interface extends from Writing and thus requires objects to have at least both Novella's pages and Writing's title members:

```
interface Writing {
    title: string;
}

interface Novella extends Writing {
    pages: number;
}

// Ok
let myNovella: Novella = {
    pages: 195,
    title: "Ethan Frome",
};

let missingPages: Novella = {
//  ~~~~~~~~~~~~
// Error: Property 'pages' is missing in type
```

```
    // '{ title: string; }' but required in type 'Novella'.
    title: "The Awakening",
}

let extraProperty: Novella = {
    // ~~~~~~~~~~~~~
    // Error: Type '{ genre: string; name: string; strategy: string; }'
    // is not assignable to type 'Novella'.
    //   Object literal may only specify known properties,
    //   and 'strategy' does not exist in type 'Novella'.
    pages: 300,
    strategy: "baseline",
    style: "Naturalism"
};
```

Interface extensions are a nifty way to represent that one type of entity in your project is a superset (it includes all the members of) another entity. They allow you to avoid having to type out the same code repeatedly across multiple interfaces to represent that relationship.

Overridden Properties

Derived interfaces may *override*, or replace, properties from their base interface by declaring the property again with a different type. TypeScript's type checker will enforce that an overridden property must be assignable to its base property. It does so to ensure that instances of the derived interface type stay assignable to the base interface type.

Most derived interfaces that redeclare properties do so either to make those properties a more specific subset of a type union or to make the properties a type that extends from the base interface's type.

For example, this WithNullableName type is properly made non-nullable in WithNonNullableName. WithNumericName, however, is not allowed as number | string and is not assignable to string | null:

```
interface WithNullableName {
    name: string | null;
}

interface WithNonNullableName extends WithNullableName {
    name: string;
}

interface WithNumericName extends WithNullableName {
    name: number | string;
}
// Error: Interface 'WithNumericName' incorrectly
// extends interface 'WithNullableName'.
//   Types of property 'name' are incompatible.
```

```
//      Type 'string | number' is not assignable to type 'string | null'.
//          Type 'number' is not assignable to type 'string'.
```

Extending Multiple Interfaces

Interfaces in TypeScript are allowed to be declared as extending multiple other interfaces. Any number of interface names separated by commas may be used after the extends keyword following the derived interface's name. The derived interface will receive all members from all base interfaces.

Here, the GivesBothAndEither has three methods: one on its own, one from GivesNumber, and one from GivesString:

```
interface GivesNumber {
  giveNumber(): number;
}

interface GivesString {
  giveString(): string;
}

interface GivesBothAndEither extends GivesNumber, GivesString {
  giveEither(): number | string;
}

function useGivesBoth(instance: GivesBothAndEither) {
  instance.giveEither(); // Type: number | string
  instance.giveNumber(); // Type: number
  instance.giveString(); // Type: string
}
```

By marking an interface as extending multiple other interfaces, you can both reduce code duplication and make it easier for object shapes to be reused across different areas of code.

Interface Merging

One of the important features of interfaces is their ability to *merge* with each other. Interface merging means if two interfaces are declared in the same scope with the same name, they'll join into one bigger interface under that name with all declared fields.

This snippet declares a Merged interface with two properties: fromFirst and fromSecond:

```
interface Merged {
  fromFirst: string;
}

interface Merged {
```

```
    fromSecond: number;
}

// Equivalent to:
// interface Merged {
//   fromFirst: string;
//   fromSecond: number;
// }
```

Interface merging isn't a feature used very often in day-to-day TypeScript development. I would recommend avoiding it when possible, as it can be difficult to understand code where an interface is declared in multiple places.

However, interface merging is particularly useful for augmenting interfaces from external packages or built-in global interfaces such as Window. For example, when using the default TypeScript compiler options, declaring a Window interface in a file with a myEnvironmentVariable property makes a window.myEnvironmentVariable available:

```
interface Window {
    myEnvironmentVariable: string;
}

window.myEnvironmentVariable; // Type: string
```

I'll cover type definitions more deeply in Chapter 11, "Declaration Files" and TypeScript global type options in Chapter 13, "Configuration Options".

Member Naming Conflicts

Note that merged interfaces may not declare the same name of a property multiple times with different types. If a property is already declared in an interface, a later merged interface must use the same type.

In this MergedProperties interface, the same property is allowed because it is the same in both declarations, but different is an error for being a different type:

```
interface MergedProperties {
    same: (input: boolean) => string;
    different: (input: string) => string;
}

interface MergedProperties {
    same: (input: boolean) => string; // Ok

    different: (input: number) => string;
    // Error: Subsequent property declarations must have the same type.
    // Property 'different' must be of type '(input: string) => string',
    // but here has type '(input: number) => string'.
}
```

Merged interfaces may, however, define a method with the same name and a different signature. Doing so creates a function overload for the method.

This `MergedMethods` interface creates a `different` method that has two overloads:

```
interface MergedMethods {
  different(input: string): string;
}

interface MergedMethods {
  different(input: number): string; // Ok
}
```

Summary

This chapter introduced how object types may be described by interfaces:

- Using interfaces instead of type aliases to declare object types
- Various interface property types: optional, read-only, function, and method
- Using index signatures for catchall object properties
- Reusing interfaces using nested interfaces and `extends` inheritance
- How interfaces with the same name can merge together

Next up will be a native JavaScript syntax for setting up multiple objects to have the same properties: classes.

 Now that you've finished reading this chapter, practice what you've learned on *https://learningtypescript.com/interfaces*.

Why are interfaces good drivers?
They're great at merging.

CHAPTER 8

Classes

Some functional devs
Try to never use classes
Too intense for me

The world of JavaScript during TypeScript's creation and release in the early 2010s was quite different from today. Features such as arrow functions and let/const variables that would later be standardized in ES2015 were still distant hopes on the horizon. Babel was a few years away from its first commit; its predecessor tools such as Traceur that converted newer JavaScript syntax to old hadn't achieved full mainstream adoption.

TypeScript's early marketing and feature set were tailored to that world. In addition to its type checking, its transpiler was emphasized—with classes as a frequent example. Nowadays TypeScript's class support is just one feature among many to support all JavaScript language features. TypeScript neither encourages nor discourages class use or any other popular JavaScript pattern.

Class Methods

TypeScript generally understands methods the same way it understands standalone functions. Parameter types default to any unless given a type or default value; calling the method requires an acceptable number of arguments; return types can generally be inferred if the function is not recursive.

This code snippet defines a Greeter class with a greet class method that takes in a single required parameter of type string:

```
class Greeter {
    greet(name: string) {
        console.log(`${name}, do your stuff!`);
    }
}

new Greeter().greet("Miss Frizzle"); // Ok
```

```
new Greeter().greet();
//          ~~~~~
// Error: Expected 1 arguments, but got 0.
```

Class constructors are treated like typical class methods with regards to their parameters. TypeScript will perform type checking to make sure a correct number of arguments with correct types are provided to method calls.

This `Greeted` constructor also expects its `message: string` parameter to be provided:

```
class Greeted {
    constructor(message: string) {
        console.log(`As I always say: ${message}!`);
    }
}

new Greeted("take chances, make mistakes, get messy");

new Greeted();
// Error: Expected 1 arguments, but got 0.
```

I'll cover constructors in the context of subclasses later in this chapter.

Class Properties

To read from or write to a property on a class in TypeScript, it must be explicitly declared in the class. Class properties are declared using the same syntax as interfaces: their name followed optionally by a type annotation.

TypeScript will not attempt to deduce what members may exist on a class from their assignments in a constructor.

In this example, `destination` is allowed to be assigned to and accessed on instances of the `FieldTrip` class because it is explicitly declared as a `string`. The `this.nonexistent` assignment in the constructor is not allowed because the class does not declare a `nonexistent` property:

```
class FieldTrip {
    destination: string;

    constructor(destination: string) {
        this.destination = destination; // Ok
        console.log(`We're going to ${this.destination}!`);

        this.nonexistent = destination;
        //   ~~~~~~~~~~~
        // Error: Property 'nonexistent' does not exist on type 'FieldTrip'.
    }
}
```

Explicitly declaring class properties allows TypeScript to quickly understand what is or is not allowed to exist on instances of classes. Later, when class instances are in use, TypeScript uses that understanding to give a type error if code attempts to access a member of a class instance not known to exist, such as with this continuation's `trip.nonexistent`:

```
const trip = new FieldTrip("planetarium");

trip.destination; // Ok

trip.nonexistent;
//   ~~~~~~~~~~~
// Error: Property 'nonexistent' does not exist on type 'FieldTrip'.
```

Function Properties

Let's recap some JavaScript method scoping and syntax fundamentals for a bit, as they can be surprising if you're not accustomed to them. JavaScript contains two syntaxes for declaring a member on a class to be a callable function: *method* and *property*.

I've already shown the method approach of putting parentheses after the member name, like `myFunction() {}`. The method approach assigns a function to the class prototype, so all class instances use the same function definition.

This `WithMethod` class declares a `myMethod` method that all instances are able to refer to:

```
class WithMethod {
    myMethod() {}
}

new WithMethod().myMethod === new WithMethod().myMethod; // true
```

The other syntax is to declare a property whose value happens to be a function. This creates a new function per instance of the class, which can be useful with `() =>` arrow functions whose `this` scope should always point to the class instance (at the time and memory cost of creating a new function per class instance).

This `WithProperty` class contains a single property of name `myProperty` and type `() => void` that will be re-created for each class instance:

```
class WithProperty {
    myProperty = () => {}
}

new WithMethod().myProperty === new WithMethod().myProperty; // false
```

Function properties can be given parameters and return types using the same syntax as class methods and standalone functions. After all, they're a value assigned to a class member and the value happens to be a function.

This `WithPropertyParameters` class has a `takesParameters` property of type `(input: string) => number`:

```
class WithPropertyParameters {
    takesParameters = (input: boolean) => input ? "Yes" : "No";
}

const instance = new WithPropertyParameters();

instance.takesParameters(true); // Ok

instance.takesParameters(123);
//                       ~~~
// Error: Argument of type 'number' is not
// assignable to parameter of type 'boolean'.
```

Initialization Checking

With strict compiler settings enabled, TypeScript will check that each property declared whose type does not include `undefined` is assigned a value in the constructor. This strict initialization checking is useful because it prevents code from accidentally forgetting to assign a value to a class property.

The following `WithValue` class does not assign a value to its `unused` property, which TypeScript recognizes as a type error:

```
class WithValue {
    immediate = 0; // Ok
    later: number; // Ok (set in the constructor)
    mayBeUndefined: number | undefined; // Ok (allowed to be undefined)

    unused: number;
    // Error: Property 'unused' has no initializer
    // and is not definitely assigned in the constructor.

    constructor() {
        this.later = 1;
    }
}
```

Without strict initialization checking, a class instance could be allowed to access a value that might be `undefined` even though the type system says it can't be.

This example would compile happily if strict initialization checking didn't happen, but the resultant JavaScript would crash at runtime:

```
class MissingInitializer {
    property: string;
}

new MissingInitializer().property.length;
// TypeError: Cannot read property 'length' of undefined
```

The billion-dollar mistake strikes again!

Configuring strict property initialization checking with TypeScript's `strictPropertyInitialization` compiler option is covered in Chapter 12, "Using IDE Features".

Definitely assigned properties

Although strict initialization checking is useful most of the time, you may come across some cases where a class property is intentionally able to be unassigned after the class constructor. If you are absolutely sure a property should not have strict initialization checking applied to it, you can add a ! after its name to disable the check. Doing so asserts to TypeScript that the property will be assigned a value other than `undefined` before its first usage.

This `ActivitiesQueue` class is meant to be re-initialized any number of times separately from its constructor, so its `pending` property must be asserted with a !:

```
class ActivitiesQueue {
    pending!: string[]; // Ok

    initialize(pending: string[]) {
        this.pending = pending;
    }

    next() {
        return this.pending.pop();
    }
}

const activities = new ActivitiesQueue();

activities.initialize(['eat', 'sleep', 'learn'])
activities.next();
```

 Needing to disable strict initialization checking on a class property is often a sign of code being set up in a way that doesn't lend itself well to type checking. Instead of adding a ! assertion and reducing type safety for the property, consider refactoring the class to no longer need the assertion.

Optional Properties

Much like interfaces, classes in TypeScript may declare a property as optional by adding a ? after its declaration name. Optional properties behave roughly the same as properties whose types happen to be a union that includes | undefined. Strict initialization checking won't mind if they're not explicitly set in their constructor.

This MissingInitializer class marks its property as optional, so it's allowed to not be assigned in the class constructor regardless of strict property initialization checking:

```
class MissingInitializer {
    property?: string;
}

new MissingInitializer().property?.length; // Ok

new MissingInitializer().property.length;
// Error: Object is possibly 'undefined'.
```

Read-Only Properties

Again much like interfaces, classes in TypeScript may declare a property as read-only by adding the readonly keyword before its declaration name. The readonly keyword exists purely within the type system and is removed when compiling to JavaScript.

Properties declared as readonly may only be assigned initial values where they are declared or in a constructor. Any other location—including methods on the class itself—may only read from the properties, not write to them.

In this example, the text property on the Quote class is given a value in the constructor, but the other uses cause type errors:

```
class Quote {
    readonly text: string;

    constructor(text: string) {
        this.text = text;
    }

    emphasize() {
        this.text += "!";
        //   ~~~~
        // Error: Cannot assign to 'text' because it is a read-only property.
    }
}

const quote = new Quote(
    "There is a brilliant child locked inside every student."
);
```

```
quote.text = "Ha!";
// Error: Cannot assign to 'text' because it is a read-only property.
```

 External users of your code, such as consumers of any npm packages you published, might not respect readonly modifiers—especially if they're writing JavaScript and don't have type checking. If you need true read-only protection, consider using # private fields and/or get() function properties.

Properties declared as readonly with an initial value of a primitive have a slight quirk compared to other properties: they are inferred to be their value's narrowed *literal* type if possible, rather than the wider *primitive*. TypeScript feels comfortable with a more aggressive initial type narrowing because it knows the value won't be changed later; it is similar to const variables taking on narrower types than let variables.

In this example, the class properties are both initially declared as a string literal, so in order to widen one of them to string, a type annotation is needed:

```
class RandomQuote {
    readonly explicit: string = "Home is the nicest word there is.";
    readonly implicit = "Home is the nicest word there is.";

    constructor() {
        if (Math.random () > 0.5) {
            this.explicit = "We start learning the minute we're born." // Ok;

            this.implicit = "We start learning the minute we're born.";
            // Error: Type '"We start learning the minute we're born."' is
            // not assignable to type '"Home is the nicest word there is."'.
        }
    }
}

const quote = new RandomQuote();

quote.explicit; // Type: string
quote.implicit; // Type: "Home is the nicest word there is."
```

Widening a property's type explicitly is not necessary very often. Still, it can sometimes be useful in the case of conditional logic in constructors like the one in RandomQuote.

Classes as Types

Classes are relatively unique in the type system in that a class declaration creates both a runtime value—the class itself—as well as a type that can be used in type annotations.

The name of this `Teacher` class is used to annotate a `teacher` variable, telling Type-Script that it should be assigned only values that are assignable to the `Teacher` class—such as instances of the `Teacher` class itself:

```
class Teacher {
    sayHello() {
        console.log("Take chances, make mistakes, get messy!");
    }
}

let teacher: Teacher;

teacher = new Teacher(); // Ok

teacher = "Wahoo!";
// Error: Type 'string' is not assignable to type 'Teacher'.
```

Interestingly, TypeScript will consider any object type that happens to include all the same members of a class to be assignable to the class. This is because TypeScript's structural typing cares only about the shape of objects, not how they're declared.

Here, `withSchoolBus` takes in a parameter of type `SchoolBus`. That can be satisfied by any object that happens to have a `getAbilities` property of type `() => string[]`, such as an instance of the `SchoolBus` class:

```
class SchoolBus {
    getAbilities() {
        return ["magic", "shapeshifting"];
    }
}

function withSchoolBus(bus: SchoolBus) {
    console.log(bus.getAbilities());
}

withSchoolBus(new SchoolBus()); // Ok

// Ok
withSchoolBus({
    getAbilities: () => ["transmogrification"],
});

withSchoolBus({
    getAbilities: () => 123,
    //                  ~~~
    // Error: Type 'number' is not assignable to type 'string[]'.
});
```

In most real-world code, developers don't pass object values in places that ask for class types. This structural checking behavior may seem unexpected but doesn't come up very often.

Classes and Interfaces

Back in Chapter 7, "Interfaces", I showed you how interfaces allow TypeScript developers to set up expectations for object shapes in code. TypeScript allows a class to declare its instances as adhering to an interface by adding the implements keyword after the class name, followed by the name of an interface. Doing so indicates to TypeScript that instances of the class should be assignable to each of those interfaces. Any mismatches would be called out as type errors by the type checker.

In this example, the Student class correctly implements the Learner interface by including its property name and method study, but Slacker is missing a study and thus results in a type error:

```
interface Learner {
    name: string;
    study(hours: number): void;
}

class Student implements Learner {
    name: string;

    constructor(name: string) {
        this.name = name;
    }

    study(hours: number) {
        for (let i = 0; i < hours; i+= 1) {
            console.log("...studying...");
        }
    }
}

class Slacker implements Learner {
    // ~~~~~~~
    // Error: Class 'Slacker' incorrectly implements interface 'Learner'.
    //   Property 'study' is missing in type 'Slacker'
    //   but required in type 'Learner'.
    name = "Rocky";
}
```

Interfaces meant to be implemented by classes are a typical reason to use the method syntax for declaring an interface member as a function—as used by the Learner interface.

Marking a class as implementing an interface doesn't change anything about how the class is used. If the class already happened to match up to the interface, TypeScript's type checker would have allowed its instances to be used in places where an instance of the interface is required anyway. TypeScript won't even infer the types of methods or properties on the class from the interface: if we had added a study(hours) {} method to the Slacker example, TypeScript would consider the hours parameter an implicit any unless we gave it a type annotation.

This version of the Student class causes implicit any type errors because it doesn't provide type annotations on its members:

```
class Student implements Learner {
    name;
    // Error: Member 'name' implicitly has an 'any' type.

    study(hours) {
        // Error: Parameter 'hours' implicitly has an 'any' type.
    }
}
```

Implementing an interface is purely a safety check. It does not copy any interface members onto the class definition for you. Rather, implementing an interface signals your intention to the type checker and surfaces type errors in the class definition, rather than later on where class instances are used. It's similar in purpose to adding a type annotation to a variable even though it has an initial value.

Implementing Multiple Interfaces

Classes in TypeScript are allowed to be declared as implementing multiple interfaces. The list of implemented interfaces for a class may be any number of interface names with commas in-between.

In this example, both classes are required to have at least a grades property to implement Graded and a report property to implement Reporter. The Empty class has two type errors for failing to implement either of the interfaces properly:

```
interface Graded {
    grades: number[];
}

interface Reporter {
    report: () => string;
}
```

```
class ReportCard implements Graded, Reporter {
    grades: number[];

    constructor(grades: number[]) {
        this.grades = grades;
    }

    report() {
        return this.grades.join(", ");
    }
}

class Empty implements Graded, Reporter { }
 // ~~~~~
 // Error: Class 'Empty' incorrectly implements interface 'Graded'.
 //    Property 'grades' is missing in type 'Empty'
 //    but required in type 'Graded'.
 // ~~~~~
 // Error: Class 'Empty' incorrectly implements interface 'Reporter'.
 //    Property 'report' is missing in type 'Empty'
 //    but required in type 'Reporter'.
```

In practice, there may be some interfaces whose definitions make it impossible to have a class implement both. Attempting to declare a class implementing two conflicting interfaces will result in at least one type error on the class.

The following AgeIsANumber and AgeIsNotANumber interfaces declare very different types for an age property. Neither the AsNumber class nor NotAsNumber class properly implement both:

```
interface AgeIsANumber {
    age: number;
}

interface AgeIsNotANumber {
    age: () => string;
}

class AsNumber implements AgeIsANumber, AgeIsNotANumber {
    age = 0;
 // ~~~
 // Error: Property 'age' in type 'AsNumber' is not assignable
 // to the same property in base type 'AgeIsNotANumber'.
 //    Type 'number' is not assignable to type '() => string'.
}
```

```
class NotAsNumber implements AgeIsANumber, AgeIsNotANumber {
    age() { return ""; }
 // ~~~
 // Error: Property 'age' in type 'NotAsNumber' is not assignable
 // to the same property in base type 'AgeIsANumber'.
 //   Type '() => string' is not assignable to type 'number'.
}
```

Cases where two interfaces describe very different object shapes generally indicate you shouldn't try to implement them with the same class.

Extending a Class

TypeScript adds type checking onto the JavaScript concept of a class extending, or subclassing, another class. To start, any method or property declared on a base class will be available on the subclass, also known as the derived class.

In this example, Teacher declares a teach method that may be used by instances of the StudentTeacher subclass:

```
class Teacher {
    teach() {
        console.log("The surest test of discipline is its absence.");
    }
}

class StudentTeacher extends Teacher {
    learn() {
        console.log("I cannot afford the luxury of a closed mind.");
    }
}

const teacher = new StudentTeacher();
teacher.teach(); // Ok (defined on base)
teacher.learn(); // Ok (defined on subclass)

teacher.other();
 //      ~~~~~
 // Error: Property 'other' does not exist on type 'StudentTeacher'.
```

Extension Assignability

Subclasses inherit members from their base class much like derived interfaces extend base interfaces. Instances of subclasses have all the members of their base class and thus may be used wherever an instance of the base is required. If a base class doesn't have all the members a subclass does, then it can't be used when the more specific subclass is required.

Instances of the following `Lesson` class may not be used where instances of its derived `OnlineLesson` are required, but derived instances may be used to satisfy either the base or subclass:

```
class Lesson {
    subject: string;

    constructor(subject: string) {
        this.subject = subject;
    }
}

class OnlineLesson extends Lesson {
    url: string;

    constructor(subject: string, url: string) {
        super(subject);
        this.url = url;
    }
}

let lesson: Lesson;
lesson = new Lesson("coding"); // Ok
lesson = new OnlineLesson("coding", "oreilly.com"); // Ok

let online: OnlineLesson;
online = new OnlineLesson("coding", "oreilly.com"); // Ok

online = new Lesson("coding");
// Error: Property 'url' is missing in type
// 'Lesson' but required in type 'OnlineLesson'.
```

Per TypeScript's structural typing, if all the members on a subclass already exist on its base class with the same type, then instances of the base class are still allowed to be used in place of the subclass.

In this example, `LabeledPastGrades` only adds an optional property to `PastGrades`, so instances of the base class may be used in place of the subclass:

```
class PastGrades {
    grades: number[] = [];
}

class LabeledPastGrades extends PastGrades {
    label?: string;
}

let subClass: LabeledPastGrades;

subClass = new LabeledPastGrades(); // Ok
subClass = new PastGrades(); // Ok
```

In most real-world code, subclasses generally add new required type information on top of their base class. This structural checking behavior may seem unexpected but doesn't come up very often.

Overridden Constructors

As with vanilla JavaScript, subclasses are not required by TypeScript to define their own constructor. Subclasses without their own constructor implicitly use the constructor from their base class.

In JavaScript, if a subclass does declare its own constructor, then it must call its base class constructor via the super keyword. Subclass constructors may declare any parameters regardless of what their base class requires. TypeScript's type checker will make sure that the call to the base class constructor uses the correct parameters.

In this example, PassingAnnouncer's constructor correctly calls the base constructor with a number argument, while FailingAnnouncer gets a type error for forgetting to make that call:

```
class GradeAnnouncer {
    message: string;

    constructor(grade: number) {
        this.message = grade < 65 ? "Maybe next time..." : "You pass!";
    }
}

class PassingAnnouncer extends GradeAnnouncer {
    constructor() {
        super(100);
    }
}

class FailingAnnouncer extends GradeAnnouncer {
    constructor() { }
//  ~~~~~~~~~~~~~~~~~
// Error: Constructors for subclasses must contain a 'super' call.
}
```

As per JavaScript rules, the constructor of a subclass must call the base constructor before accessing this or super. TypeScript will report a type error if it sees a this or super being accessed before super().

The following ContinuedGradesTally class erroneously refers to this.grades in its constructor before calling to super():

```
class GradesTally {
    grades: number[] = [];

    addGrades(...grades: number[]) {
        this.grades.push(...grades);
        return this.grades.length;
    }
}

class ContinuedGradesTally extends GradesTally {
    constructor(previousGrades: number[]) {
        this.grades = [...previousGrades];
        // Error: 'super' must be called before accessing
        // 'this' in the constructor of a subclass.

        super();

        console.log("Starting with length", this.grades.length); // Ok
    }
}
```

Overridden Methods

Subclasses may redeclare new methods with the same names as the base class, as long as the method on the subclass method is assignable to the method on the base class. Remember, since subclasses can be used wherever the original class is used, the types of the new methods must be usable in place of the original methods.

In this example, FailureCounter's countGrades method is permitted because it has the same first parameter and return type as the base GradeCounter's countGrades method. AnyFailureChecker's countGrades causes a type error for having the wrong return type:

```
class GradeCounter {
    countGrades(grades: string[], letter: string) {
        return grades.filter(grade => grade === letter).length;
    }
}

class FailureCounter extends GradeCounter {
    countGrades(grades: string[]) {
        return super.countGrades(grades, "F");
    }
}

class AnyFailureChecker extends GradeCounter {
    countGrades(grades: string[]) {
        // Property 'countGrades' in type 'AnyFailureChecker' is not
        // assignable to the same property in base type 'GradeCounter'.
        //    Type '(grades: string[]) => boolean' is not assignable
        //    to type '(grades: string[], letter: string) => number'.
```

```
    //      Type 'boolean' is not assignable to type 'number'.
        return super.countGrades(grades, "F") !== 0;
    }
}

const counter: GradeCounter = new AnyFailureChecker();
//      ~~~~~~~
// Type 'AnyFailureChecker' is not assignable to type 'GradeCounter'.
//   The types returned by 'countGrades(...)' are incompatible between these types.
//      Type 'boolean' is not assignable to type 'number'.(2322)

// Expected type: number
// Actual type: boolean
const count = counter.countGrades(["A", "C", "F"], "C");
```

Overridden Properties

Subclasses may also explicitly redeclare properties of their base class with the same name, as long as the new type is assignable to the type on the base class. As with overridden methods, subclasses must structurally match up with base classes.

Most subclasses that redeclare properties do so either to make those properties a more specific subset of a type union or to make the properties a type that extends from the base class property's type.

In this example, the base class Assignment declares its grade to be number | undefined, while the subclass GradedAssignment declares it as a number that must always exist:

```
class Assignment {
    grade?: number;
}

class GradedAssignment extends Assignment {
    grade: number;

    constructor(grade: number) {
        super();
        this.grade = grade;
    }
}
```

Expanding the allowed set of values of a property's union type is not allowed, as doing so would make the subclass property no longer assignable to the base class property's type.

In this example, VagueGrade's value tries to add | string on top of the base class NumericGrade's number type, causing a type error:

```
class NumericGrade {
    value = 0;
```

```
    }

class VagueGrade extends NumericGrade {
    value = Math.random() > 0.5 ? 1 : "...";
    // Error: Property 'value' in type 'VagueGrade' is not
    // assignable to the same property in base type 'JustNumber'.
    //   Type 'string | number' is not assignable to type 'number'.
    //      Type 'string' is not assignable to type 'number'.
}

const instance: NumericGrade = new VagueGrade();

// Expected type: number
// Actual type: number | string
instance.value;
```

Abstract Classes

It can sometimes be useful to create a base class that doesn't itself declare the implementation of some methods, but instead expects a subclass to provide them. Marking
a class as abstract is done by adding TypeScript's `abstract` keyword in front of
the class name and in front of any method intended to be abstract. Those abstract
method declarations skip providing a body in the abstract base class; instead, they are
declared the same way an interface would be.

In this example, the `School` class and its `getStudentTypes` method are marked as
abstract. Its subclasses—`Preschool` and `Absence`—are therefore expected to implement `getStudentTypes`:

```
abstract class School {
    readonly name: string;

    constructor(name: string) {
        this.name = name;
    }

    abstract getStudentTypes(): string[];
}

class Preschool extends School {
    getStudentTypes() {
        return ["preschooler"];
    }
}

class Absence extends School { }
    // ~~~~~~~
    // Error: Nonabstract class 'Absence' does not implement
    // inherited abstract member 'getStudentTypes' from class 'School'.
```

An abstract class cannot be instantiated directly, as it doesn't have definitions for some methods that its implementation may assume do exist. Only nonabstract ("concrete") classes can be instantiated.

Continuing the `School` example, attempting to call `new School` would result in a TypeScript type error:

```
let school: School;

school = new Preschool("Sunnyside Daycare"); // Ok

school = new School("somewhere else");
// Error: Cannot create an instance of an abstract class.
```

Abstract classes are often used in frameworks where consumers are expected to fill out details of a class. The class may be used as a type annotation to indicate values must adhere to the class—as with the earlier example of `school: School`—but creating new instances must be done with subclasses.

Member Visibility

JavaScript includes the ability to start the name of a class member with # to mark it as a "private" class member. Private class members may only be accessed by instances of that class. JavaScript runtimes enforce that privacy by throwing an error if an area of code outside the class tries to access the private method or property.

TypeScript's class support predates JavaScript's true # privacy, and while TypeScript supports private class members, it also allows a slightly more nuanced set of privacy definitions on class methods and properties that exist solely in the type system. TypeScript's member visibilities are achieved by adding one of the following keywords before the declaration name of a class member:

`public` *(default)*
　　Allowed to be accessed by anybody, anywhere

`protected`
　　Allowed to be accessed only by the class itself and its subclasses

`private`
　　Allowed to be accessed only by the class itself

These keywords exist purely within the type system. They're removed along with all other type system syntax when the code is compiled to JavaScript.

Here, `Base` declares two `public` members, one `protected`, one `private`, and one true private with `#truePrivate`. `Subclass` is allowed to access the `public` and `protected` members but not `private` or `#truePrivate`:

```
class Base {
    isPublicImplicit = 0;
    public isPublicExplicit = 1;
    protected isProtected = 2;
    private isPrivate = 3;
    #truePrivate = 4;
}

class Subclass extends Base {
    examples() {
        this.isPublicImplicit; // Ok
        this.isPublicExplicit; // Ok
        this.isProtected; // Ok

        this.isPrivate;
        // Error: Property 'isPrivate' is private
        // and only accessible within class 'Base'.

        this.#truePrivate;
        // Property '#truePrivate' is not accessible outside
        // class 'Base' because it has a private identifier.
    }
}

new Subclass().isPublicImplicit; // Ok
new Subclass().isPublicExplicit; // Ok

new Subclass().isProtected;
//             ~~~~~~~~~~~
// Error: Property 'isProtected' is protected
// and only accessible within class 'Base' and its subclasses.

new Subclass().isPrivate;
//             ~~~~~~~~~~~
// Error: Property 'isPrivate' is private
// and only accessible within class 'Base'.
```

The key difference between TypeScript's member visibilities and JavaScript's true private declarations is that TypeScript's exist only in the type system, while JavaScript's also exist at runtime. A TypeScript class member declared as protected or private will compile to the same JavaScript code as if they were declared public explicitly or implicitly. As with interfaces and type annotations, visibility keywords are erased when outputting JavaScript. Only # private fields are truly private in runtime JavaScript.

Visibility modifiers may be marked along with readonly. To declare a member both as readonly and with an explicit visibility, the visibility comes first.

This TwoKeywords class declares its name member as both private and readonly:

```
class TwoKeywords {
    private readonly name: string;

    constructor() {
        this.name = "Anne Sullivan"; // Ok
    }

    log() {
        console.log(this.name); // Ok
    }
}

const two = new TwoKeywords();

two.name = "Savitribai Phule";
 // ~~~~
 // Error: Property 'name' is private and
 // only accessible within class 'TwoKeywords'.
 // ~~~~
 // Error: Cannot assign to 'name'
 // because it is a read-only property.
```

Note that it is not permitted to mix TypeScript's old member visibility keyword with JavaScript's new # private fields. Private fields are always private by default, so there's no need to additionally mark them with the private keyword.

Static Field Modifiers

JavaScript allows declaring members on a class itself—rather than its instances—using the static keyword. TypeScript supports using the static keyword on its own and/or with readonly and/or with one of the visibility keywords. When combined, the visibility keyword comes first, then static, then readonly.

This Question class puts them all together to make its static prompt and answer properties both readonly and protected:

```
class Question {
    protected static readonly answer: "bash";
    protected static readonly prompt =
        "What's an ogre's favorite programming language?";

    guess(getAnswer: (prompt: string) => string) {
        // Ok
        const answer = getAnswer(Question.prompt);

        // Ok
```

```
        if (answer === Question.answer) {
            console.log("You got it!");
        } else {
            console.log("Try again...")
        }
    }
}

Question.answer;
//       ~~~~~~
// Error: Property 'answer' is protected and only
// accessible within class 'Question' and its subclasses.
```

Using read-only and/or visibility modifiers to static class fields is useful for restricting those fields from being accessed or modified outside their class.

Summary

This chapter introduced a plethora of type system features and syntaxes around classes:

- Declaring and using class methods and properties
- Marking properties readonly and/or optional
- Using class names as types in type annotations
- Implementing interfaces to enforce class instance shapes
- Extending classes, along with assignability and override rules for subclasses
- Marking classes and methods as abstract
- Adding type system modifiers to class fields

Now that you've finished reading this chapter, practice what you've learned on *https://learningtypescript.com/classes*.

_____

Why do object-oriented programming developers always wear suits?
Because they've got class.

CHAPTER 9

Type Modifiers

Types of types from types.
"It's turtles all the way down,"
Anders likes to say.

By now you've read all about how the TypeScript type system works with existing JavaScript constructs such as arrays, classes, and objects. For this chapter and Chapter 10, "Generics", I'm going to take a step further into the type system itself and show features that focus on writing more precise types, as well as types based on other types.

Top Types

I mentioned the concept of a *bottom type* back in Chapter 4, "Objects" to describe a type that can have no possible values and can't be reached. It stands to reason that the opposite might also exist in type theory. It does!

A *top type*, or universal type, is a type that can represent any possible value in a system. Values of all other types can be provided to a location whose type is a top type. In other words, all types are assignable to a top type.

any, Again

The any type can act as a top type, in that any type can be provided to a location of type any. any is generally used when a location is allowed to accept data of any type, such as the parameters to `console.log`:

```
let anyValue: any;
anyValue = "Lucille Ball"; // Ok
anyValue = 123; // Ok

console.log(anyValue); // Ok
```

The problem with any is that it explicitly tells TypeScript not to perform type checking on that value's assignability or members. That lack of safety is useful if you'd like to quickly bypass TypeScript's type checker, but the disabling of type checking reduces TypeScript's usefulness for that value.

For example, the `name.toUpperCase()` call below definitely will crash, but because `name` is declared as `any`, TypeScript does not report a type complaint:

```
function greetComedian(name: any) {
    // No type error...
    console.log(`Announcing ${name.toUpperCase()}!`);
}

greetComedian({ name: "Bea Arthur" });
    // Runtime error: name.toUpperCase is not a function
```

If you want to indicate that a value can be anything, the `unknown` type is much safer.

unknown

The `unknown` type in TypeScript is its true top type. `unknown` is similar to `any` in that all objects may be passed to locations of type `unknown`. The key difference with `unknown` is that TypeScript is much more restrictive about values of type `unknown`:

- TypeScript does not allow directly accessing properties of `unknown` typed values.

- `unknown` is not assignable to types that are not a top type (`any` or `unknown`).

Attempting to access a property of an `unknown` typed value, as in the following snippet, will cause TypeScript to report a type error:

```
function greetComedian(name: unknown) {
    console.log(`Announcing ${name.toUpperCase()}!`);
    //                         ~~~~
    // Error: Object is of type 'unknown'.
}
```

The only way TypeScript will allow code to access members on a name of type `unknown` is if the value's type is narrowed, such as using `instanceof` or `typeof`, or with a type assertion.

This code snippet uses `typeof` to narrow `name` from `unknown` to `string`:

```
function greetComedianSafety(name: unknown) {
    if (typeof name === "string") {
        console.log(`Announcing ${name.toUpperCase()}!`); // Ok
    } else {
        console.log("Well, I'm off.");
    }
}

greetComedianSafety("Betty White"); // Logs: Announcing BETTY WHITE!
greetComedianSafety({}); // Logs: Well, I'm off.
```

Those two restrictions make unknown a much safer type to use than any. You should generally prefer using unknown instead of any when possible.

Type Predicates

I've previously shown you how JavaScript constructs such as `instanceof` and `typeof` can be used to narrow types. That's all fine and good for directly using that limited set of checks, but it gets lost if you wrap the logic with a function.

For example, this `isNumberOrString` function takes in a value and returns a boolean indicating whether the value is a `number` or `string`. We as humans can infer that the `value` inside the `if` statement must therefore be one of those two types since `isNumberOrString(value)` returned true, but TypeScript does not. All it knows is that `isNumberOrString` returns a boolean—not that it's meant to narrow the type of an argument:

```
function isNumberOrString(value: unknown) {
    return ['number', 'string'].includes(typeof value);
}

function logValueIfExists(value: number | string | null | undefined) {
    if (isNumberOrString(value)) {
        // Type of value: number | string | null | undefined
        value.toString();
        // Error: Object is possibly undefined.
    } else {
        console.log("Value does not exist:", value);
    }
}
```

TypeScript has a special syntax for functions that return a boolean meant to indicate whether an argument is a particular type. This is referred to as a *type predicate*, also sometimes called a "user-defined type guard": you the developer are creating your own type guard akin to `instanceof` or `typeof`. Type predicates are commonly used to indicate whether an argument passed in as a parameter is a more specific type than the parameter's.

Type predicate's return types can be declared as the name of a parameter, the `is` keyword, and some type:

```
function typePredicate(input: WideType): input is NarrowType;
```

We can change the previous example's helper function to have an explicit return type that explicitly states `value is number | string`. TypeScript will then be able to infer that blocks of code only reachable if `value is number | string` is true must have a value of type `number | string`. Additionally, blocks of code only reachable if `value is number | string` is false must have a value of type `null | undefined`:

```
function isNumberOrString(value: unknown): value is number | string {
    return ['number', 'string'].includes(typeof value);
}

function logValueIfExists(value: number | string | null | undefined) {
    if (isNumberOrString(value)) {
        // Type of value: number | string
        value.toString(); // Ok
    } else {
        // Type of value: null | undefined
        console.log("value does not exist:", value);
    }
}
```

You can think of a type predicate as returning not just a boolean, but also an indication that the argument was that more specific type.

Type predicates are often used to check whether an object already known to be an instance of one interface is an instance of a more specific interface.

Here, the StandupComedian interface contains additional information on top of Comedian. The isStandupComedian type guard can be used to check whether a general Comedian is specifically a StandupComedian:

```
interface Comedian {
    funny: boolean;
}

interface StandupComedian extends Comedian {
    routine: string;
}

function isStandupComedian(value: Comedian): value is StandupComedian {
    return 'routine' in value;
}

function workWithComedian(value: Comedian) {
    if (isStandupComedian(value)) {
        // Type of value: StandupComedian
        console.log(value.routine); // Ok
    }

    // Type of value: Comedian
    console.log(value.routine);
    //                 ~~~~~~~
    // Error: Property 'routine' does not exist on type 'Comedian'.
}
```

Be warned: because type predicates also narrow types in the false case, you might get surprising results if a type predicate checks more than just the type of its input.

This `isLongString` type predicate returns `false` if its `input` parameter is `undefined` or a `string` with a length less than 7. As a result, the `else` statement (its false case) is narrowed to thinking `text` must be type `undefined`:

```
function isLongString(input: string | undefined): input is string {
    return !!(input && input.length >= 7);
}

function workWithText(text: string | undefined) {
    if (isLongString(text)) {
        // Type of text: string
        console.log("Long text:", text.length);
    } else {
        // Type of text: undefined
        console.log("Short text:", text?.length);
        //                         ~~~~~~
        // Error: Property 'length' does not exist on type 'never'.
    }
}
```

Type predicates that do more than verify the type of a property or value are easy to misuse. I generally recommend avoiding them when possible. Simpler type predicates are sufficient for most cases.

Type Operators

Not all types can be represented using only a keyword or a name of an existing type. It can sometimes be necessary to create a new type that combines both, performing some transformation on the properties of an existing type.

keyof

JavaScript objects can have members retrieved using dynamic values, which are commonly (but not necessarily) `string` typed. Representing these keys in the type system can be tricky. Using a catchall primitive such as `string` would allow invalid keys for the container value.

That's why TypeScript when using stricter configuration settings—covered in Chapter 13, "Configuration Options"—would report an error on the `ratings[key]` as seen in the next example. Type `string` allows values not allowed as properties on the `Ratings` interface, and `Ratings` doesn't declare an index signature to allow any `string` keys:

```
interface Ratings {
    audience: number;
    critic: number;
}
```

```
function getRating(ratings: Ratings, key: string): number {
    return ratings[key];
    //     ~~~~~~~~~~~
    // Error: Element implicitly has an 'any' type because expression
    // of type 'string' can't be used to index type 'Ratings'.
    //   No index signature with a parameter of
    //   type 'string' was found on type 'Ratings'.
}

const ratings: Ratings = { audience: 66, critic: 84 };

getRating(ratings, 'audience'); // Ok

getRating(ratings, 'not valid'); // Ok, but shouldn't be
```

Another option would be to use a type union of literals for the allowed keys. That would be more accurate in properly restricting to only the keys that exist on the container value:

```
function getRating(ratings: Ratings, key: 'audience' | 'critic'): number {
    return ratings[key]; // Ok
}

const ratings: Ratings = { audience: 66, critic: 84 };

getRating(ratings, 'audience'); // Ok

getRating(ratings, 'not valid');
//                  ~~~~~~~~~~~
// Error: Argument of type '"not valid"' is not
// assignable to parameter of type '"audience" | "critic"'.
```

However, what if the interface has dozens or more members? You would have to type out each of those members' keys into the union type and keep them up-to-date. What a pain.

TypeScript instead provides a keyof operator that takes in an existing type and gives back a union of all the keys allowed on that type. Place it in front of the name of a type wherever you might use a type, such as a type annotation.

Here, keyof Ratings is equivalent to 'audience' | 'critic' but is much quicker to write out and won't need to be manually updated if the Ratings interface ever changes:

```
function getCountKeyof(ratings: Ratings, key: keyof Ratings): number {
    return ratings[key]; // Ok
}

const ratings: Ratings = { audience: 66, critic: 84 };

getCountKeyof(ratings, 'audience'); // Ok
```

```
getCountKeyof(ratings, 'not valid');
//                      ~~~~~~~~~~~
// Error: Argument of type '"not valid"' is not
// assignable to parameter of type 'keyof Ratings'.
```

keyof is a great feature for creating union types based on the keys of existing types. It also combines well with other type operators in TypeScript, allowing for some very nifty patterns you'll see later in this chapter and Chapter 15, "Type Operations".

typeof

Another type operator provided by TypeScript is typeof. It gives back the type of a provided value. This can be useful if the value's type would be annoyingly complex to write manually.

Here, the adaptation variable is declared as being the same type as original:

```
const original = {
    medium: "movie",
    title: "Mean Girls",
};

let adaptation: typeof original;

if (Math.random() > 0.5) {
    adaptation = { ...original, medium: "play" }; // Ok
} else {
    adaptation = { ...original, medium: 2 };
    //                          ~~~~~~
    // Error: Type 'number' is not assignable to type 'string'.
}
```

Although the typeof *type* operator visually looks like the *runtime* typeof operator used to return a string description of a value's type, the two are different. They only coincidentally use the same word. Remember: the JavaScript operator is a runtime operator that returns the string name of a type. The TypeScript version, because it's a type operator, can only be used in types and won't appear in compiled code.

keyof typeof

typeof retrieves the type of a value, and keyof retrieves the allowed keys on a type. TypeScript allows the two keywords to be chained together to succinctly retrieve the allowed keys on a value's type. Putting them together, the typeof type operator becomes wonderfully useful for working with keyof type operations.

In this example, the logRating function is meant to take in one of the keys of the ratings value. Instead of creating an interface, the code uses keyof typeof to indicate key must be one of the keys on the type of the ratings value:

```
const ratings = {
    imdb: 8.4,
    metacritic: 82,
};

function logRating(key: keyof typeof ratings) {
    console.log(ratings[key]);
}

logRating("imdb"); // Ok

logRating("invalid");
//         ~~~~~~~~~
// Error: Argument of type '"invalid"' is not assignable
// to parameter of type '"imdb" | "metacritic"'.
```

By combining keyof and typeof, we get to save ourselves the pain of writing out—and having to update—types representing the allowed keys on objects that don't have an explicit interface type.

Type Assertions

TypeScript works best when your code is "strongly typed": all the values in your code have precisely known types. Features such as top types and type guards provide ways to wrangle complex code into being understood by TypeScript's type checker. However, sometimes it's not reasonably possible to be 100% accurate in telling the type system how your code is meant to work.

For example, JSON.parse intentionally returns the top type any. There's no way to safely inform the type system that a particular string value given to JSON.parse should return any particular value type. (As we will see in Chapter 10, "Generics", adding a generic type to parse that is only used once for a return type would violate a best practice known as The Golden Rule of Generics.)

TypeScript provides a syntax for overriding the type system's understanding of a value's type: a "type assertion," also known as a "type cast." On a value that is meant to be a different type, you can place the as keyword followed by a type. TypeScript will defer to your assertion and treat the value as that type.

In this snippet, it is possible that the returned result from JSON.parse is meant to be a type such as string[], [string, string], or ["grace", "frankie"]. The snippet uses type assertions for three of the lines of code to switch the type from any to one of those:

```
const rawData = `["grace", "frankie"]`;

// Type: any
JSON.parse(rawData);
```

```
// Type: string[]
JSON.parse(rawData) as string[];

// Type: [string, string]
JSON.parse(rawData) as [string, string];

// Type: ["grace", "frankie"]
JSON.parse(rawData) as ["grace", "frankie"];
```

Type assertions exist only in the TypeScript type system. They're removed along with all other pieces of type system syntax when compiled to JavaScript. The previous code would look like this when compiled to JavaScript:

```
const rawData = `["grace", "frankie"]`;

// Type: any
JSON.parse(rawData);

// Type: string[]
JSON.parse(rawData);

// Type: [string, string]
JSON.parse(rawData);

// Type: ["grace", "frankie"]
JSON.parse(rawData);
```

If you're working with older libraries or code, you may see a different casting syntax that looks like <type>item instead of item as type. Because this syntax is incompatible with JSX syntax and therefore does not work in *.tsx* files, it is discouraged.

TypeScript best practice is generally to avoid using type assertions when possible. It's best for your code to be fully typed and to not need to interfere with TypeScript's understanding of its types using assertions. But occasionally there will be cases where type assertions are useful, even necessary.

Asserting Caught Error Types

Error handling is another place where type assertions may come in handy. It is generally impossible to know what type a caught error in a catch block will be because the code in the try block may unexpectedly throw any object different from what you expect. Furthermore, although JavaScript best practice is to always throw an instance of the Error class, some projects instead throw string literals or other surprising values.

If you are absolutely confident that an area of code will only throw an instance of the Error class, you can use a type assertion to treat a caught assertion as an Error. This snippet accesses the message property of a caught error that it assumes is an instance of the Error class:

```
try {
    // (code that may throw an error)
} catch (error) {
    console.warn("Oh no!", (error as Error).message);
}
```

It is generally safer to use a form of type narrowing such as an instanceof check to ensure the thrown error is the expected error type. This snippet checks whether the thrown error is an instance of the Error class to know whether to log that message or the error itself:

```
try {
    // (code that may throw an error)
} catch (error) {
    console.warn("Oh no!", error instanceof Error ? error.message : error);
}
```

Non-Null Assertions

Another common use case for type assertions is to remove null and/or undefined from a variable that only theoretically, not practically, might include them. That situation is so common that TypeScript includes a shorthand for it. Instead of writing out as and the full type of whatever a value is excluding null and undefined, you can use a ! to signify the same thing. In other words, the ! non-null assertion asserts that the type is not null or undefined.

The following two type assertions are identical in that they both result in Date and not Date | undefined:

```
// Inferred type: Date | undefined
let maybeDate = Math.random() > 0.5
    ? undefined
    : new Date();

// Asserted type: Date
maybeDate as Date;

// Asserted type: Date
maybeDate!;
```

Non-null assertions are particularly useful with APIs such as Map.get that return a value or undefined if it doesn't exist.

Here, seasonCounts is a general Map<string, number>. We know that it contains an "I Love Lucy" key so the knownValue variable can use a ! to remove | undefined from its type:

```
const seasonCounts = new Map([
    ["I Love Lucy", 6],
    ["The Golden Girls", 7],
]);

// Type: number | undefined
const maybeValue = seasonCounts.get("I Love Lucy");

console.log(maybeValue.toPrecision());
//          ~~~~~~~~~~
// Error: Object is possibly 'undefined'.

// Type: number
const knownValue = seasonCounts.get("I Love Lucy")!;

console.log(knownValue.toPrecision()); // Ok
```

Type Assertion Caveats

Type assertions, like the any type, are a necessary escape hatch for TypeScript's type system. Therefore, also like the any type, they should be avoided whenever reasonably possible. It is often better to have more accurate types representing your code than it is to make it easier to assert on a value's type. Those assertions are often wrong—either already so at the time of writing, or they become wrong later on as the codebase changes.

For example, suppose the seasonCounts example were to change over time to have different values in the map. Its non-null assertion might still make the code pass TypeScript type checking, but there might be a runtime error:

```
const seasonCounts = new Map([
    ["Broad City", 5],
    ["Community", 6],
]);

// Type: string
const knownValue = seasonCounts.get("I Love Lucy")!;

console.log(knownValue.toPrecision()); // No type error, but...
// Runtime TypeError: Cannot read property 'toPrecision' of undefined.
```

Type assertions should generally be used sparingly, and only when you're absolutely certain it is safe to do so.

Assertions versus declarations

There is a difference between using a type annotation to declare a variable's type versus using a type assertion to change the type of a variable with an initial value. TypeScript's type checker performs assignability checking on a variable's initial value against the variable's type annotation when both exist. A type assertion, however, explicitly tells TypeScript to skip some of its type checking.

The following code creates two objects of type `Entertainer` with the same flaw: a missing `acts` member. TypeScript is able to catch the error in the `declared` variable because of its `: Entertainer` type annotation. It is not able to catch the error on the `asserted` variable because of the type assertion:

```
interface Entertainer {
    acts: string[];
    name: string;
}

const declared: Entertainer = {
    name: "Moms Mabley",
};
// Error: Property 'acts' is missing in type
// '{ name: string; }' but required in type 'Entertainer'.

const asserted = {
    name: "Moms Mabley",
} as Entertainer; // Ok, but...

// Both of these statements would fail at runtime with:
// Runtime TypeError: Cannot read properties of undefined (reading 'join')
console.log(declared.acts.join(", "));
console.log(asserted.acts.join(", "));
```

It is therefore strongly preferable to either use a type annotation or allow TypeScript to infer a variable's type from its initial value.

Assertion assignability

Type assertions are meant to be only a small escape hatch, for situations where some value's type is slightly incorrect. TypeScript will only allow type assertions between two types if one of the types is assignable to the other. If the type assertion is between two completely unrelated types, then TypeScript will notice and report a type error.

For example, switching from one primitive to another is not allowed, as primitives have nothing to do with each other:

```
let myValue = "Stella!" as number;
//                ~~~~~~~~~~~~~~~~~~~
// Error: Conversion of type 'string' to type 'number'
// may be a mistake because neither type sufficiently
// overlaps with the other. If this was intentional,
// convert the expression to 'unknown' first.
```

If you absolutely must switch a value from one type to a totally unrelated type, you can use a double type assertion. First cast the value to a top type—any or unknown—and then cast that result to the unrelated type:

```
let myValueDouble = "1337" as unknown as number; // Ok, but... eww.
```

as unknown as... double type assertions are dangerous and almost always a sign of something incorrect in the types of the surrounding code. Using them as an escape hatch from the type system means the type system may not be able to save you when changes to surrounding code would cause an issue with previously working code. I teach double type assertions only as a precautionary tale to help explain the type system, not to encourage their use.

Const Assertions

Back in Chapter 6, "Arrays", I introduced an as const syntax for changing a mutable array type to a read-only tuple type and promised to use it more later in the book. That time is now!

Const assertions can generally be used to indicate that any value—array, primitive, value, you name it—should be treated as the constant, immutable version of itself. Specifically, as const applies the following three rules to whatever type it receives:

- Arrays are treated as readonly tuples, not mutable arrays.
- Literals are treated as literals, not their general primitive equivalents.
- Properties on objects are considered readonly.

You've already seen arrays become tuples, as with this array being asserted as a tuple:

```
// Type: (number | string)[]
[0, ''];

// Type: readonly [0, '']
[0, ''] as const;
```

Let's dig into the other two changes as const produces.

Literals to Primitives

It can be useful for the type system to understand a literal value to be that specific literal, rather than widening it to its general primitive.

For example, similar to functions that return tuples, it might be useful for a function to be known to produce a specific literal instead of a general primitive. These functions also return values that can be made more specific—here, getNameConst's return type is the more specific "Maria Bamford" instead of the general string:

```
// Type: () => string
const getName = () => "Maria Bamford";

// Type: () => "Maria Bamford"
const getNameConst = () => "Maria Bamford" as const;
```

It may also be useful to have specific fields on a value be more specific literals. Many popular libraries ask that a discriminant field on a value be a specific literal so the types of their code can more specifically make inferences on the value. Here, the narrowJoke variable has a style of type "one-liner" instead of string, so it can be provided in a location that needs type Joke:

```
interface Joke {
    quote: string;
    style: "story" | "one-liner";
}

function tellJoke(joke: Joke) {
    if (joke.style === "one-liner") {
        console.log(joke.quote);
    } else {
        console.log(joke.quote.split("\n"));
    }
}

// Type: { quote: string; style: "one-liner" }
const narrowJoke = {
    quote: "If you stay alive for no other reason do it for spite.",
    style: "one-liner" as const,
};

tellJoke(narrowJoke); // Ok

// Type: { quote: string; style: string }
const wideObject = {
    quote: "Time flies when you are anxious!",
    style: "one-liner",
};

tellJoke(wideObject);
// Error: Argument of type '{ quote: string; style: string; }'
// is not assignable to parameter of type 'Joke'.
//   Types of property 'style' are incompatible.
//     Type 'string' is not assignable to type '"story" | "one-liner"'.
```

Read-Only Objects

Object literals such as those used as the initial value of a variable generally widen the types of properties the same way the initial values of `let` variables widen. String values such as `'apple'` become primitives such as `string`, arrays are typed as arrays instead of tuples, and so on. This can be inconvenient when some or all of those values are meant to later be used in a place that requires their specific literal type.

Asserting a value literal with `as const`, however, switches the inferred type to be as specific as possible. All member properties become `readonly`, literals are considered their own literal type instead of their general primitive type, arrays become read-only tuples, and so on. In other words, applying a const assertion to a value literal makes that value literal immutable and recursively applies the same const assertion logic to all its members.

As an example, the `preferencesMutable` value that follows is declared without an `as const`, so its names are the primitive type `string` and it's allowed to be modified. `preferencesReadonly`, however, is declared with an `as const`, so its member values are literals and not allowed to be modified:

```
function describePreference(preference: "maybe" | "no" | "yes") {
    switch (preference) {
        case "maybe":
            return "I suppose...";
        case "no":
            return "No thanks.";
        case "yes":
            return "Yes please!";
    }
}

// Type: { movie: string, standup: string }
const preferencesMutable = {
    movie: "maybe"
    standup: "yes",
};

describePreference(preferencesMutable.movie);
//                 ~~~~~~~~~~~~~~~~~~~~~~~~
// Error: Argument of type 'string' is not assignable
// to parameter of type '"maybe" | "no" | "yes"'.

preferencesMutable.movie = "no"; // Ok

// Type: readonly { readonly movie: "maybe", readonly standup: "yes" }
const preferencesReadonly = {
    movie: "maybe"
    standup: "yes",
} as const;
```

```
describePreference(preferencesReadonly.movie); // Ok

preferencesReadonly.movie = "no";
//                ~~~~~
// Error: Cannot assign to 'movie' because it is a read-only property.
```

Summary

In this chapter, you used type modifiers to take existing objects and/or types and turn them into new types:

- Top types: the highly permissive any and the highly restrictive unknown
- Type operators: using keyof to grab the keys of a type and/or typeof to grab the type of a value
- Using—and when not to use—type assertions to sneakily change the type of a value
- Narrowing types using as const assertions

 Now that you've finished reading this chapter, practice what you've learned on *https://learningtypescript.com/type-modifiers*.

Why was the literal type being stubborn?
It had a narrow mind.

CHAPTER 10

Generics

*Variables you
declare in the type system?
A whole new (typed) world!*

All the type syntaxes you've learned about so far are meant to be used with types that are completely known when they're being written. Sometimes, however, a piece of code may be intended to work with various different types depending on how it's called.

Take this `identity` function in JavaScript meant to receive an input of any possible type and return that same input as output. How would you describe its parameter type and return type?

```
function identity(input) {
    return input;
}

identity("abc");
identity(123);
identity({ quote: "I think your self emerges more clearly over time." });
```

We could declare `input` as any, but then the return type of the function would also be any:

```
function identity(input: any) {
    return input;
}

let value = identity(42); // Type of value: any
```

Given that `input` is allowed to be any input, we need a way to say that there is a relationship between the `input` type and the type the function returns. TypeScript captures relationships between types using *generics*.

In TypeScript, constructs such as functions may declare any number of generic *type parameters*: types that are determined for each usage of the generic construct. These type parameters are used as types in the construct to represent some type that can be different in each instance of the construct. Type parameters may be provided with different types, referred to as *type arguments*, for each instance of the construct but will remain consistent within that instance.

Type parameters typically have single-letter names like T and U or PascalCase names like Key and Value. In all of the constructs covered in this chapter, generics may be declared using < and > brackets, like someFunction<T> or SomeInterface<T>.

Generic Functions

A function may be made generic by placing an alias for a type parameter, wrapped in angle brackets, immediately before the parameters parentheses. That type parameter will then be available for usage in parameter type annotations, return type annotations, and type annotations inside the function's body.

The following version of identity declares a type parameter T for its input parameter, which allows TypeScript to infer that the return type of the function is T. TypeScript can then infer a different type for T every time identity is called:

```
function identity<T>(input: T) {
    return input;
}

const myString = identity("me"); // Type: "me"
const myNumber = identity(123); // Type: 123
```

Arrow functions can be generic too. Their generic declarations are also placed immediately before the (before their list of parameters.

The following arrow function is functionally the same as the previous declaration:

```
const identity = <T>(input: T) => input;

identity(123); // Type: 123
```

The syntax for generic arrow functions has some restrictions in *.tsx* files, as it conflicts with JSX syntax. See Chapter 13, "Configuration Options" for workarounds as well as configuring JSX and React support.

Adding type parameters to functions in this way allows them to be reused with different inputs while still maintaining type safety and avoiding any types.

Explicit Generic Call Types

Most of the time when calling generic functions, TypeScript will be able to infer type arguments based on how the function is being called. For example, in the previous examples' identity functions, TypeScript's type checker used an argument provided to identity to infer the corresponding function parameter's type argument.

Unfortunately, as with class members and variable types, sometimes there isn't enough information from a function's call to inform TypeScript what its type argument should resolve to. This will commonly happen if a generic construct is provided another generic construct whose type arguments aren't known.

TypeScript will default to assuming the unknown type for any type argument it cannot infer.

For example, the following logWrapper function takes in a callback with a parameter type set to logWrapper's type parameter Input. TypeScript can infer the type argument if logWrapper is called with a callback that explicitly declares its parameter type. If the parameter type is implicit, however, TypeScript has no way of knowing what Input should be:

```
function logWrapper<Input>(callback: (input: Input) => void) {
    return (input: Input) => {
        console.log("Input:", input);
        callback(input);
    };
}

// Type: (input: string) => void
logWrapper((input: string) => {
    console.log(input.length);
});

// Type: (input: unknown) => void
logWrapper((input) => {
    console.log(input.length);
    //                ~~~~~~
    // Error: Property 'length' does not exist on type 'unknown'.
});
```

To avoid defaulting to unknown, functions may be called with an explicit generic type argument that explicitly tells TypeScript what that type argument should be instead. TypeScript will perform type checking on the generic call to make sure the parameter being requested matches up to what's provided as a type argument.

Here, the logWrapper seen previously is provided with an explicit string for its Input generic. TypeScript can then infer that the callback's input parameter of generic type Input resolves to type string:

```
// Type: (input: string) => void
logWrapper<string>((input) => {
    console.log(input.length);
});

logWrapper<string>((input: boolean) => {
    //              ~~~~~~~~~~~~~~~~~~~~~~~
    // Argument of type '(input: boolean) => void' is not
    // assignable to parameter of type '(input: string) => void'.
    //    Types of parameters 'input' and 'input' are incompatible.
    //       Type 'string' is not assignable to type 'boolean'.
});
```

Much like explicit type annotations on variables, explicit type arguments may always be specified on a generic function but often aren't necessary. Many TypeScript developers generally only specify them when needed.

The following logWrapper usage explicitly specifies string both as a type argument and as a function parameter type. Either could be removed:

```
// Type: (input: string) => void
logWrapper<string>((input: string) => { /* ... */ });
```

The Name<Type> syntax for specifying a type argument will be the same for other generic constructs throughout this chapter.

Multiple Function Type Parameters

Functions may define any number of type parameters, separated by commas. Each call of the generic function may resolve its own set of values for each of the type parameters.

In this example, makeTuple declares two type parameters and returns a value typed as a read-only tuple with one, then the other:

```
function makeTuple<First, Second>(first: First, second: Second) {
    return [first, second] as const;
}

let tuple = makeTuple(true, "abc"); // Type of value: readonly [boolean, string]
```

Note that if a function declares multiple type parameters, calls to that function must explicitly declare either none of the generic types or all of them. TypeScript does not yet support inferring only some of the types of a generic call.

Here, makePair also takes in two type parameters, so either neither of them or both of them must be explicitly specified:

```
function makePair<Key, Value>(key: Key, value: Value) {
    return { key, value };
}

// Ok: neither type argument provided
makePair("abc", 123); // Type: { key: string; value: number }

// Ok: both type arguments provided
makePair<string, number>("abc", 123); // Type: { key: string; value: number }
makePair<"abc", 123>("abc", 123); // Type: { key: "abc"; value: 123 }

makePair<string>("abc", 123);
//       ~~~~~~
// Error: Expected 2 type arguments, but got 1.
```

 Try not to use more than one or two type parameters in any generic construct. As with runtime function parameters, the more you use, the harder it is to read and understand the code.

Generic Interfaces

Interfaces may be declared as generic as well. They follow similar generic rules to functions: they may have any number of type parameters declared between a < and > after their name. That generic type may later be used elsewhere in their declaration, such as on member types.

The following Box declaration has a T type parameter for a property. Creating an object declared to be a Box with a type argument enforces that the inside: T property matches that type argument:

```
interface Box<T> {
    inside: T;
}

let stringyBox: Box<string> = {
    inside: "abc",
};

let numberBox: Box<number> = {
    inside: 123,
}

let incorrectBox: Box<number> = {
    inside: false,
    // Error: Type 'boolean' is not assignable to type 'number'.
}
```

Fun fact: the built-in `Array` methods are defined in TypeScript as a generic interface! `Array` uses a type parameter T to represent the type of data stored within an array. Its pop and push methods look roughly like so:

```
interface Array<T> {
    // ...

    /**
     * Removes the last element from an array and returns it.
     * If the array is empty, undefined is returned and the array is not modified.
     */
    pop(): T | undefined;

    /**
     * Appends new elements to the end of an array,
     * and returns the new length of the array.
     * @param items new elements to add to the array.
     */
    push(...items: T[]): number;

    // ...
}
```

Inferred Generic Interface Types

As with generic functions, generic interface type arguments may be inferred from usage. TypeScript will do its best to infer type arguments from the types of values provided to a location declared as taking in a generic type.

This `getLast` function declares a type parameter `Value` that is then used for its `node` parameter. TypeScript can then infer `Value` based on the type of whatever value is passed in as an argument. It can even report a type error when an inferred type argument doesn't match the type of a value. Providing `getLast` with an object that doesn't include `next`, or whose inferred `Value` type argument is the same type, is allowed. Mismatching the provided object's `value` and `next.value`, though, is a type error:

```
interface LinkedNode<Value> {
    next?: LinkedNode<Value>;
    value: Value;
}

function getLast<Value>(node: LinkedNode<Value>): Value {
    return node.next ? getLast(node.next) : node.value;
}

// Inferred Value type argument: Date
let lastDate = getLast({
    value: new Date("09-13-1993"),
});
```

```
// Inferred Value type argument: string
let lastFruit = getLast({
    next: {
        value: "banana",
    },
    value: "apple",
});

// Inferred Value type argument: number
let lastMismatch = getLast({
    next: {
        value: 123
    },
    value: false,
//      ~~~~~
// Error: type 'boolean' is not assignable to type 'number'.
});
```

Note that if an interface declares type parameters, any type annotations referring to that interface must provide corresponding type arguments. Here, the usage of CrateLike is incorrect for not including a type argument:

```
interface CrateLike<T> {
    contents: T;
}

let missingGeneric: CrateLike = {
    //              ~~~~~~~~~~
    // Error: Generic type 'CrateLike<T>' requires 1 type argument(s).
    contents: "??"
};
```

Later in this chapter, I'll show how to provide default values for type parameters to get around this requirement.

Generic Classes

Classes, like interfaces, can also declare any number of type parameters to be later used on members. Each instance of the class may have a different set of type arguments for its type parameters.

This Secret class declares Key and Value type parameters, then uses them for member properties, constructor parameter types, and a method's parameter and return types:

```
class Secret<Key, Value> {
    key: Key;
    value: Value;

    constructor(key: Key, value: Value) {
```

```
        this.key = key;
        this.value = value;
    }

    getValue(key: Key): Value | undefined {
        return this.key === key
            ? this.value
            : undefined;
    }
}

const storage = new Secret(12345, "luggage"); // Type: Secret<number, string>

storage.getValue(1987); // Type: string | undefined
```

As with generic interfaces, type annotations using a class must indicate to TypeScript what any generic types on that class are. Later in this chapter, I'll show how to provide default values for type parameters to get around this requirement for classes too.

Explicit Generic Class Types

Instantiating generic classes goes by the same type arguments inference rules as calling generic functions. If the type argument can be inferred from the type of a parameter to the class constructor, such as the new Secret(12345, "luggage") earlier, TypeScript will use the inferred type. Otherwise, if a class type argument can't be inferred from the arguments passed to its constructor, the type argument will default to unknown.

This CurriedCallback class declares a constructor that takes in a generic function. If the generic function has a known type—such as from an explicit type argument type annotation—then the class instance's Input type argument can be informed by it. Otherwise, the class instance's Input type argument will default to unknown:

```
class CurriedCallback<Input> {
    #callback: (input: Input) => void;

    constructor(callback: (input: Input) => void) {
        this.#callback = (input: Input) => {
            console.log("Input:", input);
            callback(input);
        };
    }

    call(input: Input) {
        this.#callback(input);
    }
}

// Type: CurriedCallback<string>
new CurriedCallback((input: string) => {
```

```
    console.log(input.length);
});

// Type: CurriedCallback<unknown>
new CurriedCallback((input) => {
    console.log(input.length);
    //                ~~~~~~
    // Error: Property 'length' does not exist on type 'unknown'.
});
```

Class instances may also avoid defaulting to unknown by providing explicit type argument(s) the same way other generic function calls do.

Here, CurriedCallback from before is now being provided with an explicit string for its Input type argument, so TypeScript can infer that the callback's Input type parameter resolves to string:

```
// Type: CurriedCallback<string>
new CurriedCallback<string>((input) => {
    console.log(input.length);
});

new CurriedCallback<string>((input: boolean) => {
    //                       ~~~~~~~~~~~~~~~~~~~~~~~
    // Argument of type '(input: boolean) => void' is not
    // assignable to parameter of type '(input: string) => void'.
    //    Types of parameters 'input' and 'input' are incompatible.
    //       Type 'string' is not assignable to type 'boolean'.
});
```

Extending Generic Classes

Generic classes can be used as the base class following an extends keyword. TypeScript will not attempt to infer type arguments for the base class from usage. Any type arguments without defaults will need to be specified using an explicit type annotation.

The following SpokenQuote class provides string[] as the T type argument for its base class Quote<T>:

```
class Quote<T> {
    lines: T;

    constructor(lines: T) {
        this.lines = lines;
    }
}

class SpokenQuote extends Quote<string[]> {
    speak() {
        console.log(this.lines.join("\n"));
```

```
        }
    }

    new Quote("The only real failure is the failure to try.").lines; // Type: string
    new Quote([4, 8, 15, 16, 23, 42]).lines; // Type: number[]

    new SpokenQuote([
        "Greed is so destructive.",
        "It destroys everything",
    ]).lines; // Type: string[]

    new SpokenQuote([4, 8, 15, 16, 23, 42]);
    //              ~~~~~~~~~~~~~~~~~~~~~~~
    // Error: Argument of type 'number' is not
    // assignable to parameter of type 'string'.
```

Generic derived classes can alternately pass their own type argument through to their base class. The type names don't have to match; just for fun, this AttributedQuote passes a differently named Value type argument to the base class Quote<T>:

```
    class AttributedQuote<Value> extends Quote<Value> {
        speaker: string

        constructor(value: Value, speaker: string) {
            super(value);
            this.speaker = speaker;
        }
    }

    // Type: AttributedQuote<string>
    // (extending Quote<string>)
    new AttributedQuote(
        "The road to success is always under construction.",
        "Lily Tomlin",
    );
```

Implementing Generic Interfaces

Generic classes may also implement generic interfaces by providing them any necessary type parameters. This works similarly to extending a generic base class: any type parameters on the base interface must be declared by the class.

Here, the MoviePart class specifies the ActingCredit interface's Role type argument as string. The IncorrectExtension class causes a type complaint because its role is type boolean despite it providing string[] as a type argument to ActingCredit:

```
    interface ActingCredit<Role> {
        role: Role;
    }

    class MoviePart implements ActingCredit<string> {
```

```
        role: string;
        speaking: boolean;

        constructor(role: string, speaking: boolean) {
            this.role = role;
            this.speaking = speaking;
        }
    }

    const part = new MoviePart("Miranda Priestly", true);

    part.role; // Type: string

    class IncorrectExtension implements ActingCredit<string> {
        role: boolean;
        //   ~~~~~~~
        // Error: Property 'role' in type 'IncorrectExtension' is not
        // assignable to the same property in base type 'ActingCredit<string>'.
        //   Type 'boolean' is not assignable to type 'string'.
    }
```

Method Generics

Class methods may declare their own generic types separate from their class instance. Each call to a generic class method may have a different type argument for each of its type parameters.

This generic `CreatePairFactory` class declares a `Key` type and includes a `createPair` method that also declares a separate `Value` generic type. The return type for `create Pair` is then inferred to be `{ key: Key, value: Value }`:

```
    class CreatePairFactory<Key> {
        key: Key;

        constructor(key: Key) {
            this.key = key;
        }

        createPair<Value>(value: Value) {
            return { key: this.key, value };
        }
    }

    // Type: CreatePairFactory<string>
    const factory = new CreatePairFactory("role");

    // Type: { key: string, value: number }
    const numberPair = factory.createPair(10);

    // Type: { key: string, value: string }
    const stringPair = factory.createPair("Sophie");
```

Static Class Generics

Static members of a class are separate from instance members and aren't associated with any particular instance of the class. They don't have access to any class instances or type information specific to any class instances. As a result, while static class methods can declare their own type parameters, they can't access any type parameters declared on a class.

Here, a `BothLogger` class declares an `OnInstance` type parameter for its `instanceLog` method and a separate `OnStatic` type parameter for its static `staticLog` method. The static method is not able to access the instance `OnInstance` because `OnInstance` is declared for class instances:

```
class BothLogger<OnInstance> {
    instanceLog(value: OnInstance) {
        console.log(value);
        return value;
    }

    static staticLog<OnStatic>(value: OnStatic) {
        let fromInstance: OnInstance;
        //               ~~~~~~~~~~
        // Error: Static members cannot reference class type arguments.

        console.log(value);
        return value;
    }
}

const logger = new BothLogger<number[]>;
logger.instanceLog([1, 2, 3]); // Type: number[]

// Inferred OnStatic type argument: boolean[]
BothLogger.staticLog([false, true]);

// Explicit OnStatic type argument: string
BothLogger.staticLog<string>("You can't change the music of your soul.");
```

Generic Type Aliases

One last construct in TypeScript that can be made generic with type arguments is type aliases. Each type alias may be given any number of type parameters, such as this `Nullish` type receiving a T:

```
type Nullish<T> = T | null | undefined;
```

Generic type aliases are commonly used with functions to describe the type of a generic function:

```
type CreatesValue<Input, Output> = (input: Input) => Output;

// Type: (input: string) => number
let creator: CreatesValue<string, number>;

creator = text => text.length; // Ok

creator = text => text.toUpperCase();
//                ~~~~~~~~~~~~~~~~~~~
// Error: Type 'string' is not assignable to type 'number'.
```

Generic Discriminated Unions

I mentioned back in Chapter 4, "Objects" that discriminated unions are my favorite
feature in all of TypeScript because they beautifully combine a common elegant Java-
Script pattern with TypeScript's type narrowing. My favorite use for discriminated
unions is to add a type argument to create a generic "result" type that represents
either a successful result with data or a failure with an error.

This `Result` generic type features a `succeeded` discriminant that must be used to
narrow a result to whether it's a success or failure. This means any operation that
returns a `Result` can indicate an error or data result, and be assured that consumers
will need to check whether the result succeeded:

```
type Result<Data> = FailureResult | SuccessfulResult<Data>;

interface FailureResult {
    error: Error;
    succeeded: false;
}

interface SuccessfulResult<Data> {
    data: Data;
    succeeded: true;
}

function handleResult(result: Result<string>) {
    if (result.succeeded) {
        // Type of result: SuccessfulResult<string>
        console.log(`We did it! ${result.data}`);
    } else {
        // Type of result: FailureResult
        console.error(`Awww... ${result.error}`);
    }

    result.data;
    //     ~~~~
    // Error: Property 'data' does not exist on type 'Result<string>'.
    //   Property 'data' does not exist on type 'FailureResult'.
}
```

Put together, generic types and discriminated types provide a wonderful way to model reusable types like Result.

Generic Modifiers

TypeScript includes syntax that allows you to modify the behavior of generic type parameters.

Generic Defaults

I have stated so far that if a generic type is used in a type annotation or as the base of a class extends or implements, it must provide a type argument for each type parameter. You can get around explicitly providing type arguments by placing an = sign followed by a default type after the type parameter's declaration. The default will be used in any subsequent type where the type argument isn't explicitly declared and can't be inferred.

Here, the Quote interface takes in a T type parameter that defaults to string if not provided. The explicit variable explicitly sets T to number while implicit and mismatch both resolve to string:

```
interface Quote<T = string> {
    value: T;
}

let explicit: Quote<number> = { value: 123 };

let implicit: Quote = { value: "Be yourself. The world worships the original." };

let mismatch: Quote = { value: 123 };
//                              ~~~
// Error: Type 'number' is not assignable to type 'string'.
```

Type parameters can default to earlier type parameters in the same declaration too. Since each type parameter introduces a new type for the declaration, they are available as defaults for later type parameters in that declaration.

This KeyValuePair type can have different types for its Key and Value generics but defaults to keeping them the same—though because Key doesn't have a default, it does still need to be inferrable or provided:

```
interface KeyValuePair<Key, Value = Key> {
    key: Key;
    value: Value;
}

// Type: KeyValuePair<string, number>
let allExplicit: KeyValuePair<string, number> = {
    key: "rating",
```

```
    value: 10,
};

// Type: KeyValuePair<string, string>
let oneDefaulting: KeyValuePair<string> = {
    key: "rating",
    value: "ten",
};

let firstMissing: KeyValuePair = {
    //            ~~~~~~~~~~~~
    // Error: Generic type 'KeyValuePair<Key, Value>'
    // requires between 1 and 2 type arguments.
    key: "rating",
    value: 10,
};
```

Keep in mind that all default type parameters must come last in their declaration list, similar to default function parameters. Generic types without a default may not follow generic types with a default.

Here, `inTheEnd` is allowed because all generic types without defaults come before generic types with defaults. `inTheMiddle` is a problem because a generic type without a default follows types with defaults:

```
function inTheEnd<First, Second, Third = number, Fourth = string>() {} // Ok

function inTheMiddle<First, Second = boolean, Third = number, Fourth>() {}
//                                                            // ~~~~~~
// Error: Required type parameters may not follow optional type parameters.
```

Constrained Generic Types

Generic types by default can be given any type in the world: classes, interfaces, primitives, unions, you name it. However, some functions are only meant to work with a limited set of types.

TypeScript allows for a type parameter to declare itself as needing to *extend* a type: meaning it's only allowed to alias types that are assignable to that type. The syntax to constrain a type parameter is to place the `extends` keyword after the type parameter's name, followed by a type to constrain it to.

For example, by creating a `WithLength` interface to describe anything that has a `length: number`, we can then allow our generic function to take in any type that has a `length` for its `T` generic. Strings, arrays, and now even objects that just so happen to have a `length: number` are allowed, while type shapes such as `Date` missing that numeric `length` result in a type error:

```
interface WithLength {
    length: number;
}

function logWithLength<T extends WithLength>(input: T) {
    console.log(`Length: ${input.length}`);
    return input;
}

logWithLength("No one can figure out your worth but you."); // Type: string
logWithLength([false, true]); // Type: boolean[]
logWithLength({ length: 123 }); // Type: { length: number }

logWithLength(new Date());
//            ~~~~~~~~~~
// Error: Argument of type 'Date' is not
// assignable to parameter of type 'WithLength'.
//   Property 'length' is missing in type
//   'Date' but required in type 'WithLength'.
```

I'll cover more type operations you can perform with generics in Chapter 15, "Type Operations".

keyof and Constrained Type Parameters

The keyof operator introduced in Chapter 9, "Type Modifiers" also works well with constrained type parameters. Using extends and keyof together allows a type parameter to be constrained to the keys of a previous type parameter. It is also the only way to specify the key of a generic type.

Take this simplified version of the get method from the popular library Lodash. It takes in a container value, typed as T, and a key name of one of the keys of T to retrieve from container. Because the Key type parameter is constrained to be a keyof T, TypeScript knows this function is allowed to return T[Key]:

```
function get<T, Key extends keyof T>(container: T, key: Key) {
    return container[key];
}

const roles = {
    favorite: "Fargo",
    others: ["Almost Famous", "Burn After Reading", "Nomadland"],
};

const favorite = get(roles, "favorite"); // Type: string
const others = get(roles, "others"); // Type: string[]

const missing = get(roles, "extras");
//                          ~~~~~~~~
// Error: Argument of type '"extras"' is not assignable
// to parameter of type '"favorite" | "others"'.
```

Without `keyof`, there would have been no way to correctly type the generic key parameter.

Note the importance of the `Key` type parameter in the previous example. If only `T` is provided as a type parameter, and the key parameter is allowed to be any `keyof T`, then the return type will be the union type of all property values in `Container`. This less-specific function declaration doesn't indicate to TypeScript that each call can have a specific key via a type argument:

```
function get<T>(container: T, key: keyof T) {
    return container[key];
}

const roles = {
    favorite: "Fargo",
    others: ["Almost Famous", "Burn After Reading", "Nomadland"],
};

const found = get(roles, "favorite"); // Type: string | string[]
```

Be sure when writing generic functions to know when a parameter's type depends on a previous parameter's type. You'll often need to use constrained type parameters for correct parameter types in those cases.

Promises

Now that you've seen how generics work, it's finally time to talk about a core feature of modern JavaScript that relies on their concepts: Promises! To recap, a Promise in JavaScript represents something that might still be pending, such as a network request. Each Promise provides methods to register callbacks in case the pending action "resolves" (completes successfully) or "rejects" (throws an error).

A Promise's ability to represent similar actions on any arbitrary value types is a natural fit for TypeScript's generics. Promises are represented in the TypeScript type system as a `Promise` class with a single type parameter representing the eventual resolved value.

Creating Promises

The `Promise` constructor is typed in TypeScript as taking in a single parameter. That parameter's type relies on a type parameter declared on the generic `Promise` class. A reduced form would look roughly like this:

```
class PromiseLike<Value> {
    constructor(
        executor: (
            resolve: (value: Value) => void,
            reject: (reason: unknown) => void,
```

```
        ) => void,
    ) { /* ... */ }
}
```

Creating a Promise intended to eventually resolve with a value generally necessitates explicitly declaring the type argument of the Promise. TypeScript would default to assuming the parameter type is unknown without that explicit generic type argument. Explicitly providing a type argument to the Promise constructor would allow Type-Script to understand the resultant Promise instance's resolved type:

```
// Type: Promise<unknown>
const resolvesUnknown = new Promise((resolve) => {
    setTimeout(() => resolve("Done!"), 1000);
});

// Type: Promise<string>
const resolvesString = new Promise<string>((resolve) => {
    setTimeout(() => resolve("Done!"), 1000);
});
```

A Promise's generic .then method introduces a new type parameter representing the resolved value of the Promise it returns.

For example, the following code creates a textEventually Promise that resolves with a string value after a second, as well as a lengthEventually that immediately resolves with a number:

```
// Type: Promise<string>
const textEventually = new Promise<string>((resolve) => {
    setTimeout(() => resolve("Done!"), 1000);
});

// Type: Promise<number>
const lengthEventually = textEventually.then((text) => text.length)
```

Async Functions

Any function declared in JavaScript with the async keyword returns a Promise. If a value returned by an async function in JavaScript isn't a Thenable (an object with a .then() method; in practice almost always a Promise), it will be wrapped in a Promise as if Promise.resolve was called on it. TypeScript recognizes this and will infer the return type of an async function to always be a Promise for whatever value is returned.

Here, lengthAfterSecond returns a Promise<number> directly, while lengthImmediately is inferred to return a Promise<number> because it is async and directly returns a number:

```
// Type: (text: string) => Promise<number>
async function lengthAfterSecond(text: string) {
```

```
    await new Promise((resolve) => setTimeout(resolve, 1000))
    return text.length;
}

// Type: (text: string) => Promise<number>
async function lengthImmediately(text: string) {
    return text.length;
}
```

Any manually declared return type on an `async` function therefore must always be a `Promise` type, even if the function doesn't explicitly mention Promises in its implementation:

```
// Ok
async function givesPromiseForString(): Promise<string> {
    return "Done!";
}

async function givesString(): string {
    //                        ~~~~~~
    // Error: The return type of an async function
    // or method must be the global Promise<T> type.
    return "Done!";
}
```

Using Generics Right

As in the `Promise<Value>` implementations earlier in this chapter, although generics can give us a lot of flexibility in describing types in code, they can become rather complex quite quickly. Programmers new to TypeScript often go through a phase of overusing generics to the point of making code confusing to read and overly complex to work with. TypeScript best practice is generally to use generics only when necessary, and to be clear about what they're used for when they are.

 Most code you write in TypeScript should not heavily use generics to the point of confusion. However, types for utility libraries, particularly general-use modules, may sometimes need to heavily use them. Understanding generics is particularly useful to be able to work effectively with those utility types.

The Golden Rule of Generics

One quick test that can help show whether a type parameter is necessary for a function is it should be used at least twice. Generics describe relationships between types, so if a generic type parameter only appears in one place, it can't possibly be defining a relationship between multiple types.

Each function type parameter should be used for a parameter and then also for at least one other parameter and/or the return type of the function.

For example, this `logInput` function uses its `Input` type parameter exactly once, to declare its `input` parameter:

```
function logInput<Input extends string>(input: Input) {
    console.log("Hi!", input);
}
```

Unlike the `identify` functions earlier in the chapter, `logInput` doesn't do anything with its type parameter such as returning or declaring more parameters. There is therefore not much use to declaring that `Input` type parameter. We can rewrite `logInput` without it:

```
function logInput(input: string) {
    console.log("Hi!", input);
}
```

Effective TypeScript by Dan Vanderkam (O'Reilly, 2019) contains several excellent tips for how to work with generics, including a section titled "The Golden Rule of Generics." I highly recommend reading *Effective TypeScript* and that section especially if you're finding yourself spending a lot of time wrestling with generics in your code.

Generic Naming Conventions

The standard naming convention for type parameters in many languages, TypeScript included, is to default to calling a first type argument "T" (for "type" or "template") and if subsequent type parameters exist, calling them "U," "V," and so on.

If some contextual information is known about how the type argument is supposed to be used, the convention sometimes extends to using the first letter of the term for that usage: for example, state management libraries might refer to a generic state as "S." "K" and "V" often refer to keys and values in data structures.

Unfortunately, naming a type argument with one letter can be just as confusing as naming a function or variable with just one character:

```
// What on earth are L and V?!
function labelBox<L, V>(l: L, v: V) { /* ... */ }
```

When the intent of a generic isn't clear from a single-letter T, it's best to use descriptive generic type names that indicate what the type is used for:

```
// Much more clear.
function labelBox<Label, Value>(label: Label, value: Value) { /* ... */ }
```

Whenever a construct has multiple type parameters, or the purpose of a single type argument isn't immediately clear, consider using fully written names for readability instead of single-letter abbreviations.

Summary

In this chapter, you made classes, functions, interfaces, and type aliases "generic" by allowing them to work with type parameters:

- Using type parameters to represent types different between uses of a construct
- Providing explicit or implicit type arguments when calling generic functions
- Using generic interfaces to represent generic object types
- Adding type parameters to classes, and how that impacts their types
- Adding type parameters to type aliases, in particular with discriminated type unions
- Modifying generic type parameters with defaults (=) and constraints (extends)
- How Promises and async functions use generics to represent asynchronous data flow
- Best practices with generics, including their Golden Rule and naming conventions

Thus concludes the *Features* section of this book. Congratulations: you now know all the most important syntax and type-checking features in the TypeScript type system for most projects!

The next section, *Usage*, covers how to configure TypeScript to run on your project, interact with external dependencies, and tweak its type checking and emitted JavaScript. Those are important features for using TypeScript on your own projects.

There are some other miscellaneous type operations available in TypeScript syntax. You don't need to fully understand them to work in most TypeScript projects—but they are interesting and useful to know. I've thrown them in Part IV, "Extra Credit" after Part III, "Usage" as a fun little treat if you have the time.

 Now that you've finished reading this chapter, practice what you've learned on *https://learningtypescript.com/generics*.

Why do generics anger developers?
They're always typing arguments.

Usage

CHAPTER 11

Declaration Files

Declaration files
Have purely type system code
No runtime constructs

Even though writing code in TypeScript is great and that's all you want to do, you'll need to be able to work with raw JavaScript files in your TypeScript projects. Many packages are written directly in JavaScript, not TypeScript. Even packages that are written in TypeScript are distributed as JavaScript files.

Moreover, TypeScript projects need a way to be told the type shapes of environment-specific features such as global variables and APIs. A project running in, say, Node.js might have access to built-in Node modules not available in browsers—and vice versa.

TypeScript allows declaring type shapes separately from their implementation. Type declarations are typically written in files whose names end with the *.d.ts* extension, known as *declaration files*. Declaration files are generally either written within a project, built and distributed with a project's compiled npm package, or shared as a standalone "typings" package.

Declaration Files

A *.d.ts* declaration file generally works similarly to a *.ts* file, except with the notable constraint of not being allowed to include runtime code. *.d.ts* files contain only descriptions of available runtime values, interfaces, modules, and general types. They cannot contain any runtime code that could be compiled down to JavaScript.

Declaration files can be imported just like any other source TypeScript file.

This *types.d.ts* file exports a `Character` interface used by an *index.ts* file:

```
// types.d.ts
export interface Character {
    catchphrase?: string;
    name: string;
}

// index.ts
import { Character } from "./types";

export const character: Character = {
    catchphrase: "Yee-haw!",
    name: "Sandy Cheeks",
};
```

 Declaration files create what's known as an *ambient context*, meaning an area of code where you can only declare types, not values.

This chapter is largely dedicated to declaration files and the most common forms of
type declarations used within them.

Declaring Runtime Values

Although definition files may not create runtime values such as functions or variables, they are able to declare that those constructs exist with the `declare` keyword.
Doing so tells the type system that some external influence—such as a `<script>` tag
in a web page—has created the value under that name with a particular type.

Declaring a variable with `declare` uses the same syntax as a normal variable declaration, except an initial value is not allowed.

This snippet successfully declares a `declared` variable but receives a type error for
trying to give a value to an `initializer` variable:

```
// types.d.ts
declare let declared: string; // Ok

declare let initializer: string = "Wanda";
//                                ~~~~~~~
// Error: Initializers are not allowed in ambient contexts.
```

Functions and classes are also declared similarly to their normal forms, but without
the bodies of functions or methods.

The following `canGrantWish` function and method are properly declared without a body, but the `grantWish` function and method are syntax errors for improperly attempting to set up a body:

```
// fairies.d.ts
declare function canGrantWish(wish: string): boolean; // Ok

declare function grantWish(wish: string) { return true; }
//                                       ~
// Error: An implementation cannot be declared in ambient contexts.

class Fairy {
    canGrantWish(wish: string): boolean; // Ok

    grantWish(wish: string) {
    //                     ~
    // Error: An implementation cannot be declared in ambient contexts.
        return true;
    }
}
```

 TypeScript's implicit any rules work the same for functions and variables declared in ambient contexts as they do in normal source code. Because ambient contexts may not provide function bodies or initial variable values, explicit type annotations—including explicit return type annotations—are generally the only way to stop them from implicitly being type any.

Although type declarations using the `declare` keyword are most common in *.d.ts* definition files, the `declare` keyword can be used outside of declaration files as well. A module or script file can use `declare` as well. This can be useful when a globally available variable is only meant to be used in that file.

Here, a `myGlobalValue` variable is defined in an *index.ts* file, so it's allowed to be used in that file:

```
// index.ts
declare const myGlobalValue: string;

console.log(myGlobalValue); // Ok
```

Note that while type shapes such as interfaces are allowed with or without a `declare` in *.d.ts* definition files, runtime constructs such as functions or variables will trigger a type complaint without a `declare`:

```
// index.d.ts
interface Writer {} // Ok
declare interface Writer {} // Ok
```

```
declare const fullName: string; // Ok: type is the primitive string
declare const firstName: "Liz"; // Ok: type is the literal "value"

const lastName = "Lemon";
// Error: Top-level declarations in .d.ts files must
// start with either a 'declare' or 'export' modifier.
```

Global Values

Because TypeScript files that have no import or export statements are treated as
scripts rather than *modules*, constructs—including types—declared in them are available globally. Definition files without any imports or exports can take advantage of
that behavior to declare types globally. Global definition files are particularly useful
for declaring global types or variables available across all files in an application.

Here, a *globals.d.ts* file declares that a const version: string exists globally. A
version.ts file is then able to refer to a global version variable despite not importing
from *globals.d.ts*:

```
// globals.d.ts
declare const version: string;

// version.ts
export function logVersion() {
    console.log(`Version: ${version}`); // Ok
}
```

Globally declared values are most often used in browser applications that use global
variables. Although most modern web frameworks generally use newer techniques
such as ECMAScript modules, it can still be useful—especially in smaller projects—to
be able to store variables globally.

If you find that you can't automatically access global types declared
in a *.d.ts* file, double-check that the *.d.ts* file isn't importing and
exporting anything. Even a single export will cause the whole file to
no longer be available globally!

Global Interface Merging

Variables aren't the only globals floating around in a TypeScript project's type system.
Many type declarations exist globally for global APIs and values. Because interfaces
merge with other interfaces of the same name, declaring an interface in a global script
context—such as a *.d.ts* declaration file without any import or export statements—
augments that interface globally.

For example, a web application that relies on a global variable set by the server might want to declare that as existing on the global `Window` interface. Interface merging would allow a file such as *types/window.d.ts* to declare a variable that exists on the global `window` variable of type `Window`:

```
<script type="text/javascript">
window.myVersion = "3.1.1";
</script>

// types/window.d.ts
interface Window {
    myVersion: string;
}

// index.ts
export function logWindowVersion() {
    console.log(`Window version is: ${window.myVersion}`);
    window.alert("Built-in window types still work! Hooray!")
}
```

Global Augmentations

It's not always feasible to refrain from `import` or `export` statements in a *.d.ts* file that needs to also augment the global scope, such as when your global definitions are simplified greatly by importing a type defined elsewhere. Sometimes types declared in a module file are meant to be consumed globally.

For those cases, TypeScript allows a syntax to `declare global` a block of code. Doing so marks the contents of that block as being in a global context even though their surroundings are not:

```
// types.d.ts
// (module context)

declare global {
    // (global context)
}

// (module context)
```

Here, a `types/data.d.ts` file exports a `Data` interface, which will later be imported by both `types/globals.d.ts` and the runtime *index.ts*:

```
// types/data.d.ts
export interface Data {
    version: string;
}
```

Additionally, `types/globals.d.ts` declares a variable of type `Data` globally inside a `declare global` block as well as a variable available only in that file:

```
// types/globals.d.ts
import { Data } from "./data";

declare global {
    const globallyDeclared: Data;
}

declare const locallyDeclared: Data;
```

index.ts then has access to the `globallyDeclared` variable without an import, and still needs to import `Data`:

```
// index.ts
import { Data } from "./types/data";

function logData(data: Data) { // Ok
    console.log(`Data version is: ${data.version}`);
}

logData(globallyDeclared); // Ok

logData(locallyDeclared);
//      ~~~~~~~~~~~~~~~
// Error: Cannot find name 'locallyDeclared'.
```

Wrangling global and module declarations to play well together can be tricky. Proper usage of TypeScript's `declare` and `global` keywords can describe which type definitions are meant to be available globally in projects.

Built-In Declarations

Now that you've seen how declarations work, it's time to unveil their hidden use in TypeScript: they've been powering its type checking the whole time! Global objects such as `Array`, `Function`, `Map`, and `Set` are examples of constructs that the type system needs to know about but aren't declared in your code. They're provided by whatever runtime(s) your code is meant to run in: Deno, Node, a web browser, etc.

Library Declarations

Built-in global objects such as `Array` and `Function` that exist in all JavaScript runtimes are declared in files with names like *lib.[target].d.ts*. *target* is the minimum support version of JavaScript targeted by your project, such as ES5, ES2020, or ESNext.

The built-in library definition files, or "lib files," are fairly large because they represent the entirety of JavaScript's built-in APIs. For example, members on the built-in `Array` type are represented by a global `Array` interface that starts like this:

```
// lib.es5.d.ts

interface Array<T> {
    /**
     * Gets or sets the length of the array.
     * This is a number one higher than the highest index in the array.
     */
    length: number;

    //
}
```

Lib files are distributed as part of the TypeScript npm package. You can find them inside the package at paths like *node_modules/typescript/lib/lib.es5.d.ts*. For IDEs such as VS Code that use their own packaged TypeScript versions to type check code, you can find the lib file being used by right-clicking on a built-in method such as an array's `forEach` in your code and selecting an option like Go to Definition (Figure 11-1).

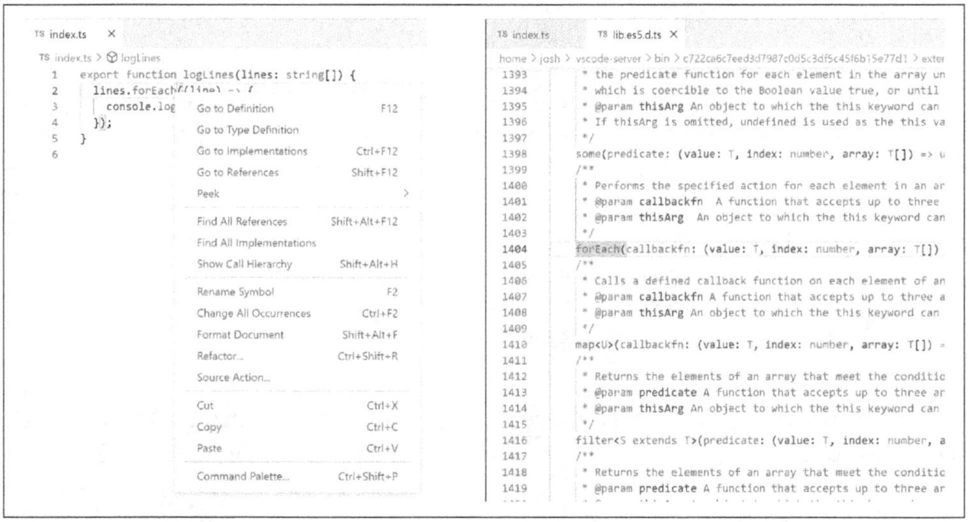

Figure 11-1. Left: going to definition on a `forEach`; right: the resultant opened lib.es5.d.ts file

Library targets

TypeScript by default will include the appropriate lib file based on the `target` setting provided to the `tsc` CLI and/or in your project's *tsconfig.json* (by default, `"es5"`). Successive lib files for newer versions of JavaScript build on each other using interface merging.

For example, static `Number` members such as `EPSILON` and `isFinite` added in ES2015 are listed in *lib.es2015.d.ts*:

```
// lib.es2015.d.ts

interface NumberConstructor {
    /**
     * The value of Number.EPSILON is the difference between 1 and the
     * smallest value greater than 1 that is representable as a Number
     * value, which is approximately:
     * 2.2204460492503130808472633361816 x 10-16.
     */
    readonly EPSILON: number;

    /**
     * Returns true if passed value is finite.
     * Unlike the global isFinite, Number.isFinite doesn't forcibly
     * convert the parameter to a number. Only finite values of the
     * type number result in true.
     * @param number A numeric value.
     */
    isFinite(number: unknown): boolean;

    // ...
}
```

TypeScript projects will include the lib files for all version targets of JavaScript up through their minimum target. For example, a project with a target of "es2016" would include *lib.es5.d.ts*, *lib.es2015.d.ts*, and *lib.es2016.d.ts*.

Language features available only in newer versions of JavaScript than your target will not be available in the type system. For example, if your target is "es5", language features from ES2015 or later such as String.prototype.startsWith will not be recognized.

Compiler options such as target are covered in more detail in Chapter 13, "Configuration Options".

DOM Declarations

Outside of the JavaScript language itself, the most commonly referenced area of type declarations is for web browsers. Web browser types, generally referred to as "DOM" types, cover APIs such as localStorage and type shapes such as HTMLElement available primarily in web browsers. DOM types are stored in a *lib.dom.d.ts* file alongside the other *lib.*.d.ts* declaration files.

Global DOM types, like many built-in globals, are often described with global interfaces. For example, the Storage interface used for localStorage and sessionStorage starts roughly like this:

```
// lib.dom.d.ts

interface Storage {
    /**
     * Returns the number of key/value pairs.
     */
    readonly length: number;

    /**
     * Removes all key/value pairs, if there are any.
     */
    clear(): void;

    /**
     * Returns the current value associated with the given key,
     * or null if the given key does not exist.
     */
    getItem(key: string): string | null;

    // ...
}
```

TypeScript includes DOM types by default in projects that don't override the `lib` compiler option. That can sometimes be confusing for developers working on projects meant to be run in nonbrowser environments such as Node, as they shouldn't be able to access the global APIs such as `document` and `localStorage` that the type system would then claim to exist. Compiler options such as `lib` are covered in more detail in Chapter 13, "Configuration Options".

Module Declarations

One more important feature of declaration files is their ability to describe the shapes of modules. The `declare` keyword can be used before a string name of a module to inform the type system of the contents of that module.

Here, the `"my-example-lib"` module is declared as being in existence in a `modules.d.ts` declaration script file, then used in an *index.ts* file:

```
// modules.d.ts
declare module "my-example-lib" {
    export const value: string;
}
// index.ts
import { value } from "my-example-lib";

console.log(value); // Ok
```

You shouldn't have to use `declare module` often, if ever, in your own code. It's mostly used with the following section's wildcard module declarations and with package types covered later in this chapter. Additionally, see Chapter 13, "Configuration Options" for information on `resolveJsonModule`, a compiler option that allows TypeScript to natively recognize imports from *.json* files.

Wildcard Module Declarations

A common use of module declarations is to tell web applications that a particular non-JavaScript/TypeScript file extension is available to `import` into code. Module declarations may contain a single * wildcard to indicate that any module matching that pattern looks the same.

For example, many web projects such as those preconfigured in popular React starters such as create-react-app and create-next-app support CSS modules to import styles from CSS files as objects that can be used at runtime. They would define modules with a pattern such as `"*.module.css"` that default exports an object of type `{ [i: string]: string }`:

```
// styles.d.ts
declare module "*.module.css" {
    const styles: { [i: string]: string };
    export default styles;
}

// component.ts
import styles from "./styles.module.css";

styles.anyClassName; // Type: string
```

Using wildcard modules to represent local files isn't completely type safe. TypeScript does not provide a mechanism to ensure the imported module path matches a local file. Some projects use a build system such as Webpack and/or generate *.d.ts* files from local files to make sure imports match up.

Package Types

Now that you've seen how to declare typings within a project, it's time to cover consuming types between packages. Projects written in TypeScript still generally distribute packages containing compiled *.js* outputs. They typically use *.d.ts* files to declare the backing TypeScript type system shapes behind those JavaScript files.

declaration

TypeScript provides a `declaration` option to create *.d.ts* outputs for input files alongside JavaScript outputs.

For example, given the following *index.ts* source file:

```
// index.ts
export const greet = (text: string) => {
    console.log(`Hello, ${text}!`);
};
```

Using `declaration`, a `module` of "es2015", and a `target` of "es2015", the following outputs would be generated:

```
// index.d.ts
export declare const greet: (text: string) => void;
```

```
// index.js
export const greet = (text) => {
    console.log(`Hello, ${text}!`);
};
```

Auto-generated *.d.ts* files are the best way for a project to create type definitions to be used by consumers. It's generally recommended that most packages written in TypeScript that produce *.js* file outputs should also bundle *.d.ts* alongside those files.

Compiler options such as `declaration` are covered in more detail in Chapter 13, "Configuration Options".

Dependency Package Types

TypeScript is able to detect and utilize *.d.ts* files bundled inside a project's `node_modules` dependencies. Those files will inform the type system about the type shapes exported by that package as if they were written inside the same project or declared with a `declare module` block.

A typical npm module that comes with its own *.d.ts* declaration files might have a file structure something like:

```
lib/
    index.js
    index.d.ts
package.json
```

As an example, the ever-popular test runner Jest is written in TypeScript and provides its own bundled *.d.ts* files in its `jest` package. It has a dependency on the `@jest/globals` package that provides functions such as `describe` and `it`, which `jest` then makes available globally:

```
// package.json
{
    "devDependencies": {
        "jest": "^32.1.0"
    }
}
```

```
// using-globals.d.ts
describe("MyAPI", () => {
    it("works", () => { /* ... */ });
});

// using-imported.d.ts
import { describe, it } from "@jest/globals";

describe("MyAPI", () => {
    it("works", () => { /* ... */ });
});
```

If we were to re-create a very limited subset of the Jest typings packages from scratch, they might look something like these files. The `@jest/globals` package exports the `describe` and `it` functions. Then, the `jest` package imports those functions and augments the global scope with `describe` and `it` variables of their corresponding function's type:

```
// node_modules/@jest/globals/index.d.ts
export function describe(name: string, test: () => void): void;
export function it(name: string, test: () => void): void;

// node_modules/jest/index.d.ts
import * as globals from "@jest/globals";

declare global {
    const describe: typeof globals.describe;
    const it: typeof globals.it;
}
```

This structure allows projects that use Jest to refer to global versions of `describe` and `it`. Projects can alternatively choose to import those functions from the `@jest/globals` package.

Exposing Package Types

If your project is meant to be distributed on npm and provide types for consumers, add a `"types"` field in the package's *package.json* file to point to the root declaration file. The `types` field works similarly to the `main` field—and often will look the same but with the *.d.ts* extension instead of *.js*.

For example, in this `fictional` package file, the *./lib/index.js* main runtime file is paralleled by the *./lib/index.d.ts* types file:

```
{
    "author": "Pendant Publishing",
    "main": "./lib/index.js",
    "name": "coffeetable",
    "types": "./lib/index.d.ts",
    "version": "0.5.22",
}
```

TypeScript would then use the contents of the *./lib/index.d.ts* as what should be provided for consuming files that import from the `utilitarian` package.

 If the `types` field does not exist in a package's *package.json*, Type-Script will assume a default value of *./index.d.ts*. This mirrors the default npm behavior of assuming an *./index.js* file as the `main` entry point for a package if not specified.

Most packages use TypeScript's `declaration` compiler option to create *.d.ts* files alongside *.js* outputs from source files. Compiler options are covered in Chapter 13, "Configuration Options".

DefinitelyTyped

Sadly, not all projects are written in TypeScript. Some unfortunate developers are still writing their projects in plain old JavaScript without a type checker to aide them. Horrifying.

Our TypeScript projects still need to be informed of the type shapes of the modules from those packages. The TypeScript team and community created a giant repository called DefinitelyTyped (*https://github.com/DefinitelyTyped/DefinitelyTyped*) to house community-authored definitions for packages. DefinitelyTyped, or DT for short, is one of the most active repositories on GitHub. It contains thousands of packages of *.d.ts* definitions, along with automation around reviewing change proposals and publishing updates.

DT packages are published on npm under the `@types` scope with the same name as the package they provide types for. For example, as of 2022, `@types/react` provides type definitions for the `react` package.

 `@types` are generally installed as either `dependencies` or `devDependencies`, though the distinction between those two has become blurred in recent years. In general, if your project is meant to be distributed as an npm package, it should use `dependencies` so consumers of the package also bring in the type definitions used within. If your project is a standalone application such as one built and run on a server, it should use `devDependencies` to convey that the types are just a development-time tool.

For example, for a utility package that relies on `lodash`—which as of 2022 has a separate `@types/lodash` package—the *package.json* would contain lines similar to:

```
// package.json
{
    "dependencies": {
        "@types/lodash": "^4.14.182",
        "lodash": "^4.17.21",
    }
}
```

The *package.json* for a standalone app built on React might contain lines similar to:

```
// package.json
{
    "dependencies": {
        "react": "^18.1.0"
    },
    "devDependencies": {
        "@types/react": "^18.0.9"
    },
}
```

Note that semantic versioning ("semver") numbers do not necessarily match between @types/ packages and the packages they represent. You may often find some that are off by a patch version as with React earlier, a minor version as with Lodash earlier, or even major versions.

 As these files are authored by the community, they may lag behind the parent project or have small inaccuracies. If your project compiles successfully yet you get runtime errors when calling libraries, investigate if the signatures of the APIs you are accessing have changed. This is less common, but still not unheard of, for mature projects with stable API surfaces.

Type Availability

Most popular JavaScript packages either ship with their own typings or have typings available via DefinitelyTyped.

If you'd like to get types for a package that doesn't yet have types available, your three most common options would be:

- Send a pull request to DefinitelyTyped to create its @types/ package.
- Use the declare module syntax introduced earlier to write the types within your project.
- Disable noImplicitAny as covered—and strongly warned against—in Chapter 13, "Configuration Options".

I'd recommend contributing types to DefinitelyTyped if you have the time. Doing so helps out other TypeScript developers who may also want to use that package.

 See aka.ms/types (*https://aka.ms/types*) to display whether a package has types bundled or via a separate @types/ package.

Summary

In this chapter, you used declaration files and value declarations to inform TypeScript about modules and values not declared in your source code:

- Creating declaration files with *.d.ts*
- Declaring types and values with the `declare` keyword
- Changing global types using global values, global interface merges, and global augmentations
- Configuring and using TypeScript's built-in target, library, and DOM declarations
- Declaring types of modules, including wildcard modules
- How TypeScript picks up types from packages
- Using DefinitelyTyped to acquire types for packages that don't include their own

 Now that you've finished reading this chapter, practice what you've learned on *https://learningtypescript.com/declaration-files*.

What do TypeScript types say in the American South?
"Why, I do dec lare!"

CHAPTER 12

Using IDE Features

*Programming with an
IDE the first time feels
like superpowers.*

No popular programming language would be complete without syntax highlighting and other IDE features to help developing in it. One of TypeScript's greatest strengths is that its language service provides a suite of powerful development helpers for JavaScript and TypeScript code. This chapter will cover some of the most useful items.

I highly recommend you try these IDE features out on the TypeScript projects you've built alongside this book. Although all the examples and screenshots in this chapter are of VS Code, my favorite editor, any IDE with TypeScript support will support most or all of this chapter. As of 2022 that includes the native support or TypeScript plugins for at least all of: Atom, Emacs, Vim, Visual Studio, and WebStorm.

This chapter is a nonexhaustive list of some of the more commonly useful TypeScript IDE features, along with any default shortcuts for them in VS Code. You'll likely find more as you keep writing TypeScript code.

Many IDE features are generally made available in the context menu surfaced by right-clicking on a name in code. IDEs such as VS Code generally show keyboard shortcuts in the context menu too. Getting comfortable with your IDE's keyboard shortcuts can help you write code and execute refactors much more quickly.

This screenshot shows the list of commands and their shortcuts in VS Code for a variable in TypeScript (Figure 12-1).

```
TS index.ts
1    import { data } from "./data";
2
3    console.log(data.message);
4
5
6
```

Go to Definition	F12
Go to Type Definition	
Go to Implementations	Ctrl+F12
Go to References	Shift+F12
Peek	>
Find All References	Shift+Alt+F12
Find All Implementations	
Show Call Hierarchy	Shift+Alt+H
Rename Symbol	F2
Change All Occurrences	Ctrl+F2
Format Document	Shift+Alt+F
Refactor...	Ctrl+Shift+R
Source Action...	
Cut	Ctrl+X
Copy	Ctrl+C
Paste	Ctrl+V
Command Palette...	Ctrl+Shift+P

Figure 12-1. VS Code showing a list of commands in the right-click context menu for a variable

In VS Code, as with most applications, up and down arrows select drop-down options, and Enter activates one.

Navigating Code

Developers generally spend much more time reading code rather than actively writing it. Tools that assist in navigating code are supremely useful for speeding that time up. Many of the features provided by the TypeScript language service are geared toward learning about code: in particular, jumping between type definitions or values in code and where they're used.

I'll now go through commonly used navigation options from the context menu along with their VS Code shortcuts.

Finding Definitions

TypeScript can start from a reference to a type definition or value and navigate you back to its original location in code. VS Code also provides a couple of ways to backtrace in that way:

- Go to Definition (F12) navigates directly to where a requested name was originally defined.
- Cmd (Mac) / Ctrl (Windows) + clicking a name triggers going to definition as well.
- Peek > Peek Definition (Option (Mac) / Alt (Windows) + F12) brings up a Peek box showing the definition instead.

Go to Type Definition is a specialized version of Go to Definition that goes to the definition of whatever type a value is. For an instance of a class or interface, it will reveal the class or interface itself instead of where the instance is defined.

These screenshots show finding the definition of a `data` variable imported into a file with Go to Definition (Figure 12-2).

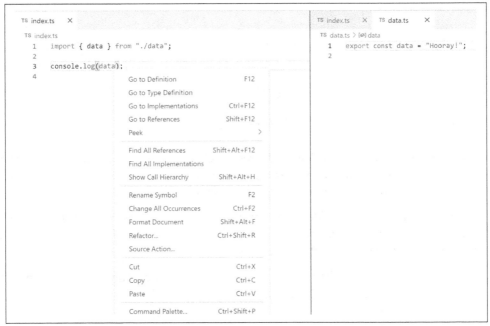

Figure 12-2. Left: going to definition on a variable name; right: the resultant opened data.ts file

When the definition is declared in your own code, such as a relative file, the editor will bring you to that file. Modules outside your code such as npm packages will commonly use *.d.ts* declaration files instead.

Finding References

Given a type definition or value, TypeScript can show you a list of all the references to it, or places it's used in the project. VS Code provides a couple ways to visualize that list.

Go to References (Shift + F12) shows a list of references to that type definition or value—starting with itself—in an expandable Peek box just below the right-clicked name.

For example, here's a Go to References of a `data` variable's declaration in one file, *data.ts*, that shows both the declaration and its usage in another file, *index.ts* (Figure 12-3).

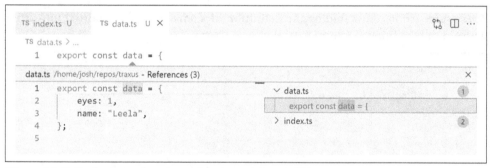

Figure 12-3. Peek menu showing references to a variable

That Peek box contains a file view of the referencing file. You can use that file—type, run editor commands, and so on—as if it were a regularly opened file. You can also double-click in the Peek box's view of a file to open that file.

Clicking through the list of file names on the right of the Peek box will switch the Peek box's file view to the clicked file. Double-clicking a line of a file from the list will open the file and select its matched reference.

Here, VS Code is showing the same `data` variable's declaration and usage, but expanded in the sidebar view on the right (Figure 12-4).

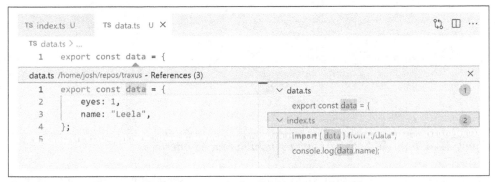

Figure 12-4. Peek menu showing an opened reference to a variable

Find All References (Option (Mac) / Alt (Windows) + Shift + F12) also shows a list of references, but in a sidebar view that stays visible after code navigation. This can be useful for opening or performing actions on more than just one reference at a time (Figure 12-5).

REFERENCES   ○ ≡x ⊟   TS index.ts U   TS data.ts   U ✕

3 results in 2 files   TS data.ts 〉 [@] data

∨   TS data.ts   U   1   export const data = {
                                     2   eyes: 1,
    export const data = {   3   name: "Leela",
∨   TS index.ts   ✕ U   4   };
                                     5
    import { data } from "./data";
    console.log(data.name);

Figure 12-5. Find All References menu for a variable

Finding Implementations

Go to Implementations (Cmd (Mac) / Ctrl (Windows) + F12) and Find All Implementations are specialized versions of Go To / Find All References made for interfaces and abstract class methods. They find all implementations of an interface or abstract method in code (Figure 12-6).

Figure 12-6. Find All Implementations menu for an AI interface

These are particularly helpful when you're specifically searching for how values typed as a type such as class or interface are used. Find All References might be too noisy, as it will also show definitions of and other type references to the class or interface.

Writing Code

IDE language services such as VS Code's TypeScript service run in the background of your editor and react to actions taken in files. They see edits to files as you type them—even before changes are saved to files. Doing so enables a slew of features that help automate common tasks when writing TypeScript code.

Completing Names

TypeScript's APIs can be used by editors to fill in names that exist in the same file as well. When you start typing a name, such as when providing a previously declared variable as a function argument, editors using TypeScript will often suggest autocompletions with a list of variables with matching names. Clicking the name in the list with your mouse or hitting the Enter key will complete the name (Figure 12-7).

Figure 12-7. Left: autocompletions on a variable typed as dat; right: the result of autocompleting to an imported data

Automatic import additions will be offered for package dependencies as well. These screenshots show a TypeScript file's imports and module code before and after `sortBy` is imported from the "`lodash`" package (Figure 12-8).

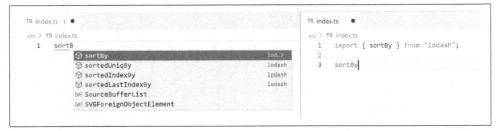

Figure 12-8. Left: autocompletions on a variable typed as `sortBy`; right: the result of autocompleting to an imported `sortBy` from `lodash`

Automatic imports are one of my favorite features of the TypeScript experience. They greatly expedite the often laborious processes of figuring out where imports come from and then explicitly typing them out.

Similarly, if you start typing the name of a property from a typed value, editors powered by TypeScript will offer to autocomplete to known properties of the value's type (Figure 12-9).

Figure 12-9. Left: autocompletions on a property typed as `forE`; right: the result of autocompleting to `.forEach`

Automatic Import Updates

If you rename a file or move it from one folder to another, you may need to update potentially many import statements for the file. Updates may need to be made both in that file itself and in any other file that imports from it.

If you drag and drop a file or rename it to a nested folder path using the VS Code file explorer, VS Code will offer to use TypeScript to update file paths for you.

These screenshots show a *src/logging.ts* file being renamed to a *src/shared/logging.ts* location, and file imports getting updated in a corresponding manner (Figure 12-10).

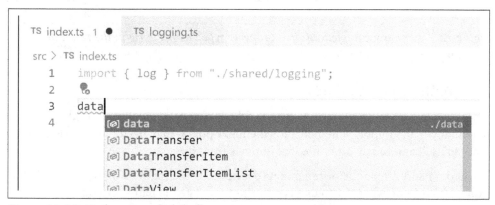

Figure 12-10. Left: a src/index.ts file importing from "./logging"; middle: renaming src/logging.ts to src/shared/logging.ts; right: src/index.ts with an updated import path

 Multifile edits may leave changes to files unsaved. Remember to save any changed files after running edits on them.

Code Actions

Many of TypeScript's IDE utilities are provided as actions you can trigger. While some of these modify only the current file being edited, some can modify many files at once. Using these code actions is a great way to direct TypeScript to do many of your manual code writing tasks such as calculating import paths and common refactors for you.

Code actions are generally represented with some kind of icon in editors when available. VS Code, for example, shows a clickable light bulb next to your text cursor when at least one code action is available (Figure 12-11).

Figure 12-11. Code actions lightbulb next to a name causing a type error

Editors generally expose keyboard shortcuts to operate their code actions menu or equivalent, allowing you to trigger any action in this chapter without using a mouse. VS Code's default shortcut to open a code actions menu is Cmd + . on Mac and Ctrl + . on Linux/Windows. Up and down arrows select drop-down options, and Enter activates one.

These code actions—in particular renames and refactors—are especially powerful by virtue of being informed by TypeScript's type system. When applying an action to a type, TypeScript will understand which values across all files are of that type, and can then apply any needed changes to those values.

Renaming

Changing a name that already exists, such as that of a function, interface, or variable can be cumbersome to perform manually. TypeScript can perform a renaming for a name that also updates all references to the name.

The Rename Symbol (F2) context menu option creates a text box where you can type in a new name. Triggering a rename on a function's name, for example, would provide a text box to rename that function and all calls to it. Hit Enter to apply that name (Figure 12-12).

```
TS logging.ts  ✕

src > shared > TS logging.ts > ◈ log
   1    export function log(...data: unknown[]) {
   2      console.log("[ logData
   3    }                        Enter to Rename, Shift+Enter to Preview
   4
```

Figure 12-12. Box for renaming a log *function, with* logData *inserted*

If you'd like to see what would happen before you apply the new name, press Shift + Enter to open a Refactor Preview pane that lists all the text changes that would happen (Figure 12-13).

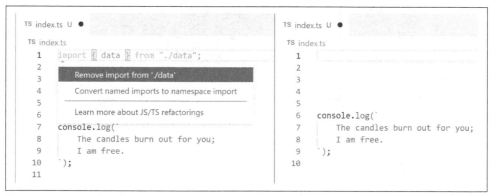

```
TS logging.ts  ✕      TS tsconfig.json

src > shared > TS logging.ts > ⊘ log
  1    export function log(...data: unknown[]) {
  2    │ 💡console.log("[log]", ...data);
  3    }
  4

REFACTOR PREVIEW      PROBLEMS      OUTPUT      DEBUG CONSOLE      TERMINAL

∨  ☑ TS index.ts  src
      ☑ import { loglogData } from "./shared/logging";
      ☑ loglogData(data);
∨  ☑ TS logging.ts  src/shared
      ☑ export function loglogData(...data: unknown[]) {
```

Figure 12-13. Refactor preview for renaming a `log` function, with `logData` previewed across two files

Removing unused code

Many IDEs subtly change the visual appearance of code that is unused, such as imported values and variables that are never referenced. VS Code, for example, reduces their opacity by about a third.

TypeScript provides code actions to delete unused code. (Figure 12-14) shows the result of asking TypeScript to remove an unused `import` statement.

```
TS index.ts U ●                              TS index.ts U ●

TS index.ts                                  TS index.ts
  1  import { data } from "./data";            1
  2                                            2
  3    ┌──────────────────────────────┐        3
  4    │ Remove import from './data'   │        4
  5    │ Convert named imports to      │        5
  6    │ namespace import              │        6  console.log(`
  7  co│ Learn more about JS/TS        │        7      The candles burn out for you;
  8    │ refactorings                  │        8      I am free.
  9    │ I am free.                    │        9  `);
 10  `);                                       10
 11
```

Figure 12-14. Left: selecting an unused import and opening the refactors menu; right: the file after TypeScript deletes it

Other quick fixes

Many TypeScript error messages are for code problems that can be quickly rectified, such as minor typos in keywords or variable names. Other commonly useful TypeScript quick fixes include:

- Declaring a missing property on a class or interface
- Correcting a mistyped field name
- Filling in missing properties of a variable declared as a type

I recommend checking the list of quick fixes whenever you spot an error message you haven't seen before. You never know what useful utilities TypeScript has made available to resolve it!

Refactoring

The TypeScript language service provides a plethora of handy code changes for different structures of code. Some are as simple as moving lines of code around, while others are as complex as creating new functions for you.

When you've selected an area of code, VS Code will display a lightbulb icon next to your selection. Click it to see the list of refactors available.

Here's a developer extracting an inline array literal to a `const` variable (Figure 12-15).

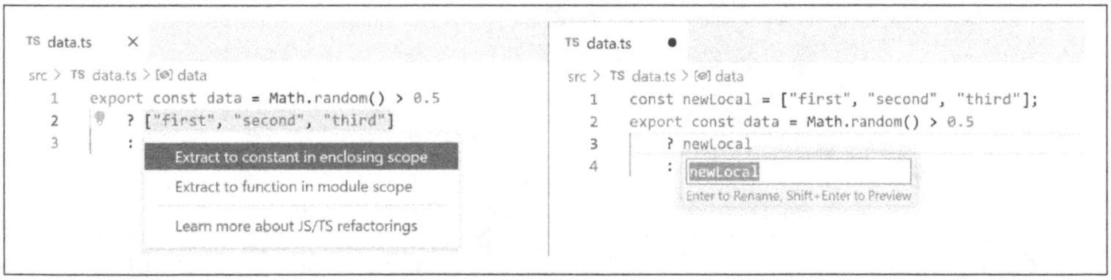

Figure 12-15. Left: selecting an array literal and opening the refactors menu; right: extracting to a constant variable

Working Effectively with Errors

Reading and taking action on error messages is a fact of life for working in any programming language. Every developer, regardless of proficiency with the TypeScript language, will trigger a plethora of TypeScript compiler errors each time they write TypeScript code. Using IDE features to enhance your ability to work effectively with TypeScript compiler errors will help you become much more productive in the language.

Language Service Errors

Editors generally surface any errors reported by the TypeScript language service as red squigglies underneath the troublesome code. Hovering your mouse over underlined characters will show a hover box next to them with the text of the error (Figure 12-16).

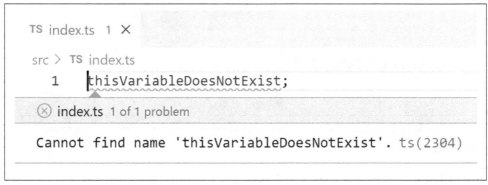

Figure 12-16. Hover information on a variable that does not exist

VS Code also shows errors for any open files in a Problems tab in its Panels section. The bottom left View Problem link in the mouse hover box for an error will open an inline display of the message inserted after the problem's line and before any subsequent lines (Figure 12-17).

```
TS index.ts  1  X

src  >  TS index.ts
  1     thisVariableDoesNotExist;

  ⊗ index.ts  1 of 1 problem

  Cannot find name 'thisVariableDoesNotExist'. ts(2304)
```

Figure 12-17. View Problem inline display for a variable that does not exist

When multiple problems exist in the same source file, their displays will include up and down arrows that you can use to switch between them. F8 and Shift + F8 will work as shortcuts to go forward and backward through that list of problems, respectively (Figure 12-18).

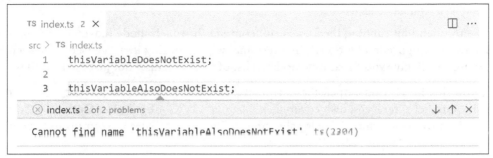

Figure 12-18. One of two View Problem inline displays for variables that do not exist

Problems tab

VS Code includes a Problems tab in its panel that, as its name suggests, surfaces any problems in your workspace. That includes errors reported by the TypeScript language service.

This screenshot shows a Problems tab showing two problems in a TypeScript file (Figure 12-19).

Figure 12-19. Problems tab showing two errors in a file

Clicking any error within the Problems tab will bring your text cursor to the offending line and column in its file.

Note that VS Code will only list problems for files that are currently open. If you want a real-time updated list of all TypeScript compiler problems, you'll need to run the TypeScript compiler in a terminal.

Running a terminal compiler

I recommending running the TypeScript compiler in watch mode (covered in Chapter 13, "Configuration Options") in a terminal while working in a TypeScript project. Doing so will give you a real-time updated list of all problems—not just those in files.

To do this in VS Code, open the Terminal panel and run `tsc -w` (or `tsc -b -w` if using project references, also covered in Chapter 13, "Configuration Options"). You should now see a terminal display showing all TypeScript issues in your project, as in this screenshot (Figure 12-20).

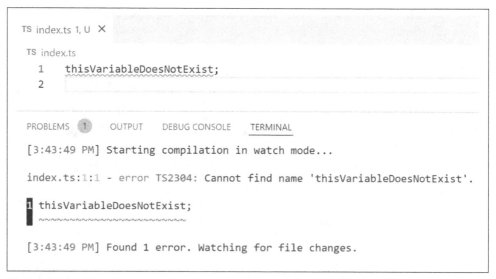

Figure 12-20. Running `tsc -w` in a terminal to report a problem in a file

Cmd (Mac) / Ctrl (Windows) + clicking a file name will bring your text cursor to the offending line and column in its file as well.

 Some projects use VS Code launch.json configurations to start a terminal with TypeScript compiler in watch mode for you. See code.visualstudio.com/docs/editor/tasks (*https://code.visualstu dio.com/docs/editor/tasks*) for a full reference on VS Code tasks.

Understanding types

You will sometimes find that you need to learn the type of something that's set up in a way that the type isn't apparent. For any value, you can hover your mouse over its name to see a hover box showing its type.

This screenshot shows the hover box for a variable (Figure 12-21).

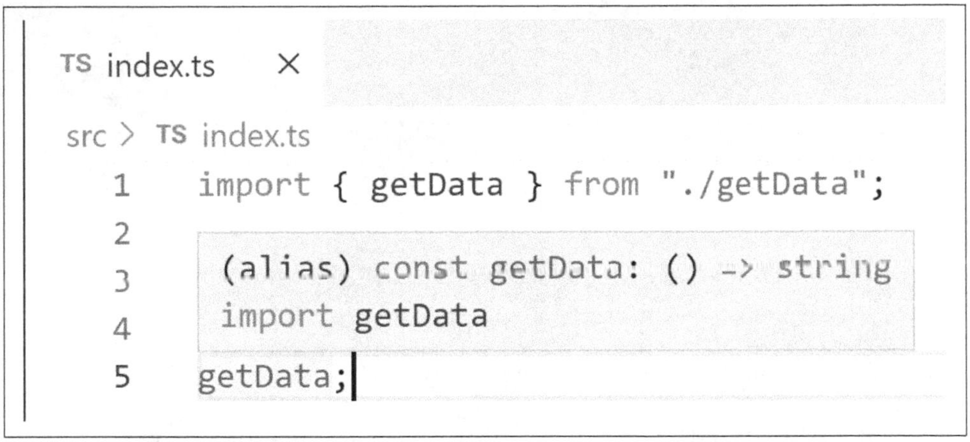

```
TS index.ts        ✕

src > TS index.ts
    1       import { getData } from "./getData";
    2
    3       (alias) const getData: () -> string
    4       import getData
    5     getData;
```

Figure 12-21. Hover information on a variable

Hold Ctrl while hovering to also show where the name is declared.

This screenshot shows the Ctrl hover box for the same variable as before
(Figure 12-22).

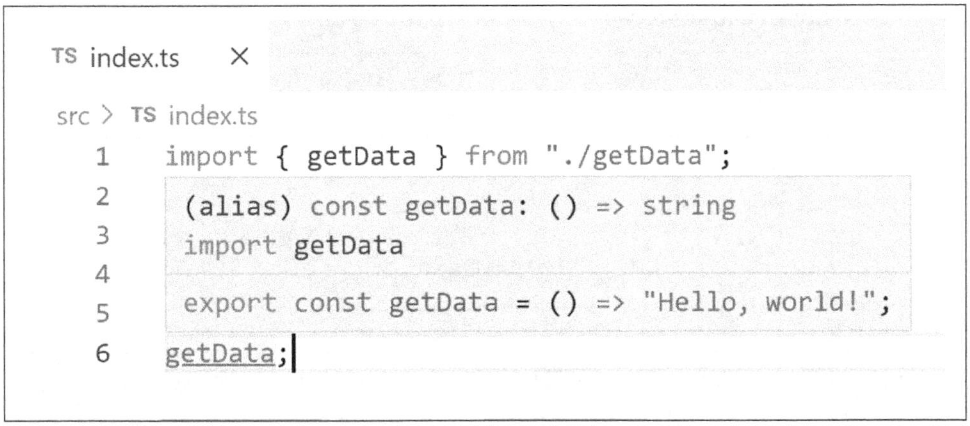

```
TS index.ts      ✕

src > TS index.ts
    1       import { getData } from "./getData";
    2
    3       (alias) const getData: () => string
            import getData
    4
    5       export const getData = () => "Hello, world!";
    6     getData;
```

Figure 12-22. Expanded hover information on a variable

Hover info boxes are also available on types, such as type aliases. This screenshot
shows hovering over a keyof typeof type to see its equivalent union of string literals
(Figure 12-23).

```
TS types.ts    ×

src > TS types.ts > [●] FruitName
  1    const fruits = {
  2        apple: 1,
  3        broccoli: 2,
  4        cherry: 3,
  5    };
                    type FruitName = "apple" | "broccoli" | "cherry"
  6
  7    export type FruitName = keyof typeof fruits;
```

Figure 12-23. Expanded hover information on a type

One strategy I've found to be helpful when trying to understand components of complex types is to create a type alias that represents just one component of the type. You will then be able to hover your mouse over that type alias to see what its type result is.

For the `FruitsType` type from before as an example, its `typeof fruits` portion could be extracted into a separate intermediary type with a refactor. That intermediary type can then be hovered to see type information (Figure 12-24).

```
TS types.ts    ×                                      TS types.ts    ×

src > TS types.ts > [●] FruitName                     src > TS types.ts > [●] NewType
  1    const fruits = {                                 1    const fruits = {
  2        apple: 1,                                     2      a   type NewType = {
  3        broccoli: 2,                                  3      b       apple: number;
  4        cherry: 3,                                    4      c       broccoli: number;
  5    };                                                5    };          cherry: number;
  6    ☀                                                 6    ☀       }
  7    export type FruitName = keyof typeof fruits;      7    type NewType = typeof fruits;
                                                         8
              Extract to type alias                      9    export type FruitName = keyof NewType;

           Learn more about JS/TS refactorings
```

Figure 12-24. Left: extracting part of the `FruitsType` type; right: hovering over that extracted type

The intermediary type alias strategy is particularly useful for debugging the type operations covered in Chapter 15, "Type Operations".

Summary

In this chapter, you explored using TypeScript's IDE integrations to level up your ability to write TypeScript code:

- Opening context menus on types and values to list their available commands
- Navigating code by finding definitions, references, and implementations
- Automating writing code with name completions and automatic imports
- More code actions including renames and refactors
- Strategies for viewing and understanding language service errors
- Strategies for understanding types

 Now that you've finished reading this chapter, practice what you've learned on *https://learningtypescript.com/using-ide-features*.

What do IDEs in love say to each other?
"You complete me!"

CHAPTER 13

Configuration Options

Compiler options:
Types and modules and oh my!
tsc your way.

TypeScript is highly configurable and made to adapt to all common JavaScript usage patterns. It can work for projects ranging from legacy browser code to the most modern server environments.

Much of TypeScript's configurability comes from its cornucopia of over 100 configuration options that can be provided via either:

- Command-line (CLI) flags passed to `tsc`
- "TSConfig" TypeScript configuration files

This chapter is not intended as a full reference for all TypeScript configuration options. Instead, I'd suggest treating this chapter as a tour of the most common options you'll find yourself using. I've included just the ones that tend to be more useful and widely used for most TypeScript project setups. See aka.ms/tsc (*https:// aka.ms/tsc*) for a full reference on each of these options and more.

tsc Options

Back in Chapter 1, "From JavaScript to TypeScript", you used `tsc index.ts` to compile an *index.ts* file. The `tsc` command can take in most of TypeScript's configuration options as - - flags.

For example, to run `tsc` on an *index.ts* file and skip emitting an *index.js* file (so, only run type checking), pass the - -noEmit flag:

```
tsc index.ts --noEmit
```

You can run `tsc --help` to get a list of commonly used CLI flags. The full list of `tsc` configuration options from aka.ms/tsc (*https://aka.ms/tsc*) is viewable with `tsc --all`.

Pretty Mode

The `tsc` CLI has the ability to output in a "pretty" mode: stylized with colors and spacing to make them easier to read. It defaults to pretty mode if it detects that the output terminal supports colorful text.

Here's an example of what `tsc` looks like printing two type errors from a file (Figure 13-1).

```
~/learningtypescript$ tsc index.ts
index.ts:1:12 - error TS2322: Type 'string' is not assignable to type 'number'.

1 export let notNumeric: number = "Gotcha!";
                                  ~~~~~~~~~~


index.ts:3:12 - error TS2322: Type 'number' is not assignable to type 'string'.

3 export let notString: string = 1337;
                                 ~~~~~~~~~


Found 2 errors in the same file, starting at: index.ts:1
```

Figure 13-1. `tsc` *reporting two errors with blue file names, yellow line and column numbers, and red squigglies*

If you'd prefer CLI output that is more condensed and/or doesn't have different colors, you can explicitly provide `--pretty false` to tell TypeScript to use a more terse, uncolored format (Figure 13-2).

```
~/learningtypescript$ tsc index.ts --pretty false
index.ts(1,12): error TS2322: Type 'string' is not assignable to type 'number'.
index.ts(3,12): error TS2322: Type 'number' is not assignable to type 'string'.
```

Figure 13-2. `tsc` *reporting two errors in plain text*

Watch Mode

My favorite way to use the `tsc` CLI is with its `-w`/`--watch` mode. Instead of exiting once completed, watch mode will keep TypeScript running indefinitely and continuously updates your terminal with a real-time list of all the errors it sees.

Running in watch mode on a file that contains two errors is shown in Figure 13-3.

```
[8:48:40 AM] Starting compilation in watch mode...

index.ts:1:12 - error TS2322: Type 'string' is not assignable to type 'number'.

1 export let notNumeric: number = "Gotcha!";
                         ~~~~~~~~~~

index.ts:3:12 - error TS2322: Type 'number' is not assignable to type 'string'.

3 export let notString: string = 1337;
                        ~~~~~~~~

[8:48:41 AM] Found 2 errors. Watching for file changes.
```

Figure 13-3. tsc reporting two errors in watch mode

Figure 13-4 shows tsc updating console output to indicate that the file was changed in a way to fix all errors.

```
[8:49:18 AM] File change detected. Starting incremental compilation...

[8:49:18 AM] Found 0 errors. Watching for file changes.
```

Figure 13-4. tsc reporting no errors in watch mode

Watch mode is particularly useful when you're working on large changes such as refactors across many files. You can use TypeScript's type errors as a checklist of sorts to see what still needs to be cleaned up.

TSConfig Files

Instead of always providing all file names and configuration options to tsc, most configuration options may be specified in a *tsconfig.json* ("TSConfig") file in a directory.

The existence of a *tsconfig.json* indicates that the directory is the root of a TypeScript project. Running tsc in a directory will read in any configuration options in that *tsconfig.json* file.

You can also pass -p/--project to tsc with a path to a directory containing a *tsconfig.json* or any file to have tsc use that instead:

```
tsc -p path/to/tsconfig.json
```

TSConfig files are generally strongly recommended to be used for TypeScript projects whenever possible. IDEs such as VS Code will respect their configuration when giving you IntelliSense features.

See aka.ms/tsconfig.json (*https://aka.ms/tsconfig.json*) for the full list of configuration options available in TSConfig files.

 If you don't set an option in your *tsconfig.json*, don't worry that TypeScript's default setting for it may change and interfere with your project's compilation settings. This almost never happens and if it did, it would require a major version update to TypeScript and be called out in the release notes.

tsc --init

The `tsc` command line includes an `--init` command to create a new *tsconfig.json* file. That newly created TSConfig file will contain a link to the configuration docs as well as most of the allowed TypeScript configuration options with one-line comments briefly describing their use.

Running this command:

```
tsc --init
```

will generate a fully commented *tsconfig.json* file:

```
{
  "compilerOptions": {
    /* Visit https://aka.ms/tsconfig.json to read more about this file */
    // ...
  }
}
```

I recommend using `tsc --init` to create your configuration file on your first few TypeScript projects. Its default values are applicable to most projects, and its documentation comments are helpful in understanding them.

CLI Versus Configuration

Looking through the TSConfig file created by `tsc --init`, you may notice that configuration options in that file are within a `"compilerOptions"` object. Most options available in both the CLI and in TSConfig files fall into one of two categories:

Compiler
How each included file is compiled and/or type checked by TypeScript

File
Which files will or will not have TypeScript run on them

Other settings that we'll talk about after those two categories, such as project references, generally are only available in TSConfig files.

If a setting is provided to the tsc CLI, such as a one-off change for a CI or production build, it will generally override any value specified in a TSConfig file. Because IDEs generally read from the *tsconfig.json* in a directory for TypeScript settings, it's recommended to put most configuration options in a *tsconfig.json* file.

File Inclusions

By default, tsc will run on all nonhidden *.ts* files (those whose names do not start with a .) in the current directory and any child directories, ignoring hidden directories and directories named *node_modules*. TypeScript configurations can change that list of files to run on.

include

The most common way to include files is with a top-level "include" property in a *tsconfig.json*. It allows an array of strings that describes what directories and/or files to include in TypeScript compilation.

For example, this configuration file recursively includes all TypeScript source files in a *src/* directory relative to the *tsconfig.json*:

```
{
  "include": ["src"]
}
```

Glob wildcards are allowed in include strings for more fine-grained control of files to include:

- * matches zero or more characters (excluding directory separators).
- ? matches any one character (excluding directory separators).
- **/ matches any directory nested to any levels.

This configuration file allows only *.d.ts* files nested in a *typings/* directory and *src/* files with at least two characters in their name before an extension:

```
{
  "include": [
    "typings/**/*.d.ts",
    "src/**/*??.*"
  ]
}
```

For most projects, a simple include compiler option such as ["src"] is generally sufficient.

exclude

The `include` list of files for a project sometimes includes files not meant for compilation by TypeScript. TypeScript allows a TSConfig file to omit paths from `include` by specifying them in a top-level `"exclude"` property. Similar to `include`, it allows an array of strings that describes what directories and/or files to exclude from TypeScript compilation.

The following configuration includes all files in *src/* except for those within any nested *external/* directory and a *node_modules* directory:

```
{
  "exclude": ["**/external", "node_modules"],
  "include": ["src"]
}
```

By default, exclude contains `["node_modules", "bower_components", "jspm_pack ages"]` to avoid running the TypeScript compiler on compiled third-party library files.

> If you're writing your own `exclude` list, you typically won't need to re-add `"bower_components"` or `"jspm_packages"`. Most JavaScript projects that install node modules to a folder within the project only install to `"node_modules"`.

Keep in mind, `exclude` only acts to remove files from the starting list in `include`. TypeScript will run on any file imported by any included file, even if the imported file is explicitly listed in `exclude`.

Alternative Extensions

TypeScript is by default able to read in any file whose extension is *.ts*. However, some projects require being able to read in files with different extensions, such as JSON modules or JSX syntax for UI libraries such as React.

JSX Syntax

JSX syntax like `<Component />` is often used in UI libraries such as Preact and React. JSX syntax is not technically JavaScript. Like TypeScript's type definitions, it's an extension to JavaScript syntax that compiles down to regular JavaScript:

```
const MyComponent = () => {
  // Equivalent to:
  //   return React.createElement("div", null, "Hello, world!");
  return <div>Hello, world!</div>;
};
```

In order to use JSX syntax in a file, you must do two things:

- Enable the "jsx" compiler option in your configuration options
- Name that file with a *.tsx* extension

jsx

The value used for the "jsx" compiler option determines how TypeScript emits Java-Script code for *.tsx* files. Projects generally use one of these three values (Table 13-1).

Table 13-1. JSX compiler option inputs and outputs

Value	Input code	Output code	Output file extension
"preserve"	<div />	<div />	.jsx
"react"	<div />	React.createElement("div")	.js
"react-native"	<div />	<div />	.js

Values for jsx may be provided to the tsc CLI and/or in a TSConfig file.

```
tsc --jsx preserve

{
  "compilerOptions": {
    "jsx": "preserve"
  }
}
```

If you're not directly using TypeScript's built-in transpiler, which is the case when you're transpiling code with a separate tool such as Babel, you most likely can use any of the allowed values for "jsx". Most web apps built on modern frameworks such as Next.js or Remix handle React configuration and compiling syntax. If you're using one of those frameworks you probably won't have to directly configure TypeScript's built-in transpiler.

Generic arrow functions in .tsx files

Chapter 10, "Generics" mentioned that the syntax for generic arrow functions conflicts with JSX syntax. Attempting to write a type argument <T> for an arrow function in a *.tsx* file will give a syntax error for there not being a closing tag for that opening T element:

```
const identity = <T>(input: T) => input;
//                ~~~
// Error: JSX element 'T' has no corresponding closing tag.
```

To work around this syntax ambiguity, you can add an `= unknown` constraint to the type argument. Type arguments default to the `unknown` type so this doesn't change code behavior at all. It just indicates to TypeScript to read a type argument, not a JSX element:

```
const identity = <T = unknown>(input: T) => input; // Ok
```

resolveJsonModule

TypeScript will allow reading in *.json* files if the `resolveJsonModule` compiler option is set to `true`. When it is, *.json* files may be imported from as if they were *.ts* files exporting an object. TypeScript will infer the type of that object as if it were a `const` variable.

For JSON files that contain an object, destructuring imports may be used. This pair of files defines an `"activist"` string in an *activist.json* file and imports it into a *usesActivist.ts* file:

```
// activist.json
{
  "activist": "Mary Astell"
}

// usesActivist.ts
import { activist } from "./activist.json";

// Logs: "Mary Astell"
console.log(activist);
```

Default imports may be used as well if the `esModuleInterop` compiler option—covered later in this chapter—is enabled:

```
// useActivist.ts
import data from "./activist.json";
```

For JSON files that contain other literal types, such as arrays or numbers, you'll have to use the `* as` import syntax. This pair of files defines an array of strings in an *activists.json* file that is then imported into a *useActivists.ts* file:

```
// activists.json
[
  "Ida B. Wells",
  "Sojourner Truth",
  "Tawakkul Karmān"
]

// useActivists.ts
import * as activists from "./activists.json";

// Logs: "3 activists"
console.log(`${activists.length} activists`);
```

Emit

Although the rise of dedicated compiler tools such as Babel has reduced TypeScript's role in some projects to solely type checking, many other projects still rely on TypeScript for compiling TypeScript syntax to JavaScript. It's quite useful for projects to be able to take in a single dependency on `typescript` and use its `tsc` command to output the equivalent JavaScript.

outDir

By default, TypeScript places output files alongside their corresponding source files. For example, running `tsc` on a directory containing *fruits/apple.ts* and *vegetables/zucchini.ts* would result with output files *fruits/apple.js* and *vegetables/zucchini.js*:

```
fruits/
  apple.js
  apple.ts
vegetables/
  zucchini.js
  zucchini.ts
```

Sometimes it may be preferable to place output files in a different folder. Many Node projects, for example, put transformed outputs in a *dist* or *lib* directory.

TypeScript's `outDir` compiler option allows specifying a different root directory for outputs. Output files are kept in the same relative directory structure as input files.

For example, running `tsc --outDir dist` on the previous directory would place outputs within a *dist/* folder:

```
dist/
  fruits/
    apple.js
  vegetables/
    zucchini.js
fruits/
  apple.ts
vegetables/
  zucchini.ts
```

TypeScript calculates the root directory to place output files into by finding the longest common subpath of all input files (excluding *.d.ts* declaration files). That means that projects that place all input source files in a single directory will have that directory treated as the root.

For example, if the above example put all inputs in a *src/* directory and compiled with --outDir lib, *lib/fruits/apple.js* would be created instead of *lib/src/fruits/apple.js*:

```
lib/
  fruits/
    apple.js
  vegetables/
    zucchini.js
src/
  fruits/
    apple.ts
  vegetables/
    zucchini.ts
```

A `rootDir` compiler option does exist to explicitly specify that root directory, but it's rarely necessary or used with values other than . or `src`.

target

TypeScript is able to produce output JavaScript that can run in environments as old as ES3 (circa 1999!). Most environments are able to support syntax features from much newer versions of JavaScript.

TypeScript includes a `target` compiler option to specify how far back in syntax support JavaScript code needs to be transpiled. Although `target` defaults to `"es3"` for backward compatibility reasons when not specified and `tsc --init` defaults to specifying `"es2016"`, it's generally advisable to use the newest JavaScript syntax possible per your target platform(s). Supporting newer JavaScript features in older environments necessitates creating more JavaScript code, which causes slightly larger file sizes and slightly worse runtime performance.

> As of 2022, all releases within the last year of browsers serving > 0.1% of worldwide users support at least all of ECMAScript 2019 and nearly all of ECMAScript 2020–2021, while the LTS-supported versions of Node.js support all of ECMAScript 2021. There's very little reason not to have a `target` at least as high as `"es2019"`.

For example, take this TypeScript source containing ES2015 `const`s and ES2020 `??` nullish coalescing:

```
function defaultNameAndLog(nameMaybe: string | undefined) {
  const name = nameMaybe ?? "anonymous";
  console.log("From", nameMaybe, "to", name);
  return name;
}
```

With `tsc --target es2020` or newer, both `const` and `??` are supported syntax features, so TypeScript would only need to remove the `: string | undefined` from that snippet:

```
function defaultNameAndLog(nameMaybe) {
  const name = nameMaybe ?? "anonymous";
  console.log("From", nameMaybe, "to", name);
  return name;
}
```

With `tsc --target es2015` through `es2019`, the `??` syntax sugar would be compiled down to its equivalent in older versions of JavaScript:

```
function defaultNameAndLog(nameMaybe) {
    const name = nameMaybe !== null && nameMaybe !== void 0
      ? nameMaybe
      : "anonymous";
    console.log("From", nameMaybe, "to", name);
    return name;
}
```

With `tsc --target es3` or `es5`, the `const` would additionally need to be converted to its equivalent `var`:

```
function defaultNameAndLog(nameMaybe) {
    var name = nameMaybe !== null && nameMaybe !== void 0
      ? nameMaybe
      : "anonymous";
    console.log("From", nameMaybe, "to", name);
    return name;
}
```

Specifying the `target` compiler option to a value that matches the oldest environment your code runs will ensure code is emitted as modern, terse syntax that can still run without syntax errors.

Emitting Declarations

Chapter 11, "Declaration Files" covered how *.d.ts* declaration files may be distributed in a package to indicate code types to consumers. Most packages use TypeScript's `declaration` compiler option to emit *.d.ts* output files from source files:

```
tsc --declaration

{
  "compilerOptions": {
    "declaration": true
  }
}
```

.d.ts output files are emitted under the same output rules as *.js* files, including respecting `outDir`.

For example, running `tsc --declaration` on a directory containing *fruits/apple.ts* and *vegetables/zucchini.ts* would result in output declaration files *fruits/apple.d.ts* and *vegetables/zucchini.d.ts* alongside output *.js* files:

```
fruits/
  apple.d.ts
  apple.js
  apple.ts
vegetables/
  zucchini.d.ts
  zucchini.js
  zucchini.ts
```

emitDeclarationOnly

An `emitDeclarationOnly` compiler option exists, as a specialized addition to the `declaration` compiler option, that directs TypeScript to only emit declaration files: no *.js*/.jsx* files at all. This is useful for projects that use an external tool to generate output JavaScript but still want to use TypeScript to generate output definition files:

```
tsc --emitDeclarationOnly

{
  "compilerOptions": {
    "emitDeclarationOnly": true
  }
}
```

If `emitDeclarationOnly` is enabled, either `declaration` or the `composite` compiler option covered later in this chapter must be enabled.

For example, running `tsc --declaration --emitDeclarationOnly` on a directory containing *fruits/apple.ts* and *vegetables/zucchini.ts* would result with output declaration files *fruits/apple.d.ts* and *vegetables/zucchini.d.ts* without any output *.js* files:

```
fruits/
  apple.d.ts
  apple.ts
vegetables/
  zucchini.d.ts
  zucchini.ts
```

Source Maps

Source maps are descriptions of how the contents of output files match up to original source files. They allow developer tools such as debuggers to display original source code when navigating through the output file. They're particularly useful for visual debuggers such as those used in browser developer tools and IDEs to let you see original source file contents while debugging. TypeScript includes the ability to output source maps alongside output files.

sourceMap

TypeScript's `sourceMap` compiler option enables outputting *.js.map* or *.jsx.map* sourcemaps alongside *.js* or *.jsx* output files. Sourcemap files are otherwise given the same name as their corresponding output JavaScript file and placed in the same directory.

For example, running `tsc --sourceMap` on a directory containing *fruits/apple.ts* and *vegetables/zucchini.ts* would result with output sourcemap files *fruits/apple.js.map* and *vegetables/zucchini.js.map* alongside output *.js* files:

```
fruits/
  apple.js
  apple.js.map
  apple.ts
vegetables/
  zucchini.js
  zucchini.js.map
  zucchini.ts
```

declarationMap

TypeScript is also able to generate source maps for *.d.ts* declaration files. Its `declarationMap` compiler option directs it to generate a *.d.ts.map* source map for each *.d.ts* that maps back to the original source file. Declaration maps enable IDEs such as VS Code to go to the original source file when using editor features such as Go to Definition.

 `declarationMap` is particularly useful when working with project references, covered toward the end of this chapter.

For example, running `tsc --declaration --declarationMap` on a directory containing *fruits/apple.ts* and *vegetables/zucchini.ts* would result in output declaration sourcemap files *fruits/apple.d.ts.map* and *vegetables/zucchini.d.ts.map* alongside output *.d.ts* and *.js* files:

```
fruits/
  apple.d.ts
  apple.d.ts.map
  apple.js
  apple.ts
vegetables/
  zucchini.d.ts
  zucchini.d.ts.map
  zucchini.js
  zucchini.ts
```

noEmit

For projects that completely rely on other tools to compile source files to output JavaScript, TypeScript can be told to skip emitting files altogether. Enabling the noEmit compiler option directs TypeScript to act purely as a type checker.

Running `tsc --noEmit` on any of the previous examples would result in no new files created. TypeScript would only report any syntax or type errors it finds.

Type Checking

Most of TypeScript's configuration options control its type checker. You can configure it to be gentle and forgiving, only emitting type-checking complaints when it's completely certain of an error, or harsh and strict, requiring nearly all code be well typed.

lib

To start, which global APIs TypeScript assumes to be present in the runtime environment is configurable with the lib compiler option. It takes in an array of strings that defaults to your target compiler option, as well as dom to indicate including browser types.

Most of the time, the only reason to customize lib would be to remove the dom inclusion for a project that doesn't run in the browser:

```
tsc --lib es2020

{
  "compilerOptions": {
    "lib": ["es2020"]
  }
}
```

Alternately, for a project that uses polyfills to support newer JavaScript APIs, lib can include dom and any ECMAScript version:

```
tsc --lib dom,es2021

{
  "compilerOptions": {
    "lib": ["dom", "es2021"]
  }
}
```

Be wary of modifying lib without providing all the right runtime polyfills. A project with a lib set to "es2021" running on a platform that only supports up through ES2020 might have no type-checking errors but still experience runtime errors attempting to use APIs defined in ES2021 or later, such as String.replaceAll:

```
const value = "a b c";

value.replaceAll(" ", ", ");
// Uncaught TypeError: value.replaceAll is not a function
```

 Think of the lib compiler option as indicating what built-in language APIs are available, whereas the target compiler option indicates what syntax features exist.

skipLibCheck

TypeScript provides a skipLibCheck compiler option that indicates to skip type checking in declaration files not explicitly included in your source code. This can be useful for applications that rely on many dependencies that may rely on different, conflicting definitions of shared libraries:

```
tsc --skipLibCheck

{
  "compilerOptions": {
    "skipLibCheck": true
  }
}
```

skipLibCheck speeds up TypeScript performance by allowing it to skip some type checking. For this reason, it is generally a good idea to enable it on most projects.

Strict Mode

Most of TypeScript's type-checking compiler options are grouped into what TypeScript refers to as *strict mode*. Each strictness compiler option defaults to false, and when enabled, directs the type checker to turn on some additional checks.

I'll cover the most commonly used strict options in alphabetical order later in this chapter. From those options, noImplicitAny and strictNullChecks are particularly useful and impactful in enforcing type-safe code.

You can enable all strict mode checks by enabling the strict compiler option:

```
tsc --strict

{
  "compilerOptions": {
    "strict": true
  }
}
```

If you want to enable all strict mode checks except for certain ones, you can both enable `strict` and explicitly disable certain checks. For example, this configuration enables all strict modes except for `noImplicitAny`:

```
tsc --strict --noImplicitAny false

{
  "compilerOptions": {
    "noImplicitAny": false,
    "strict": true
  }
}
```

 Future versions of TypeScript may introduce new strict type-checking compiler options under `strict`. Using `strict` may therefore cause new type-checking complaints when you update TypeScript versions. You can always opt out of specific settings in your TSConfig.

noImplicitAny

If TypeScript cannot infer the type of a parameter or property, then it will fall back to assuming the `any` type. It is generally best practice to not allow these implicit `any` types in code as the `any` type is allowed to bypass much of TypeScript's type checking.

The `noImplicitAny` compiler option directs TypeScript to issue a type-checking complaint when it has to fall back to an implicit `any`.

For example, writing the following function parameter without a type declaration would cause a type error under `noImplicitAny`:

```
const logMessage = (message) => {
  //                 ~~~~~~~
  // Error: Parameter 'message' implicitly has an 'any' type.
  console.log(`Message: ${message}!`);
};
```

Most of the time, a `noImplicitAny` complaint can be resolved either by adding a type annotation on the complaining location:

```
const logMessage = (message: string) => { // Ok
  console.log(`Message: ${message}!`);
}
```

Or, in the case of function parameters, putting the parent function in a location that indicates the type of the function:

```
type LogsMessage = (message: string) => void;

const logMessage: LogsMessage = (message) => { // Ok
  console.log(`Message: ${message}!`);
}
```

 noImplicitAny is an excellent flag for ensuring type safety across a project. I highly recommend striving to turn it on in projects written completely in TypeScript. However, if a project is still transitioning from JavaScript to TypeScript, it may be easier to finish converting all files to TypeScript first.

strictBindCallApply

When TypeScript was first released, it didn't have rich enough type system features to be able to represent the built-in Function.apply, Function.bind, or Function.call function utilities. Those functions by default had to take in any for their list of arguments. That's not very type safe!

As an example, without strictBindCallApply, the following variations on get Length all include any in their types:

```
function getLength(text: string, trim?: boolean) {
  return trim ? text.trim().length : text.length;
}

// Function type: (thisArg: Function, argArray?: any) => any
getLength.apply;

// Returned type: any
getLength.bind(undefined, "abc123");

// Returned type: any
getLength.call(undefined, "abc123", true);
```

Now that TypeScript's type system features are powerful enough to represent those functions' generic rest arguments, TypeScript allows opting in to using more restrictive types for the functions.

Enabling strictBindCallApply enables much more precise types for the getLength variations:

```
function getLength(text: string, trim?: boolean) {
  return trim ? text.trim().length : text;
}

// Function type:
// (thisArg: typeof getLength, args: [text: string, trim?: boolean]) => number;
getLength.apply;
```

```
// Returned type: (trim?: boolean) => number
getLength.bind(undefined, "abc123");

// Returned type: number
getLength.call(undefined, "abc123", true);
```

TypeScript best practice is to enable `strictBindCallApply`. Its improved type check-ing for built-in function utilities helps improve type safety for projects that utilize them.

strictFunctionTypes

The `strictFunctionTypes` compiler option causes function parameter types to be checked slightly more strictly. A function type is no longer considered assignable to another function type if its parameters are not subtypes of that other type's parame-ters.

As a concrete example, the `checkOnNumber` function here takes in a function that should be able to receive a `number | string`, but is provided with a `stringContainsA` function that expects to take in a parameter only of type `string`. TypeScript's default type checking would allow it—and the program would crash from trying to call `.match()` on a `number`:

```
function checkOnNumber(containsA: (input: number | string) => boolean) {
  return containsA(1337);
}

function stringContainsA(input: string) {
  return !!input.match(/a/i);
}

checkOnNumber(stringContainsA);
```

Under `strictFunctionTypes`, `checkOnNumber(stringContainsA)` would cause a type-checking error:

```
// Argument of type '(input: string) => boolean' is not assignable
// to parameter of type '(input: string | number) => boolean'.
//   Types of parameters 'input' and 'input' are incompatible.
//     Type 'string | number' is not assignable to type 'string'.
//       Type 'number' is not assignable to type 'string'.
checkOnNumber(stringContainsA);
```

In technical terms, function parameters switch from being *bivar-iant* to *contravariant*. You can read more about the difference in the TypeScript 2.6 release notes (*https://www.typescriptlang.org/docs/handbook/release-notes/typescript-2-6.html*).

strictNullChecks

Back in Chapter 3, "Unions and Literals", I discussed the billion-dollar mistake of languages: allowing empty types such as `null` and `undefined` to be assignable to nonempty types. Disabling TypeScript's `strictNullChecks` flag roughly adds `null | undefined` to every type in your code, thereby allowing any variable to receive `null` or `undefined`.

This code snippet would cause a type error for assigning `null` to a string typed value only when `strictNullChecks` is enabled:

```
let value: string;

value = "abc123"; // Always ok

value = null;
// With strictNullChecks enabled:
// Error: Type 'null' is not assignable to type 'string'.
```

TypeScript best practice is to enable `strictNullChecks`. Doing so helps prevent crashes and eliminates the billion-dollar mistake.

Refer to Chapter 3, "Unions and Literals" for more details.

strictPropertyInitialization

Back in Chapter 8, "Classes", I discussed strict initialization checking in classes: making sure that each property on a class is definitely assigned in the class constructor. TypeScript's `strictPropertyInitialization` flag causes a type error to be issued on class properties that have no initializer and are not definitely assigned in the constructor.

TypeScript best practice is generally to enable `strictPropertyInitialization`. Doing so helps prevent crashes from mistakes in class initialization logic.

Refer to Chapter 8, "Classes" for more details.

useUnknownInCatchVariables

Error handling in any language is an inherently unsafe concept. Any function can in theory throw any number of errors from edge cases such as reading properties on `undefined` or user-written `throw` statements. In fact, there's no guarantee a thrown error is even an instance of the `Error` class: code can always `throw "something-else"`.

As a result, TypeScript's default behavior for errors is to give them type `any`, as they could be anything. That allows flexibility in error handling at the cost of relying on the not-very-type-safe `any` by default.

The following snippet's `error` is typed `any` because there's no way for TypeScript to know what all the possible errors thrown by `someExternalFunction()` could be:

```
try {
  someExternalFunction();
} catch (error) {
  error; // Default type: any
}
```

As with most `any` uses, it would be more technically sound—at the cost of often necessitating explicit type assertions or narrowing—to treat errors as `unknown` instead. Catch clause errors are allowed to be annotated as the `any` or `unknown` types.

This snippet correction adds an explicit `: unknown` to `error` to switch it to the `unknown` type:

```
try {
  someExternalFunction();
} catch (error: unknown) {
  error; // Type: unknown
}
```

The strict area flag `useUnknownInCatchVariables` changes TypeScript's default catch clause error type to `unknown`. With `useUnknownInCatchVariables` enabled, both snippets would have type of `error` set to be `unknown`.

TypeScript best practice is generally to enable `useUnknownInCatchVariables`, as it's not always safe to assume errors will be any particular type.

Modules

JavaScript's various systems for exporting and importing module contents—AMD, CommonJS, ECMAScript, and so on—are one of the most convoluted module systems in any modern programming language. JavaScript is relatively unusual in that the way files import each other's contents is often driven by user-written frameworks such as Webpack. TypeScript does its best to provide configuration options that represent most reasonable user-land module configurations.

Most new TypeScript projects are written with the standardized ECMAScript modules syntax. To recap, here is how ECMAScript modules import a value (`value`) from another module (`"my-example-lib"`) and export their own value (`logValue`):

```
import { value } from "my-example-lib";

export const logValue = () => console.log(value);
```

module

TypeScript provides a `module` compiler option to direct which module system transpiled code will use. When writing source code with ECMAScript modules, TypeScript may transpile the `export` and `import` statements to a different module system based on the `module` value.

For example, directing that a project written in ECMAScript be output as CommonJS modules in either the command line:

```
tsc --module commonjs
```

or in a TSConfig:

```
{
  "compilerOptions": {
    "module": "commonjs"
  }
}
```

The previous code snippet would roughly be output as:

```
const my_example_lib = require("my-example-lib");
exports.logValue = () => console.log(my_example_lib.value);
```

If your `target` compiler option is `"es3"` or `"es5"`, module's default value will be `"commonjs"`. Otherwise, `module` will default to `"es2015"` to specify outputting ECMAScript modules.

moduleResolution

Module resolution is the process by which the imported path in an import is mapped to a module. TypeScript provides a `moduleResolution` option that you can use to specify the logic for that process. You'll typically want to provide it one of two logic strategies:

- node: The behavior used by CommonJS resolvers such as traditional Node.js
- nodenext: Aligning to the behavior specified for ECMAScript modules

The two strategies are similar. Most projects could use either of them and not notice a difference. You can read more on the intricacies behind the scenes of module resolution on *https://www.typescriptlang.org/docs/handbook/module-resolution.html*.

> `moduleResolution` does not change how TypeScript emits code at all. It's only used to describe the runtime environment your code is meant to be run in.

Both the following CLI snippet and JSON file snippet would work to specify the `moduleResolution` compiler option:

```
tsc --moduleResolution nodenext

{
  "compilerOptions": {
    "moduleResolution": "nodenext"
  }
}
```

 For backward compatibility reasons, TypeScript keeps the default `moduleResolution` value to a `classic` value that was used for projects years ago. You almost certainly do not want the `classic` strategy in any modern project.

Interoperability with CommonJS

When working with JavaScript modules, there is a difference between the "default" export of a module and its "namespace" output. The *default* export of a module is the `.default` property on its exported object. The *namespace* export of a module is the exported object itself.

Table 13-2 recaps the differences between default and namespace exports and imports.

Table 13-2. CommonJS and ECMAScript module export and import forms

Area of syntax	CommonJS	ECMAScript modules
Default export	`module.exports.default = value;`	`export default value;`
Default import	`const { default: value } = require("...");`	`import value from "...";`
Namespace export	`module.exports = value;`	Not supported
Namespace import	`const value = require("...");`	`import * as value from "...";`

TypeScript's type system builds its understanding of file imports and exports in terms of ECMAScript modules. If your project depends on npm packages as most do, however, it's likely some of those dependencies are still published as CommonJS modules. Furthermore, although some packages that comply with ECMAScript modules rules avoid including a default export, many developers prefer the more succinct default-style imports over namespace-style imports. TypeScript includes a few compiler options that improve interoperability between module formats.

esModuleInterop

The `esModuleInterop` configuration option adds a small amount of logic to Java-Script code emitted by TypeScript when `module` is not an ECMAScript module format such as `"es2015"` or `"esnext"`. That logic allows ECMAScript modules to import from modules even if they don't happen to adhere to ECMAScript modules' rules around default or namespace imports.

One common reason to enable `esModuleInterop` is for packages such as `"react"` that do not ship a default export. If a module attempts to use a default-style import from the `"react"` package, TypeScript would report a type error without `esModuleInterop` enabled:

```
import React from "react";
//     ~~~~~
// Module '"file:///node_modules/@types/react/index"' can
// only be default-imported using the 'esModuleInterop' flag.
```

Note that `esModuleInterop` only directly changes how emitted JavaScript code works with imports. The following `allowSyntheticDefaultImports` configuration option is what informs the type system about import interoperability.

allowSyntheticDefaultImports

The `allowSyntheticDefaultImports` compiler option informs the type system that ECMAScript modules may default import from files that are otherwise incompatible CommonJS namespace exports.

It defaults to `true` only if either of the following is true:

- `module` is `"system"` (an older, rarely used module format not covered in this book).
- `esModuleInterop` is `true` and `module` is not an ECMAScript modules format such as `"es2015"` or `"esnext"`.

In other words, if `esModuleInterop` is `true` but `module` is `"esnext"`, TypeScript will assume output compiled JavaScript code is not using import interoperability helpers. It would report a type error for a default import from packages such as `"react"`:

```
import React from "react";
// Module '"file:///node_modules/@types/react/index"' can only be
// default-imported using the 'allowSyntheticDefaultImports' flag`.
```

isolatedModules

External transpilers such as Babel that only operate on one file at a time cannot use type system information to emit JavaScript. As a result, TypeScript syntax features that rely on type information to emit JavaScript aren't generally supported in those transpilers. Enabling the `isolatedModules` compiler tells TypeScript to report an error on any instance of a syntax that is likely to cause issues in those transpilers:

- Const enums, covered in Chapter 14, "Syntax Extensions"
- Script (nonmodule) files
- Standalone type exports, covered in Chapter 14, "Syntax Extensions"

I generally recommend enabling `isolatedModules` if your project uses a tool other than TypeScript to transpile to JavaScript.

JavaScript

While TypeScript is lovely and I hope you want to always write code in it, you don't have to write all your source files in TypeScript. Although TypeScript by default ignores files with a *.js* or *.jsx* extension, using its `allowJs` and/or `checkJs` compiler options will allow it to read from, compile, and even—in a limited capacity—type check JavaScript files.

A common strategy for converting an existing JavaScript project to TypeScript is to start off with only a few files initially converted to TypeScript. More files may be added over time until there are no more JavaScript files left. You don't have to go all-in on TypeScript until you're ready to!

allowJs

The `allowJs` compiler option allows constructs declared in JavaScript files to factor into type checking TypeScript files When combined with the `jsx` compiler option, *.jsx* files are also allowed.

For example, take this *index.ts* importing a `value` declared in a *values.js* file:

```
// index.ts
import { value } from "./values";

console.log(`Quote: '${value.toUpperCase()}'`);

// values.js
export const value = "We cannot succeed when half of us are held back.";
```

Without `allowJs` enabled, the `import` statement would not have a known type. It would be implicitly `any` by default or trigger a type error like "Could not find a declaration file for module `"./values"`."

`allowJs` also adds JavaScript files to the list of files compiled to the ECMAScript target and emitted as JavaScript. Source maps and declaration files will be produced as well if the options to do so are enabled:

```
tsc --allowJs

{
  "compilerOptions": {
    "allowJs": true
  }
}
```

With `allowJs` enabled, the imported `value` would be type `string`. No type errors would be reported.

checkJs

TypeScript can do more than just factor JavaScript files into type checking TypeScript files: it can type check JavaScript files too. The `checkJs` compiler option serves two purposes:

- Defaulting `allowJs` to `true` if it wasn't already
- Enabling the type checker on *.js* and *.jsx* files

Enabling `checkJs` will make TypeScript treat JavaScript files as if they were Type-Script files that don't have any TypeScript-specific syntax. Type mismatches, misspelled variable names, and so on will all cause type errors as they normally would in a TypeScript file:

```
tsc --checkJs

{
  "compilerOptions": {
    "checkJs": true
  }
}
```

With `checkJs` enabled, this JavaScript file would cause a type-checking complaint for an incorrect variable name:

```
// index.js
let myQuote = "Each person must live their life as a model for others.";

console.log(quote);
//          ~~~~~
// Error: Cannot find name 'quote'. Did you mean 'myQuote'?
```

Without `checkJs` enabled, TypeScript would not have reported a type error for that likely bug.

@ts-check

Alternately, `checkJs` can be enabled on a file-by-file basis by including a `// @ts-check` comment on top of the file. Doing so enables the `checkJs` option for just that JavaScript file:

```
// index.js
// @ts-check
let myQuote = "Each person must live their life as a model for others.";

console.log(quote);
//          ~~~~~~~
// Error: Cannot find name 'quote'. Did you mean 'myQuote'?
```

JSDoc Support

Because JavaScript doesn't have TypeScript's rich type syntax, the types of values declared in JavaScript files are often not as precise as those declared in TypeScript files. For example, while TypeScript can infer the value of an object declared as a variable in a JavaScript file, there's no native JavaScript way to declare in that file that the value adheres to any particular interface.

I mentioned back in Chapter 1, "From JavaScript to TypeScript" that the JSDoc community standard provides some ways to describe types using comments. When `allowJs` and/or `checkJs` are enabled, TypeScript will recognize any JSDoc definitions in code.

For example, this snippet declares in JSDoc that the `sentenceCase` function takes in a `string`. TypeScript can then infer that it returns a `string`. With `checkJs` enabled, TypeScript would know to report a type error for passing it a `string[]` later:

```
// index.js

/**
 * @param {string} text
 */
function sentenceCase(text) {
    return `${text[0].toUpperCase()} ${text.slice(1)}.`;
}

sentenceCase("hello world");// Ok

sentenceCase(["hello", "world"]);
//           ~~~~~~~~~~~~~~~~~~
// Error: Argument of type 'string[]' is not
// assignable to parameter of type 'string'.
```

TypeScript's JSDoc support is useful for incrementally adding type checking for projects that don't have the time or developer familiarity to convert to TypeScript.

The full list of supported JSDoc syntax is available on *https://
www.typescriptlang.org/docs/handbook/jsdoc-supported-types.html*.

Configuration Extensions

As you write more and more TypeScript projects, you may find yourself writing the same project settings repeatedly. Although TypeScript doesn't allow configuration files to be written in JavaScript and use `import` or `require`, it does offer a mechanism for a TSConfig file to opt into "extending," or copying in configuration values, from another configuration file.

extends

A TSConfig may extend from another TSConfig with the `extends` configuration option. `extends` takes in a path to another TSConfig file and indicates that all settings from that file should be copied over. It behaves similarly to the `extends` keyword on classes: any option declared on the derived, or child, configuration will override any option of the same name on the base, or parent, configuration.

For example, many repositories that have multiple TSConfigs, such as monorepos containing multiple *packages/** directories, by convention create a *tsconfig.base.json* file for *tsconfig.json* files to extend from:

```
// tsconfig.base.json
{
  "compilerOptions": {
    "strict": true
  }
}
// packages/core/tsconfig.json
{
  "extends": "../../tsconfig.base.json",
  "includes": ["src"]
}
```

Note that `compilerOptions` are factored in recursively. Each compiler option from a base TSConfig will copy over to a derived TSConfig unless the derived TSConfig overrides that specific option.

If the previous example were to add a TSConfig that adds the `allowJs` option, that new derived TSConfig would still have `compilerOptions.strict` set to `true`:

```
// packages/js/tsconfig.json
{
  "extends": "../../tsconfig.base.json",
```

```
  "compilerOptions": {
    "allowJs": true
  },
  "includes": ["src"]
}
```

Extending modules

The `extends` property may point to either kind of JavaScript import:

Absolute
> Starting with @ or an alphabetical letter

Relative
> A local file path starting with .

When an `extends` value is an absolute path, it indicates to extend the TSConfig from an npm module. TypeScript will use the normal Node module resolution system to find a package matching the name. If that package's `package.json` contains a `"tsconfig"` field containing a relative path string, the TSConfig file at that path will be used. Otherwise, the package's *tsconfig.json* file will be used.

Many organizations use npm packages to standardize TypeScript compiler options across repositories and/or within monorepos. The following TSConfig files are what you might set up for a monorepo in a @my-org organization. `packages/js` needs to specify the `allowJs` compiler option, while `packages/ts` does not change any compiler options:

```
// packages/tsconfig.json
{
  "compilerOptions": {
    "strict": true
  }
}
// packages/js/tsconfig.json
{
  "extends": "@my-org/tsconfig",
  "compilerOptions": {
    "allowJs": true
  },
  "includes": ["src"]
}
// packages/ts/tsconfig.json
{
  "extends": "@my-org/tsconfig",
  "includes": ["src"]
}
```

Configuration Bases

Instead of creating your own configuration from scratch or the `--init` suggestions, you can start with a premade "base" TSConfig file tailored to a particular runtime environment. These premade configuration bases are available on the npm package registry under `@tsconfig/`, such as `@tsconfig/recommended` or `@tsconfig/node16`.

For example, to install the recommended TSConfig base for deno:

```
npm install --save-dev @tsconfig/deno
# or
yarn add --dev @tsconfig/deno
```

Once a configuration base package is installed, it can be referenced like any other npm package configuration extension:

```
{
    "extends": "@tsconfig/deno/tsconfig.json"
}
```

The full list of TSConfig bases is documented on *https://github.com/tsconfig/bases*.

> It is generally a good idea to know what TypeScript configuration options your file is using, even if you aren't changing them yourself.

Project References

Each of the TypeScript configuration files I've shown so far have assumed they manage all the source files of a project. It can be useful in larger projects to use different configuration files for different areas of a project. TypeScript allows defining a system of "project references" where multiple projects can be built together. Setting up project references is a little more work than using a single TSConfig file but comes with several key benefits:

- You can specify different compiler options for certain areas of code.
- TypeScript will be able to cache build outputs for individual projects, often resulting in significantly faster build times for large projects.
- Project references enforce a "dependency tree" (only allowing certain projects to import files from certain other projects), which can help structure discrete areas of code.

Project references are generally used in larger projects that have multiple distinct areas of code, such as monorepos and modular component systems. You probably don't want to use them for small projects that don't have dozens or more files.

The following three sections show how to build up project settings to enable project references:

- `composite` mode on a TSConfig enforces that it works in ways suitable for multi-TSConfig build modes.
- `references` in a TSConfig indicate which composite TSConfigs it relies on.
- Build mode uses composite TSConfig references to orchestrate building their files.

composite

TypeScript allows a project to opt into the `composite` configuration option to indicate that its file system inputs and outputs obey constraints that make it easier for build tools to determine whether its build outputs are up-to-date compared to its build inputs. When `composite` is `true`:

- The rootDir setting, if not already explicitly set, defaults to the directory containing the TSConfig file.
- All implementation files must be matched by an include pattern or listed in the `files` array.
- `declaration` must be turned on.

This configuration snippet matches all conditions for enabling `composite` mode in a `core/` directory:

```
// core/tsconfig.json
{
  "compilerOptions": {
    "composite": true,
    "declaration": true
  },
}
```

These changes help TypeScript enforce that all input files to the project create a matching *.d.ts* file. `composite` is generally most useful in combination with the following `references` configuration option.

references

A TypeScript project can indicate it relies on the outputs generated by a composite TypeScript project with a `references` setting in its TSConfig. Importing modules from a referenced project will be seen in the type system as importing from its output *.d.ts* declaration file(s).

This configuration snippet sets up a *shell/* directory to reference a *core/* directory as its inputs:

```
// shell/tsconfig.json
{
  "references": [
    { "path": "../core" }
  ]
}
```

 The `references` configuration option will not be copied from base TSConfigs to derived TSConfigs via `extends`.

`references` is generally most useful in combination with the following build mode.

Build Mode

Once an area of code has been set up to use project references, it will be possible to use `tsc` in its alternate "build" mode via the `-b`/`--b` CLI flag. Build mode enhances `tsc` into something of a project build coordinator. It lets `tsc` rebuild only the projects that have been changed since the last build, based on when their contents and their file outputs were last generated.

More precisely, TypeScript's build mode will do the following when given a TSConfig:

1. Find that TSConfig's referenced projects.
2. Detect if they are up-to-date.
3. Build out-of-date projects in the correct order.
4. Build the provided TSConfig if it or any of its dependencies have changed.

The ability of TypeScript's build mode to skip rebuilding up-to-date projects can significantly improve build performance.

Coordinator configurations

A common handy pattern for setting up TypeScript project references in a repository is to set up a root-level `tsconfig.json` with an empty `files` array and references to all the project references in the repository. That root TSConfig won't direct TypeScript to build any files itself. Instead it will act purely to tell TypeScript to build referenced projects as needed.

This `tsconfig.json` indicates to build the `packages/core` and `packages/shell` projects in a repository:

```
// tsconfig.json
{
  "files": [],
  "references": [
    { "path": "./packages/core" },
    { "path": "./packages/shell" }
  ]
}
```

I personally like to standardize having a script in my `package.json` named `build` or `compile` that calls to `tsc -b` as a shortcut:

```
// package.json
{
  "scripts": {
    "build": "tsc -b"
  }
}
```

Build-mode options

Build mode supports a few build-specific CLI options:

- `--clean`: deletes the outputs of the specified projects (may be combined with `--dry`)
- `--dry`: shows what would be done but doesn't actually build anything
- `--force`: acts as if all projects are out of date
- `-w`/`--watch`: similar to the typical TypeScript watch mode

Because build mode supports watch mode, running a command like `tsc -b -w` can be a fast way to get an up-to-date listing of all compiler errors in a large project.

Summary

In this chapter, you went over many of the important configuration options provided by TypeScript:

- Using `tsc`, including its pretty and watch modes
- Using TSConfig files, including creating one with `tsc --init`
- Changing which files will be included by the TypeScript compiler
- Allowing JSX syntax in *.tsx* files and/or JSON syntax in *.json* files
- Changing the directory, ECMAScript version target, declaration file, and/or source map outputs with files
- Changing the built-in library types used in compilation
- Strict mode and useful strict flags such as `noImplicitAny` and `strictNullChecks`
- Supporting different module systems and changing module resolution
- Allowing including JavaScript files, and opting into type checking those files
- Using `extends` to share configuration options between files
- Using project references and build mode to orchestrate multi-TSConfig builds

 Now that you've finished reading this chapter, practice what you've learned on *https://learningtypescript.com/configuration-options*.

What is a disciplinarian's favorite TypeScript compiler option?

`strict.`

PART IV

Extra Credit

JavaScript has been around for a few decades at this point, and people have done quite a lot of odd things with it. TypeScript's syntax and type system need to be able to represent all those odd things to enable any JavaScript developer to work with TypeScript. As a result, there are some corners of the TypeScript language not seen in most day-to-day code but that are relevant, even necessary, for working with some kinds of projects.

I think of these parts of the language as "extra credit" in that you could avoid them entirely and still be a productive TypeScript developer. In fact, for the logical types introduced toward the end of the section, I would hope you wouldn't need to use them very often—if at all.

CHAPTER 14

Syntax Extensions

*"TypeScript does not add
to the JavaScript runtime."
...was that all a lie?!*

When TypeScript was first released in 2012, web applications were growing in complexity faster than plain JavaScript was adding features that supported the deep complexity. The most popular JavaScript language flavor at the time, CoffeeScript, had made its mark diverging from JavaScript by introducing new and exciting syntactic constructs.

Nowadays, extending JavaScript syntax with new runtime features specific to a superset language such as TypeScript is considered bad practice for several reasons:

- Most importantly, runtime syntax extensions might conflict with new syntax in newer versions of JavaScript.
- They make it more difficult for programmers new to the language to understand where JavaScript ends and other languages begin.
- They increase complexity of transpilers that take superset language code and emit JavaScript.

Thus, it is with a heavy heart and deep regret that I must inform you that the early TypeScript designers introduced three syntax extensions to JavaScript in the TypeScript language:

- Classes, which aligned with JavaScript classes as the spec was ratified
- Enums, a straightforward syntactic sugar akin to a plain object of keys and values
- Namespaces, a solution predating modern modules to structure and arrange code

TypeScript's "original sin" of runtime syntax extensions to JavaScript is fortunately not a design decision the language has made since its early years. TypeScript does not add new runtime syntax constructs until they have made significant progress through the ratification process to be added to JavaScript itself.

TypeScript classes ended up looking and behaving almost identical to JavaScript classes (phew!) with the exception of `useDefineForClassFields` behavior (a configuration option not covered in this book) and parameter properties (covered here). Enums are still used in some projects because they are occasionally useful. Virtually no new projects use namespaces anymore.

TypeScript also adopted an experimental proposal for JavaScript "decorators" that I'll cover as well.

Class Parameter Properties

I recommend avoiding using class parameter properties unless you're working in a project that heavily uses classes or a framework that would benefit from them.

It is common in JavaScript classes to want to take in a parameter in a constructor and immediately assign it to a class property.

This `Engineer` class takes in a single `area` parameter of type `string` and assigns it to an `area` property of type `string`:

```
class Engineer {
    readonly area: string;

    constructor(area: string) {
        this.area = area;
        console.log(`I work in the ${area} area.`);
    }
}

// Type: string
new Engineer("mechanical").area;
```

TypeScript includes a shorthand syntax for declaring these kinds of "parameter properties": properties that are assigned to a member property of the same type at the beginning of a class constructor. Placing `readonly` and/or one of the privacy modifiers—`public`, `protected`, or `private`—in front of the parameter to a constructor indicates to TypeScript to also declare a property of that same name and type.

The previous `Engineer` example could be rewritten in TypeScript using a parameter property for `area`:

```
class Engineer {
    constructor(readonly area: string) {
        console.log(`I work in the ${area} area.`);
    }
}

// Type: string
new Engineer("mechanical").area;
```

Parameter properties are assigned at the very beginning of the class constructor (or after the `super()` call if the class is derived from a base class). They can be intermixed with other parameters and/or properties on a class.

The following `NamedEngineer` class declares a regular property `fullName`, a regular parameter `name`, and a parameter property `area`:

```
class NamedEngineer {
    fullName: string;

    constructor(
        name: string,
        public area: string,
    ) {
        this.fullName = `${name}, ${area} engineer`;
    }
}
```

Its equivalent TypeScript without parameter properties looks similar, but with a couple more lines of code to explicitly assign `area`:

```
class NamedEngineer {
    fullName: string;
    area: string;

    constructor(
        name: string,
        area: string,
    ) {
        this.area = area;
        this.fullName = `${name}, ${area} engineer`;
    }
}
```

Parameter properties are a sometimes-debated issue in the TypeScript community. Most projects prefer to avoid them categorically, as they're a runtime syntax extension and therefore suffer from the same drawbacks I mentioned earlier. They also can't be used with the newer # class private fields syntax.

On the other hand, they're quite nice when used in projects that heavily favor creating classes. Parameter properties solve a convenience issue of needing to declare the parameter property name and type twice, which is inherent to TypeScript and not JavaScript.

Experimental Decorators

 I recommend avoiding decorators if at all possible until a version of ECMAScript is ratified with decorator syntax. If you're working in a version of a framework such as Angular or NestJS that recommends using TypeScript decorators, the framework's documentation will guide how to use them.

Many other languages that contain classes allow annotating, or decorating, those classes and/or their members with some kind of runtime logic to modify them. *Decorator* functions are a proposal for JavaScript to allow annotating classes and members by placing a @ and the name of a function first.

For example, the following code snippet shows just the syntax for using a decorator on a class `MyClass`:

```
@myDecorator
class MyClass { /* ... */ }
```

Decorators have not yet been ratified in ECMAScript, so TypeScript does not support them by default as of version 4.7.2. However, TypeScript does include an `experimen talDecorators` compiler option that allows for an old experimental version of them to be used in code. It can be enabled via the `tsc` CLI or in a TSConfig file, shown here, like other compiler options:

```
{
    "compilerOptions": {
        "experimentalDecorators": true
    }
}
```

Each usage of a decorator will execute once, as soon as the entity it's decorating is created. Each kind of decorator—accessor, class, method, parameter, and property—receives a different set of arguments describing the entity it's decorating.

For example, this `logOnCall` decorator used on a `Greeter` class method receives the `Greeter` class itself, the key of the property (`"greet"`), and a `descriptor` object describing the property. Modifying `descriptor.value` to log before calling the original `greet` method on the `Greeter` class "decorates" the `greet` method:

```
function logOnCall(target: any, key: string, descriptor: PropertyDescriptor) {
    const original = descriptor.value;
    console.log("[logOnCall] I am decorating", target.constructor.name);

    descriptor.value = function (...args: unknown[]) {
        console.log(`[descriptor.value] Calling '${key}' with:`, ...args);
        return original.call(this, ...args);
    }
}

class Greeter {
    @logOnCall
    greet(message: string) {
        console.log(`[greet] Hello, ${message}!`);
    }
}

new Greeter().greet("you");
// Output log:
// "[logOnCall] I am decorating", "Greeter"
// "[descriptor.value] Calling 'greet' with:", "you"
// "[greet] Hello, you!"
```

I won't delve into the nuances and specifics of how the old `experimentalDecora tors` works for each of the possible decorator types. TypeScript's decorator support is experimental and does not align with the latest drafts of the ECMAScript proposal. Writing your own decorators in particular is rarely justified in any TypeScript project.

Enums

 I recommend not to use enums unless you have a set of literals that are repeated often, can all be described by a common name, and whose code would be much easier to read if switched to an enum.

Most programming languages contain the concept of an "enum," or enumerated type, to represent a set of related values. Enums can be thought of as a set of literal values stored in an object with a friendly name for each value.

JavaScript does not include an enum syntax because traditional objects can be used in place of them. For example, while HTTP status codes can be stored and used as numbers, many developers find it more readable to store them in an object that keys them by their friendly name:

```
const StatusCodes = {
    InternalServerError: 500,
    NotFound: 404,
    Ok: 200,
    // ...
} as const;

StatusCodes.InternalServerError; // 500
```

The tricky thing with enum-like objects in TypeScript is that there isn't a great type system way to represent that a value must be one of their values. One common method is to use the `keyof` and `typeof` type modifiers from Chapter 9, "Type Modifiers" to hack one together, but that's a fair amount of syntax to type out.

The following `StatusCodeValue` type uses the previous `StatusCodes` value to create a type union of its possible status code number values:

```
// Type: 200 | 404 | 500
type StatusCodeValue = (typeof StatusCodes)[keyof typeof StatusCodes];

let statusCodeValue: StatusCodeValue;

statusCodeValue = 200; // Ok

statusCodeValue = -1;
// Error: Type '-1' is not assignable to type 'StatusCodeValue'.
```

TypeScript provides an `enum` syntax for creating an object with literal values of type `number` or `string`. Start with the `enum` keyword, then a name of an object—conventionally in PascalCase—then an `{}` object containing comma-separated keys in the enum. Each key can optionally use = before an initial value.

The previous `StatusCodes` object would look like this `StatusCode` enum:

```
enum StatusCode {
    InternalServerError = 500,
    NotFound = 404,
    Ok = 200,
}

StatusCode.InternalServerError; // 500
```

As with class names, an enum name such as `StatusCode` can be used as the type name in a type annotation. Here, the `statusCode` variable of type `StatusCode` may be given `StatusCode.Ok` or a number value:

```
let statusCode: StatusCode;

statusCode = StatusCode.Ok; // Ok
statusCode = 200; // Ok
```

TypeScript allows any number to be assigned to a numeric enum value as a convenience at the cost of a little type safety. `statusCode = -1` would have also been allowed in the previous code snippet.

Enums compile down to an equivalent object in output compiled JavaScript. Each of their members becomes an object member key with the corresponding value, and vice versa.

The previous `enum StatusCode` would create roughly the following JavaScript:

```
var StatusCode;
(function (StatusCode) {
    StatusCode[StatusCode["InternalServerError"] = 500] = "InternalServerError";
    StatusCode[StatusCode["NotFound"] = 404] = "NotFound";
    StatusCode[StatusCode["Ok"] = 200] = "Ok";
})(StatusCode || (StatusCode = {}));
```

Enums are a mildly contentious topic in the TypeScript community. On the one hand, they violate TypeScript's general mantra of never adding new runtime syntax constructs to JavaScript. They present a new non-JavaScript syntax for developers to learn and have a few quirks around options such as `preserveConstEnums`, covered later in this chapter.

On the other hand, they're quite useful for explicitly declaring known sets of values. Enums are used extensively in both the TypeScript and VS Code source repositories!

Automatic Numeric Values

Enum members don't need to have an explicit initial value. When values are omitted, TypeScript will start the first value off with 0 and increment each subsequent value by 1. Allowing TypeScript to choose the values for enum members is a good option when the value doesn't matter beyond being unique and associated with the key name.

This `VisualTheme` enum allows TypeScript to choose the values entirely, resulting in three integers:

```
enum VisualTheme {
    Dark, // 0
    Light, // 1
    System, // 2
}
```

The emitted JavaScript looks the same as if the values had been set explicitly:

```
var VisualTheme;
(function (VisualTheme) {
    VisualTheme[VisualTheme["Dark"] = 0] = "Dark";
    VisualTheme[VisualTheme["Light"] = 1] = "Light";
    VisualTheme[VisualTheme["System"] = 2] = "System";
})(VisualTheme || (VisualTheme = {}));
```

In enums with numeric values, any members missing an explicit value will be 1 greater than the previous value.

As an example, a `Direction` enum might only care that its `Top` member has a value of 1 and the remaining values are also positive integers:

```
enum Direction {
  Top = 1,
  Right,
  Bottom,
  Left,
}
```

Its output JavaScript would also look the same as if the remaining members had explicit values 2, 3, and 4:

```
var Direction;
(function (Direction) {
    Direction[Direction["Top"] = 1] = "Top";
    Direction[Direction["Right"] = 2] = "Right";
    Direction[Direction["Bottom"] = 3] = "Bottom";
    Direction[Direction["Left"] = 4] = "Left";
})(Direction || (Direction = {}));
```

 Modifying the order of an enum will cause the underlying number to change. If you persist these values somewhere, such as a database, be careful of changing the enum order or removing an entry. Your data may suddenly be corrupt because the saved number will no longer represent what your code expects.

String-Valued Enums

Enums may also use strings for their members instead of numbers.

This `LoadStyle` enum uses friendly string values for its members:

```
enum LoadStyle {
    AsNeeded = "as-needed",
    Eager = "eager",
}
```

Output JavaScript for enums with string member values looks structurally the same as enums with numeric member values:

```
var LoadStyle;
(function (LoadStyle) {
    LoadStyle["AsNeeded"] = "as-needed";
    LoadStyle["Eager"] = "eager";
})(LoadStyle || (LoadStyle = {}));
```

String valued enums are handy for aliasing shared constants under legible names. Instead of using a type union of string literals, string valued enums allow for more powerful editor autocompletions and renames of those properties—as covered in Chapter 12, "Using IDE Features".

One downside of string member values is that they cannot be computed automatically by TypeScript. Only enum members that follow a member with a numeric value are allowed to be computed automatically.

TypeScript would be able to provide an implicit value of 9001 in this enum's ImplicitNumber because the previous member value is the number 9000, but its NotAllowed member would issue an error because it follows a string member value:

```
enum Wat {
    FirstString = "first",
    SomeNumber = 9000,
    ImplicitNumber, // Ok (value 9001)
    AnotherString = "another",

    NotAllowed,
    // Error: Enum member must have initializer.
}
```

 In theory, you could make an enum with both numeric and string member values. In practice, that enum would likely be unnecessarily confusing, so you probably shouldn't.

Const Enums

Because enums create a runtime object, using them produces more code than the common alternative strategy of unions of literal values. TypeScript allows declaring enums with the const modifier in front of them to tell TypeScript to omit their objects definition and property lookups from compiled JavaScript code.

This DisplayHint enum is used as a value for a displayHint variable:

```
const enum DisplayHint {
    Opaque = 0,
    Semitransparent,
    Transparent,
}
```

```
let displayHint = DisplayHint.Transparent;
```

The output compiled JavaScript code would be missing the enum declaration altogether and would use a comment for the enum's value:

```
let displayHint = 2 /* DisplayHint.Transparent */;
```

For projects where it's still desirable to create enum object definitions, a `preserveConstEnums` compiler option does exist that would keep the enum declaration itself in existence. Values would still directly use literals instead of accessing them on the enum object.

The previous code snippet would still omit the property lookup in its compiled JavaScript output:

```
var DisplayHint;
(function (DisplayHint) {
    DisplayHint[DisplayHint["Opaque"] = 0] = "Opaque";
    DisplayHint[DisplayHint["Semitransparent"] = 1] = "Semitransparent";
    DisplayHint[DisplayHint["Transparent"] = 2] = "Transparent";
})(DisplayHint || (DisplayHint = {}));

let displayHint = 2 /* Transparent */;
```

`preserveConstEnums` can help reduce the size of emitted JavaScript code, though not all ways to transpile TypeScript code support it. See Chapter 13, "Configuration Options" for more information on the `isolatedModules` compiler option and when `const` enums may not be supported.

Namespaces

Unless you are authoring DefinitelyTyped type definitions for an existing package, do not use namespaces. Namespaces do not match up to modern JavaScript module semantics. Their automatic member assignments can make code confusing to read. I only mention them because you may come across them in .d.ts files.

Back before ECMAScript modules were ratified, it wasn't uncommon for web applications to bundle much of their output code into a single file loaded by the browser. Those giant single files often created global variables to hold references to important values across different areas of the project. It was simpler for pages to include that one file than to set up an old module loader such as RequireJS—and oftentimes more performant to load, since many servers didn't yet support HTTP/2 download streaming. Projects made for a single-file output needed a way to organize sections of code and those global variables.

The TypeScript language provided one solution with the concept of "internal modules," now referred to as namespaces. A *namespace* is a globally available object with "exported" contents available to call as members of that object. Namespaces are defined with the `namespace` keyword followed by a `{}` block of code. Everything in that namespace block is evaluated inside a function closure.

This `Randomized` namespace creates a `value` variable and uses it internally:

```
namespace Randomized {
    const value = Math.random();
    console.log(`My value is ${value}`);
}
```

Its output JavaScript creates a `Randomized` object and evaluates the contents of the block inside a function, so the `value` variable isn't available outside of the namespace:

```
var Randomized;
(function (Randomized) {
    const value = Math.random();
    console.log(`My value is ${value}`);
})(Randomized || (Randomized = {}));
```

 Namespaces and the `namespace` keyword were originally called "modules" and "module," respectively, in TypeScript. That was a regrettable choice in hindsight given the rise of modern module loaders and ECMAScript modules. The `module` keyword is still occasionally found in very old projects, but can—and should—be safely replaced with `namespace`.

Namespace Exports

The key feature of namespaces that made them useful was that a namespace could "export" contents by making them a member of the namespace object. Other areas of code can then refer to that member by name.

Here, a `Settings` namespace exports `describe`, `name`, and `version` values used internally and externally to the namespace:

```
namespace Settings {
  export const name = "My Application";
  export const version = "1.2.3";

  export function describe() {
    return `${Settings.name} at version ${Settings.version}`;
  }

  console.log("Initializing", describe());
}
```

```
    console.log("Initialized", Settings.describe());
```

The output JavaScript shows that the values are always referenced as members of
Settings (e.g., Settings.name) in both internal and external usage:

```
var Settings;
(function (Settings) {
    Settings.name = "My Application";
    Settings.version = "1.2.3";
    function describe() {
        return `${Settings.name} at version ${Settings.version}`;
    }
    Settings.describe = describe;
    console.log("Initializing", describe());
})(Settings || (Settings = {}));
console.log("Initialized", Settings.describe());
```

By using a var for the output object and referencing exported contents as members
of those objects, namespaces by design work well when split across multiple files. The
previous Settings namespace could be rewritten across multiple files:

```
// settings/constants.ts
namespace Settings {
  export const name = "My Application";
  export const version = "1.2.3";
}

// settings/describe.ts
namespace Settings {
    export function describe() {
        return `${Settings.name} at version ${Settings.version}`;
    }

    console.log("Initializing", describe());
}

// index.ts
console.log("Initialized", Settings.describe());
```

The output JavaScript, concatenated together, would look roughly like:

```
// settings/constants.js
var Settings;
(function (Settings) {
    Settings.name = "My Application";
    Settings.version = "1.2.3";
})(Settings || (Settings = {}));
// settings/describe.js
(function (Settings) {
    function describe() {
        return `${Settings.name} at version ${Settings.version}`;
    }
    Settings.describe = describe;
```

```
        console.log("Initialized", describe());
    })(Settings || (Settings = {}));
    console.log("Initialized", Settings.describe());
```

In both the single-file and multiple-file declaration forms, the output object at runtime is one with three keys. Roughly:

```
const Settings = {
    describe: function describe() {
        return `${Settings.name} at version ${Settings.version}`;
    },
    name: "My Application",
    version: "1.2.3",
};
```

The key difference with using a namespace is that it can be split across different files and members can still refer to each other under the namespace's name.

Nested Namespaces

Namespaces can be "nested" to indefinite levels by either exporting a namespace from within another namespace or putting one or more . periods inside a name.

The following two namespace declarations would behave identically:

```
namespace Root.Nested {
    export const value1 = true;
}

namespace Root {
    export namespace Nested {
        export const value2 = true;
    }
}
```

They both compile to structurally identical code:

```
(function (Root) {
    let Nested;
    (function (Nested) {
        Nested.value2 = true;
    })(Nested || (Nested = {}));
})(Root || (Root = {}));
```

Nested namespaces are a handy way to enforce more delineation between sections within larger projects organized with namespaces. Many developers opted to use a root namespace by the name of their project—perhaps inside a namespace for their company and/or organization—and child namespaces for each major area of the project.

Namespaces in Type Definitions

The only redeeming quality for namespaces today—and the only reason why I opted to include them in this book—is that they can be useful for DefinitelyTyped type definitions. Many JavaScript libraries—particularly older web application staples such as jQuery—are set up to be included in web browsers with a traditional, non-module <script> tag. Their typings need to indicate that they create a global variable available to all code—structure perfectly captured by namespaces.

Additionally, many browser-capable JavaScript libraries are set up both to be imported in more modern module systems and also to create a global namespace. TypeScript allows a module type definition to include an export as namespace, followed by a global name, to indicate the module is also available globally under that name.

For example, this declaration file for a module exports a value and is available globally:

```
// node_modules/@types/my-example-lib/index.d.ts
export const value: number;
export as namespace libExample;
```

The type system would know that both import("my-example-lib") and window.libExample would give back the module, with a value property of type number:

```
// src/index.ts
import * as libExample from "my-example-lib"; // Ok
const value = window.libExample.value; // Ok
```

Prefer Modules Over Namespaces

Instead of using namespaces, the previous examples' *settings/constants.ts* file and *settings/describe.ts* file could be rewritten for modern standards with ECMAScript modules:

```
// settings/constants.ts
export const name = "My Application";
export const version = "1.2.3";

// settings/describe.ts
import { name, version } from "./constants";

export function describe() {
    return `${name} at version ${version}`;
}

console.log("Initializing", describe());

// index.ts
import { describe } from "./settings/describe";
```

```
console.log("Initialized", describe());
```

TypeScript code structured with namespaces can't be easily tree-shaken (have unused files removed) in modern builders such as Webpack because namespaces create implicit, rather than explicitly declared, ties between files the way ECMAScript modules do. It is generally strongly preferred to write runtime code using ECMAScript modules and not TypeScript namespaces.

 As of 2022, TypeScript itself is written in namespaces, but the TypeScript team is working on migrating over to modules. Who knows, maybe by the time you're reading this, they'll have finished that conversion! Fingers crossed.

Type-Only Imports and Exports

I'd like to end this chapter on a positive note. One last set of syntax extensions, type-only imports and exports, can be quite useful and don't add any complexity to output emitted JavaScript.

TypeScript's transpiler will remove values used only in the type system from imports and exports in files because they aren't used in runtime JavaScript.

For example, the following *index.ts* file creates an `action` variable and an `ActivistArea` type, then later exports both of them with a standalone export declaration. When compiling it to *index.js*, TypeScript's transpiler would know to remove `ActivistArea` from that standalone export declaration:

```
// index.ts
const action = { area: "people", name: "Bella Abzug", role: "politician" };

type ActivistArea = "nature" | "people";

export { action, ActivistArea };
// index.js
const action = { area: "people", name: "Bella Abzug", role: "politician" };

export { action };
```

Knowing to remove re-exported types such as that `ActivistArea` requires knowledge of the TypeScript type system. Transpilers such as Babel that act on a single file at a time don't have access to the TypeScript type system to know whether each name is only used in the type system. TypeScript's `isolatedModules` compiler option, covered in Chapter 13, "Configuration Options", helps make sure code will transpile in tools other than TypeScript.

TypeScript allows adding the `type` modifier in front of individual imported names or the entire `{...}` object in `export` and `import` declarations. Doing so indicates they're only meant to be used in the type system. Marking a default import of a package as `type` is allowed as well.

In the following snippet, only the `value` import and export are kept when *index.ts* is transpiled to the output *index.js*:

```
// index.ts
import { type TypeOne, value } from "my-example-types";
import type { TypeTwo } from "my-example-types";
import type DefaultType from "my-example-types";

export { type TypeOne, value };
export type { DefaultType, TypeTwo };

// index.js
import { value } from "my-example-types";

export { value };
```

Some TypeScript developers even prefer to opt into using type-only imports to make it more clear which imports are only used as types. If an import is marked as type-only, attempting to use it as a runtime value will trigger a TypeScript error.

The following `ClassOne` is imported normally and can be used at runtime, but `ClassTwo` cannot because it is imported as a type:

```
import { ClassOne, type ClassTwo } from "my-example-types";

new ClassOne(); // Ok

new ClassTwo();
//  ~~~~~~~~
// Error: 'ClassTwo' cannot be used as a value
// because it was imported using 'import type'.
```

Instead of adding complexity to emitted JavaScript, type-only imports and exports make it clear to transpilers outside of TypeScript when it's possible to remove pieces of code. Most TypeScript developers therefore don't treat them with the distaste given to the previous syntax extensions covered in this chapter.

Summary

In this chapter, you worked with some of the JavaScript syntax extensions included in TypeScript:

- Declaring class parameter properties in class constructors
- Using decorators to augment classes and their fields
- Representing groups of values with enums
- Using namespaces to create groupings across files or in type definitions
- Type-only imports and exports

 Now that you've finished reading this chapter, practice what you've learned on *https://learningtypescript.com/syntax-extensions*.

What do you call the cost of supporting legacy JavaScript extensions in TypeScript?
"Sin tax."

CHAPTER 15

Type Operations

Conditionals, maps
With great power over types
comes great confusion

TypeScript gives us awesome levels of power to define types in the type system. Even the logical modifiers from Chapter 10, "Generics" pale in comparison to the capabilities of the type operations in this chapter. Once you've completed this chapter, you'll be able to mix, match, and modify types based on other types—giving you powerful ways to represent types in the type system.

 Most of these fancy types are techniques you generally don't want to use very frequently. You'll want to understand them for the cases where they are useful, but beware: they can be difficult to read through when overused. Have fun!

Mapped Types

TypeScript provides syntax for creating a new type based on the properties of another type: in other words, *mapping* from one type to another. A *mapped type* in TypeScript is a type that takes in another type and performs some operation on each property of that type.

Mapped types create a new type by creating a new property under each key in a set of keys. They use a syntax similar to index signatures, but instead of using a static key type with : like [i: string], they use a computed type from the other type with in like [K in OriginalType]:

```
type NewType = {
    [K in OriginalType]: NewProperty;
};
```

One common use case for mapped types is to create an object whose keys are each of the string literals in an existing union type. This AnimalCounts type creates a new object type where the keys are each of the values from the `Animals` union type and each of the values is `number`:

```
type Animals = "alligator" | "baboon" | "cat";

type AnimalCounts = {
    [K in Animals]: number;
};
// Equivalent to:
// {
//    alligator: number;
//    baboon: number;
//    cat: number;
// }
```

Mapped types based on existing literals of unions are a convenient way to save space in declaring big interfaces. But mapped types really shine when they can act on other types and even add or remove modifiers from members.

Mapped Types from Types

Mapped types commonly act on existing types using the `keyof` operator to grab the keys of that existing type. By instructing a type to map over the keys of an existing type, we can *map* from that existing type to a new one.

This `AnimalCounts` type ends up being the same as the `AnimalCounts` type from before by mapping from the `AnimalVariants` type to a new equivalent one:

```
interface AnimalVariants {
    alligator: boolean;
    baboon: number;
    cat: string;
}

type AnimalCounts = {
    [K in keyof AnimalVariants]: number;
};
// Equivalent to:
// {
//    alligator: number;
//    baboon: number;
//    cat: number;
// }
```

The new type keys mapped over a `keyof`—named K in the previous snippets—are known to be keys of the original type. That means each mapped type member value is allowed to reference the original type's corresponding member value under the same key.

If the original object is SomeName and the mapping is [K in keyof SomeName], then each member in the mapped type would be able to refer to the equivalent SomeName member's value as SomeName[K].

This NullableBirdVariants type takes an original BirdVariants type and adds | null to each member:

```
interface BirdVariants {
    dove: string;
    eagle: boolean;
}

type NullableBirdVariants = {
    [K in keyof BirdVariants]: BirdVariants[K] | null,
};
// Equivalent to:
// {
//    dove: string | null;
//    eagle: boolean | null;
// }
```

Instead of painstakingly copying each field from an original type to any number of other types, mapped types let you define a set of members once and re-create new versions of them en masse as many times as you need.

Mapped types and signatures

In Chapter 7, "Interfaces", I introduced that TypeScript provides two ways of declaring interface members as functions:

- *Method* syntax, like member(): void: declaring that a member of the interface is a function intended to be called as a member of the object
- *Property* syntax, like member: () => void: declaring that a member of the interface is equal to a standalone function

Mapped types don't distinguish between method and property syntaxes on object types. Mapped types treat methods as properties on original types.

This ResearcherProperties type contains both the property and method members of Researcher:

```
interface Researcher {
    researchMethod(): void;
    researchProperty: () => string;
}

type JustProperties<T> = {
    [K in keyof T]: T[K];
};
```

```
type ResearcherProperties = JustProperties<Researcher>;
// Equivalent to:
// {
//    researchMethod: () => void;
//    researchProperty: () => string;
// }
```

The distinction between methods and properties does not show up very often in most practical TypeScript code. It's rare to find a practical use of a mapped type that takes in a class type.

Changing Modifiers

Mapped types can also change the access control modifiers—readonly and ? optionality—on the original type's members. readonly or ? can be placed on members of mapped types using the same syntax as typical interfaces.

The following ReadonlyEnvironmentalist type makes a version of the Environmentalist interface with all members given readonly, while OptionalReadonlyEnvironmentalist goes one step further and makes another version that adds ? to all the ReadonlyEnvironmentalist members:

```
interface Environmentalist {
    area: string;
    name: string;
}

type ReadonlyEnvironmentalist = {
    readonly [K in keyof Environmentalist]: Environmentalist[K];
};
// Equivalent to:
// {
//    readonly area: string;
//    readonly name: string;
// }

type OptionalReadonlyEnvironmentalist = {
    [K in keyof ReadonlyEnvironmentalist]?: ReadonlyEnvironmentalist[K];
};
// Equivalent to:
// {
//    readonly area?: string;
//    readonly name?: string;
// }
```

The `OptionalReadonlyEnvironmentalist` type could alternately be written with `readonly [K in keyof Environmentalist]?: Environmentalist[K]`.

Removing modifiers is done by adding a - before the modifier in a new type. Instead of writing `readonly` or `?:`, you can write `-readonly` or `-?:`, respectively.

This `Conservationist` type contains ? optional and/or readonly members that are made writable In `WritableConservationist` and then also required in `RequiredWritableConservationist`:

```
interface Conservationist {
    name: string;
    catchphrase?: string;
    readonly born: number;
    readonly died?: number;
}

type WritableConservationist = {
    -readonly [K in keyof Conservationist]: Conservationist[K];
};
// Equivalent to:
// {
//    name: string;
//    catchphrase?: string;
//    born: number;
//    died?: number;
// }

type RequiredWritableConservationist = {
    [K in keyof WritableConservationist]-?: WritableConservationist[K];
};
// Equivalent to:
// {
//    name: string;
//    catchphrase: string;
//    born: number;
//    died: number;
// }
```

The `RequiredWritableConservationist` type could alternately be written with `-readonly [K in keyof Conservationist]-?: Conservationist[K]`.

Generic Mapped Types

The full power of mapped types comes from combining them with generics, allowing a single kind of mapping to be reused across different types. Mapped types are able to access the keyof any type name in their scope, including a type parameter on the mapped type itself.

Generic mapped types are frequently useful for representing how data morphs as it flows through an application. For example, it may be desirable for an area of the application to be able to take in values of existing types but not be allowed to modify the data.

This MakeReadonly generic type takes in any type and creates a new version with the readonly modifier added to all its members:

```
type MakeReadonly<T> = {
    readonly [K in keyof T]: T[K];
}

interface Species {
    genus: string;
    name: string;
}

type ReadonlySpecies = MakeReadonly<Species>;
// Equivalent to:
// {
//    readonly genus: string;
//    readonly name: string;
// }
```

Another transform developers commonly need to represent is a function that takes in any amount of an interface and returns a fully filled-out instance of that interface.

The following MakeOptional type and createGenusData function allow for providing any amount of the GenusData interface and getting back an object with the defaults filled in:

```
interface GenusData {
    family: string;
    name: string;
}

type MakeOptional<T> = {
    [K in keyof T]?: T[K];
}
// Equivalent to:
// {
//    family?: string;
//    name?: string;
// }
```

```
/**
 * Spreads any {overrides} on top of default values for GenusData.
 */
function createGenusData(overrides?: MakeOptional<GenusData>): GenusData {
    return {
        family: 'unknown',
        name: 'unknown',
        ...overrides,
    }
}
```

Some operations done by generic mapped types are so useful that TypeScript provides utility types for them out-of-the-box. Making all properties optional, for example, is achievable using the built-in `Partial<T>` type. You can find a list of those built-in types on *https://www.typescriptlang.org/docs/handbook/utility-types.html*.

Conditional Types

Mapping existing types to other types is nifty, but we haven't yet added logical conditions into the type system. Let's do that now.

TypeScript's type system is an example of a *logic programming language*. It allows creating new constructs (types) based on logically checking previous types. It does so with the concept of a *conditional type*: a type that resolves to one of two possible types, based on an existing type.

Conditional type syntax looks like ternaries:

```
LeftType extends RightType ? IfTrue : IfFalse
```

The logical check in a conditional type is always on whether the left type *extends*, or is assignable to, the right type.

The following `CheckStringAgainstNumber` conditional type checks whether `string` extends `number`—or in other words, whether the `string` type is assignable to the `number` type. It's not, so the resultant type is the "if false" case: `false`:

```
// Type: false
type CheckStringAgainstNumber = string extends number ? true : false;
```

Much of the rest of this chapter will involve combining other type system features with conditional types. As the code snippets get more complex, remember: each conditional type is purely a piece of boolean logic. Each takes in some type and results in one of two possible results.

Generic Conditional Types

Conditional types are able to check any type name in their scope, including a type parameter on the conditional type itself. That means you can write reusable generic types to create new types based on any other types.

Turning the previous `CheckStringAgainstNumber` type into a generic `CheckAgainst Number` gives a type that is either `true` or `false` based on whether the previous type is assignable to `number`. `string` is still not true, while `number` and `0 | 1` both are:

```
type CheckAgainstNumber<T> = T extends number ? true : false;

// Type: false
type CheckString = CheckAgainstNumber<'parakeet'>;

// Type: true
type CheckString = CheckAgainstNumber<1891>;

// Type: true
type CheckString = CheckAgainstNumber<number>;
```

The following `CallableSetting` type is a little more useful. It takes in a generic `T` and checks whether `T` is a function. If `T` is, then the resultant type is `T`—as with `GetNumbersSetting` where `T` is `() => number[]`. Otherwise, the resultant type is a function that returns `T`, as with `StringSetting` where `T` is `string`, and so the resultant type is `() => string`:

```
type CallableSetting<T> =
    T extends () => any
        ? T
        : () => T;

// Type: () => number[]
type GetNumbersSetting = CallableSetting<() => number[]>;

// Type: () => string
type StringSetting = CallableSetting<string>;
```

Conditional types are also able to access members of provided types with the object member lookup syntax. They can use that information both in their `extends` clause and/or in the resultant types.

One pattern used by JavaScript libraries that lends itself well to conditional generic types is to change the return type of a function based on an options object provided to the function.

For example, many database functions or equivalents might use a property like `throwIfNotFound` to change the function to throw an error instead of returning `undefined` if a value isn't found. The following `QueryResult` type models that behavior by resulting in the more narrow `string` instead of `string | undefined` if the options' `throwIfNotFound` is specifically known to be `true`:

```
interface QueryOptions {
  throwIfNotFound: boolean;
}

type QueryResult<Options extends QueryOptions> =
  Options["throwIfNotFound"] extends true ? string : string | undefined;

declare function retrieve<Options extends QueryOptions>(
    key: string,
    options?: Options,
): Promise<QueryResult<Options>>;

// Returned type: string | undefined
await retrieve("Birutė Galdikas");

// Returned type: string | undefined
await retrieve("Jane Goodall", { throwIfNotFound: Math.random() > 0.5 });

// Returned type: string
await retrieve("Dian Fossey", { throwIfNotFound: true });
```

By combining a conditional type with a generic type parameter, that `retrieve` function is more precise in telling the type system how it will change its program's control flow.

Type Distributivity

Conditional types *distribute* over unions, meaning their resultant type will be a union of applying that conditional type to each of the constituents (types in the union type). In other words, `ConditionalType<T | U>` is the same as `ConditionalType<T> | ConditionalType<U>`.

Type distributivity is a mouthful to explain but is important for how conditional types behave with unions.

Consider the following `ArrayifyUnlessString` type that converts its type parameter `T` to an array unless `T extends string`. `HalfArrayified` is equivalent to `string | number[]` because `ArrayifyUnlessString<string | number>` is the same as `ArrayifyUnlessString<string> | ArrayifyUnlessString<number>`:

```
type ArrayifyUnlessString<T> = T extends string ? T : T[];

// Type: string | number[]
type HalfArrayified = ArrayifyUnlessString<string | number>;
```

If TypeScript's conditional types didn't distribute across unions, `HalfArrayified` would be (`string` | `number`)`[]` because `string` | `number` is not assignable to `string`. In other words, conditional types apply their logic to each constituent of a union type, not the whole union type.

Inferred Types

Accessing members of provided types works well for information stored as a member of a type, but it can't capture other information such as function parameters or return types. Conditional types are able to access arbitrary portions of their condition by using an `infer` keyword within their extends clause. Placing the `infer` keyword and a new name for a type within an extends clause means that new type will be available inside the conditional type's true case.

This `ArrayItems` type takes in a type parameter `T` and checks whether the `T` is an array of some new `Item` type. If it is, the resultant type is `Item`; if not, it's `T`:

```
type ArrayItems<T> =
    T extends (infer Item)[]
        ? Item
        : T;

// Type: string
type StringItem = ArrayItems<string>;

// Type: string
type StringArrayItem = ArrayItems<string[]>;

// Type: string[]
type String2DItem = ArrayItems<string[][]>;
```

Inferred types can work to create recursive conditional types too. The `ArrayItems` type seen previously could be extended to retrieve the item type of an array of any dimensionality recursively:

```
type ArrayItemsRecursive<T> =
    T extends (infer Item)[]
        ? ArrayItemsRecursive<Item>
        : T;

// Type: string
type StringItem = ArrayItemsRecursive<string>;

// Type: string
type StringArrayItem = ArrayItemsRecursive<string[]>;

// Type: string
type String2DItem = ArrayItemsRecursive<string[][]>;
```

Note that while `ArrayItems<string[][]>` resulted in `string[]`, `ArrayItemsRecur`
`sive<string[][]>` resulted in `string`. That ability for generic types to be recursive
allows them to keep applying modifications—such as retrieving the element type of
an array here.

Mapped Conditional Types

Mapped types apply a change to every member of an existing type. Conditional
types apply a change to a single existing type. Put together, they allow for applying
conditional logic to each member of a generic template type.

This `MakeAllMembersFunctions` type turns each nonfunction member of a type into a
function:

```
type MakeAllMembersFunctions<T> = {
    [K in keyof T]: T[K] extends (...args: any[]) => any
        ? T[K]
        : () => T[K]
};

type MemberFunctions = MakeAllMembersFunctions<{
    alreadyFunction: () => string,
    notYetFunction: number,
}>;
// Type:
// {
//    alreadyFunction: () => string,
//    notYetFunction: () => number,
// }
```

Mapped conditional types are a convenient way to modify all properties of an existing
type using some logical check.

never

In Chapter 4, "Objects", I introduced the `never` type, a bottom type, which means it
can have no possible values and can't be reached. Adding a `never` type annotation
in the right place can tell TypeScript to be more aggressive about detecting never-hit
code paths in the type system as well as in the previous examples of runtime code.

never and Intersections and Unions

Another way of describing the `never` bottom type is that it's a type that can't exist.
That gives `never` some interesting behaviors with & intersection and | union types:

- `never` in an & intersection type reduces the intersection type to just `never`.
- `never` in a | union type is ignored.

These `NeverIntersection` and `NeverUnion` types illustrate those behaviors:

```
type NeverIntersection = never & string; // Type: never
type NeverUnion = never | string; // Type: string
```

In particular, the behavior of being ignored in union types makes `never` useful for filtering out values from conditional and mapped types.

never and Conditional Types

Generic conditional types commonly use `never` to filter out types from unions. Because `never` is ignored in unions, the result of a generic conditional on a union of types will only be those that are not `never`.

This `OnlyStrings` generic conditional type filters out types that aren't strings, so the `RedOrBlue` type filters out `0` and `false` from the union:

```
type OnlyStrings<T> = T extends string ? T : never;

type RedOrBlue = OnlyStrings<"red" | "blue" | 0 | false>;
// Equivalent to: "red" | "blue"
```

`never` is also commonly combined with inferred conditional types when making type utilities for generic types. Type inferences with `infer` have to be in the true case of a conditional type, so if the false case is never meant to be used, `never` is a suitable type to put there.

This `FirstParameter` type takes in a function type T, checks if it's a function with an `arg: infer Arg`, and returns that Arg if so:

```
type FirstParameter<T extends (...args: any[]) => any> =
    T extends (arg: infer Arg) => any
        ? Arg
        : never;

type GetsString = FirstParameter<
    (arg0: string) => void
>; // Type: string
```

Using `never` in the false case of the conditional type allowed `FirstParameter` to extract the type of the function's first parameter.

never and Mapped Types

The `never` behavior in unions makes it useful for filtering out members in mapped types too. It's possible to filter out keys of an object using the following three type system features:

- `never` is ignored in unions.
- Mapped types can map members of types.
- Conditional types can be used to turn types into `never` if a condition is met.

Putting the three of those together, we can create a mapped type that changes each member of the original type either to the original key or to `never`. Asking for the members of that type with [`keyof T`], then, produces a union of all those mapped type results, filtering out `never`.

The following `OnlyStringProperties` type turns each `T[K]` member into either the `K` key if that member is a string, or `never` if not:

```
type OnlyStringProperties<T> = {
  [K in keyof T]: T[K] extends string ? K : never;
}[keyof T];

interface AllEventData {
    participants: string[];
    location: string;
    name: string;
    year: number;
}

type OnlyStringEventData = OnlyStringProperties<AllEventData>;
// Equivalent to: "location" | "name"
```

Another way of reading the `OnlyStringProperties<T>` type is that it filters out all non-`string` properties (switches them to `never`), then gives back all the remaining keys ([`keyof T`]).

Template Literal Types

We've covered a lot on conditional and/or mapped types now. Let's switch to less logic-intensive types and focus on strings for a while instead. So far I've brought up two strategies for typing string values:

- The primitive `string` type: for when the value can be any string in the world
- Literal types such as `""` and `"abc"`: for when the value can only be that one type (or a union of them)

Sometimes, however, you may want to indicate that a string matches some string pattern: part of the string is known, but part of it is not. Enter *template literal types*, a TypeScript syntax for indicating that a string type adheres to a pattern. They look like template literal strings—hence their name—but with primitive types or unions of primitive types interpolated.

This template literal type indicates that the string must start with "Hello" but can end with any string (string). Names that start with "Hello" such as "Hello, world!" match, but not "World! Hello!" or "hi":

```
type Greeting = `Hello${string}`;

let matches: Greeting = "Hello, world!"; // Ok

let outOfOrder: Greeting = "World! Hello!";
//  ~~~~~~~~~~
// Error: Type '"World! Hello!"' is not assignable to type '`Hello ${string}`'.

let missingAltogether: Greeting = "hi";
//  ~~~~~~~~~~~~~~~~~
// Error: Type '"hi"' is not assignable to type '`Hello ${string}`'.
```

String literal types—and unions of them—may be used in the type interpolation instead of the catchall string primitive to restrict template literal types to more narrow patterns of strings. Template literal types can be quite useful for describing strings that must match a restricted set of allowed strings.

Here, BrightnessAndColor matches only strings that start with a Brightness, end with a Color, and have a - hyphen in-between:

```
type Brightness = "dark" | "light";
type Color  = "blue" | "red";

type BrightnessAndColor = `${Brightness}-${Color}`;
// Equivalent to: "dark-red" | "light-red" | "dark-blue" | "light-blue"

let colorOk: BrightnessAndColor = "dark-blue"; // Ok

let colorWrongStart: BrightnessAndColor = "medium-blue";
//  ~~~~~~~~~~~~~~~
// Error: Type '"medium-blue"' is not assignable to type
// '"dark-blue" | "dark-red" | "light-blue" | "light-red"'.

let colorWrongEnd: BrightnessAndColor = "light-green";
//  ~~~~~~~~~~~~~
// Error: Type '"light-green"' is not assignable to type
// '"dark-blue" | "dark-red" | "light-blue" | "light-red"'.
```

Without template literal types, we would have had to laboriously write out all four combinations of Brightness and Color. That would get cumbersome if we added more string literals to either of them!

TypeScript allows template literal types to contain any primitives (other than symbol) or a union thereof: string, number, bigint, boolean, null, or undefined.

This `ExtolNumber` type allows any string that starts with `"much "`, includes a string that looks like a number, and ends with `"wow"`:

```
type ExtolNumber = `much ${number} wow`;

function extol(extolee: ExtolNumber) { /* ... */ }

extol('much 0 wow'); // Ok
extol('much -7 wow'); // Ok
extol('much 9.001 wow'); // Ok

extol('much false wow');
//      ~~~~~~~~~~~~~~~
// Error: Argument of type '"much false wow"' is not
// assignable to parameter of type '`much ${number} wow`'.
```

Intrinsic String Manipulation Types

To assist in working with string types, TypeScript provides a small set of intrinsic (meaning: they're built into TypeScript) generic utility types that take in a string and apply some operation to the string. As of TypeScript 4.7.2, there are four:

- `Uppercase`: Converts a string literal type to uppercase.
- `Lowercase`: Converts a string literal type to lowercase.
- `Capitalize`: Converts a first character of string literal type to uppercase.
- `Uncapitalize`: Converts a first character of string literal type to lowercase.

Each of these can be used as a generic type that takes in a string. For example, using `Capitalize` to capitalize the first letter in a string:

```
type FormalGreeting = Capitalize<"hello.">; // Type: "Hello."
```

These intrinsic string manipulation types can be quite useful for manipulating property keys on object types.

Template Literal Keys

Template literal types are a half-way point between the primitive `string` and string literals, which means they're still strings. They can be used in any other place where you'd be able to use string literals.

For example, you can use them as the index signature in a mapped type. This `ExistenceChecks` type has a key for every string in `DataKey`, mapped with `check${Capitalize<DataKey>}`:

```typescript
type DataKey = "location" | "name" | "year";

type ExistenceChecks = {
    [K in `check${Capitalize<DataKey>}`]: () => boolean;
};
// Equivalent to:
// {
//    checkLocation: () => boolean;
//    checkName: () => boolean;
//    checkYear: () => boolean;
// }

function checkExistence(checks: ExistenceChecks) {
    checks.checkLocation(); // Type: boolean
    checks.checkName(); // Type: boolean

    checks.checkWrong();
    //     ~~~~~~~~~~
    // Error: Property 'checkWrong' does not exist on type 'ExistenceChecks'.
}
```

Remapping Mapped Type Keys

TypeScript allows you to create new keys for members of mapped types based on the original members using template literal types. Placing the `as` keyword followed by a template literal type for the index signature in a mapped typed changes the resultant type's keys to match the template literal type. Doing so allows the mapped type to have a different key for each mapped property while still referring to the original value.

Here, `DataEntryGetters` is a mapped type whose keys are `getLocation`, `getName`, and `getYear`. Each key is mapped to a new key with a template literal type. Each mapped value is a function whose return type is a `DataEntry` using the original `K` key as a type argument:

```typescript
interface DataEntry<T> {
    key: T;
    value: string;
}

type DataKey = "location" | "name" | "year";

type DataEntryGetters = {
    [K in DataKey as `get${Capitalize<K>}`]: () => DataEntry<K>;
};
// Equivalent to:
// {
//    getLocation: () => DataEntry<"location">;
//    getName: () => DataEntry<"name">;
```

```
//    getYear: () => DataEntry<"year">;
// }
```

Key remappings can be combined with other type operations to create mapped types that are based on existing type shapes. One fun combination is using `keyof typeof` on an existing object to make a mapped type off that object's type.

This `LazyValues` type is based on the `config` type, but each field is a function that returns the value from the const `config`, and the keys are modified from the original key:

```
const config = {
    location: "unknown",
    name: "anonymous",
    year: 0,
};

type LazyValues = {
    [K in keyof typeof config as `${K}Lazy`]: () => Promise<typeof config[K]>;
};
// Equivalent to:
// {
//    locationLazy: Promise<string>;
//    nameLazy: Promise<string>;
//    yearLazy: Promise<number>;
// }

async function withLazyValues(configGetter: LazyValues) {
    await configGetter.locationLazy; // Resultant type: string

    await configGetter.missingLazy();
    //                 ~~~~~~~~~~~
    // Error: Property 'missingLazy' does not exist on type 'LazyValues'.
};
```

Note that in JavaScript, object keys may be type `string` or `Symbol`—and `Symbol` keys aren't usable as template literal types because they're not primitives. If you try to use a remapped template literal type key in a generic type, TypeScript will issue a complaint that `symbol` can't be used in a template literal type:

```
type TurnIntoGettersDirect<T> = {
    [K in keyof T as `get${K}`]: () => T[K]
    //                   ~
    // Error: Type 'keyof T' is not assignable to type
    // 'string | number | bigint | boolean | null | undefined'.
    //    Type 'string | number | symbol' is not assignable to type
    //    'string | number | bigint | boolean | null | undefined'.
    //       Type 'symbol' is not assignable to type
    //       'string | number | bigint | boolean | null | undefined'.
};
```

To get around that restriction, you can use a `string &` intersection type to enforce that only types that can be strings are used. Because `string & symbol` results in `never`, the whole template string will reduce to `never` and TypeScript will ignore it:

```
const someSymbol = Symbol("");

interface HasStringAndSymbol {
    StringKey: string;
    [someSymbol]: number;
}

type TurnIntoGetters<T> = {
    [K in keyof T as `get${string & K}`]: () => T[K]
};

type GettersJustString = TurnIntoGetters<HasStringAndSymbol>;
// Equivalent to:
// {
//     getStringKey: () => string;
// }
```

TypeScript's behavior of filtering out `never` types from unions is proving itself useful yet again!

Type Operations and Complexity

> Debugging is twice as hard as writing the code in the first place. Therefore, if you write the code as cleverly as possible, you are, by definition, not smart enough to debug it.
>
> —Brian Kernighan

The type operations described in this chapter are among the most powerful, cutting-edge type system features in any programming language today. Most developers are not yet familiar enough with them to be able to debug errors in significantly complex uses of them. Industry-standard development tools such as IDE features I cover in Chapter 12, "Using IDE Features" aren't generally made for visualizing multilayered type operations used with each other.

If you do find a need to use type operations, please—for the sake of any developer who has to read your code, including a future you—try to keep them to a minimum if possible. Use readable names that help readers understand the code as they read it. Leave descriptive comments for anything you think future readers might struggle with.

Summary

In this chapter, you unlocked the true power of TypeScript by operating on types in its type system:

- Using mapped types to transform existing types into new ones
- Introducing logic into type operations with conditional types
- Learning how never interacts with intersections, unions, conditional types, and mapped types
- Representing patterns of string types using template literal types
- Combining template literal types and mapped types to modify type keys

 Now that you've finished reading this chapter, practice what you've learned on *https://learningtypescript.com/type-operations*.

When you're lost in the type system, what do you use?
A mapped type!

Glossary

ambient context

An area in code where you can declare types but cannot declare implementations. Generally used in reference to *.d.ts* declaration files.

See also declaration file.

any

A type that is allowed to be used anywhere and can be given anything. any can act as a top type, in that any type can be provided to a location of type any. Most of the time, you probably want to use unknown for more accurate type safety.

See also unknown, top type

argument

Something being provided as an input, used to refer to a value being passed to a function. For functions, an *argument* is the value being passed to a call, while a *parameter* is the value inside the function.

See also parameter

assertion, type assertion

An assertion to TypeScript that a value is of a different type than what TypeScript would otherwise expect.

assignable, assignability

Whether one type is allowed to be used in place of another.

billion-dollar mistake

The catchy industry term for many type systems allowing values such as null to be used in places that require a different type. Coined by Tony Hoare in reference to the amount of damage it seems to have caused.

See also strict null checking

bottom type

A type that has no possible values—the empty set of types. No type is assignable to the bottom type. TypeScript provides the never keyword to indicate a bottom type.

See also never.

call signature

Type system description of how a function may be called. Includes a list of parameters and a return type.

camel case

A naming convention where the first letter of each compound word after the first in a name is capitalized, like camelCase. The convention for names of members in many TypeScript type system constructs, including members of classes and interfaces.

class

JavaScript syntax sugar around functions that assign to a prototype. TypeScript allows working with JavaScript classes.

compile

Turning source code into another format. TypeScript includes a compiler that, in addition to type checking, turns TypeScript source code into JavaScript and/or declaration files.

See also transpile

conditional type

A type that resolves to one of two possible types, based on an existing type.

const assertion

`as const` type assertion shorthand that tells TypeScript to use the most literal, read-only possible form of a value's type.

constituent, constituent type

One of the types in an intersection or union type.

declaration file

A file with the *.d.ts* extension. Declaration files create an ambient context, meaning they can only declare types and cannot declare implementations.

See also ambient context

decorator

An experimental JavaScript proposal to allow annotating a class or class member with a function marked by a @. Doing so would have the function be run on that class or class member upon creation.

DefinitelyTyped

The massive repository of community-authored type definitions for packages (DT for short). It contains thousands of *.d.ts* definitions along with automation around reviewing change proposals and publishing updates. Those definitions are published as packages under the `@types/` organization on npm, such as `@types/react`.

derived interface

An interface that extends at least one other interface, referred to as a base interface. Doing so copies all the members of the base interface into the derived interface.

discriminant

A member of a discriminated union that has the same name but different type in each constituent.

discriminated union, discriminated type union

A union of types where a "discriminant" member exists with the same name but different value in each constituent type. Checking the value of the discriminant acts as a form of type narrowing.

distributivity

A property of TypeScript's conditional types when given union template types: their resultant type will be a union of applying that conditional type to each of the constituents (types in the union type). `Conditional<T | U>` is the same as `Conditional<T> | Conditional<U>`.

duck typed

A common phrase for how JavaScript's type system behaves. It comes from the phrase, "If it looks like a duck and quacks like a duck, it's probably a duck." It means that JavaScript allows any value to be passed anywhere; if an object is asked for a member that doesn't exist, the result will be `undefined`.

See also structurally typed

dynamically typed, dynamic typing

A classification of programming language that does not natively include a type checker. Examples of dynamically typed programming languages include JavaScript and Ruby.

emit, emitted Code

The output from a compiler, such as *.js* files often produced by running tsc. The TypeScript compiler's JavaScript and/or declaration file emits can be controlled by its compiler options.

enum

A set of literal values stored in an object with a friendly name for each value. Enums are a rare example of a TypeScript-specific syntax extension to vanilla JavaScript.

evolving any

A special case of implicit any for variables who don't have a type annotation or initial value. Their type will be evolved to whatever they are used with.

See also implicit any

extending an interface

When an interface declares that it extends another interface. Doing so copies all members of the original interface into the new one.

See also interface

function overload, overloaded function

A way to describe a function able to be called with drastically different sets of parameters.

generic

Allowing a different type to be substituted for a construct each time a new usage of the construct is created. Classes, interfaces, and type aliases may be made generic.

generic type argument, type argument

A type provided as the type parameter to a generic construct.

generic type parameter, type parameter

A substituted type for a generic. Generic type parameters may be provided with different type arguments for each instance of the construct but will remain consistent within that instance.

global variable

A variable that exists in the global scope, such as setTimeout in environments such as browsers, Deno, and Node.

IDE, Integrated Development Environment

Program that provides developer tooling on top of a text editor for source code. IDEs generally come with debuggers, syntax highlighting, and plugins that surface complaints from programming languages such as type errors. This book uses VS Code for its IDE examples, but others include Atom, Emacs, Vim, Visual Studio, and WebStorm.

implementation signature

The final signature declared on an overloaded function, used for its implementation's parameters.

See also function overload

implicit any

When TypeScript cannot immediately deduce the type of a class property, function parameter, or variable, it implicitly assumes the type to be any. Implicit any types for class properties and function parameters may be configured to be type errors using the noImplicitAny compiler option.

interface

A named set of properties. TypeScript will know a value that's declared to be of a particular interface's type will have that interface's declared properties.

interface merging

A property of interfaces that when multiple interfaces with the same name are declared in the same scope, they combine into one interface instead of causing a type error about conflicting names. This is most commonly used by definition authors to augment global interfaces such as Window.

intersection type

A type that uses the & operator to indicate it has all the properties of both its constituents.

JSDoc

A standard for /** ... */ block comments that describe pieces of code such as classes, functions, and variables. Often used in JavaScript projects to roughly describe types.

literal

A value that is known to be a distinct instance of a primitive.

mapped types

A type that takes in another type and performs some operation on each member of that type. In other words, it *maps* from members of one type into a new set of members.

module

A file with a top-level `export` or `import`. These are generally either files in your source code or files in `node_modules/` packages.

See also script.

module resolution

The set of steps used to determine what file a module import resolves to. The TypeScript compiler can have this specified by its `moduleResolution` compiler option.

namespace

An old construct in TypeScript that creates a globally available object with "exported" contents available to call as members of that object. Namespaces are a rare example of a TypeScript-specific syntax extension to vanilla JavaScript. These days, they're mostly used in *.d.ts* declaration files.

never

The TypeScript type representing the bottom type: a type that can have no possible values.

See also bottom type.

non-null assertion

A shorthand `!` that asserts a type is not `null` or `undefined`.

null

One of the two primitive types in Java-Script that represents a lack of value. `null` represents an intentional lack of value, while `undefined` represents a more general lack of value.

See also undefined.

optional

A function parameter, class property, or member of an interface or object type that doesn't need to be provided. Indicated by placing a `?` after its name, or for function parameters and class properties, alternately indicated by providing a default value with a `=`.

overload signature

One of the signatures declared on an overloaded function to describe a way it may be called.

See also function overload

override

Redeclaring a property on a subclass-derived interface object that already exists on the base.

parameter

A received input, commonly referring to what a function declares. For functions, an *argument* is the value being passed to a call, while a *parameter* is the value inside the function.

See also argument

parameter property

A TypeScript syntax extension for declaring a property assigned to a member property of the same type at the beginning of a class constructor.

Pascal case

A naming convention where the first letter of each compound word in a name is capitalized, like PascalCase. The convention for names of many TypeScript type system constructs, including generics, interfaces, and type aliases.

project references

A feature of TypeScript configuration files where they can reference other configuration files' projects as dependencies. This allows you to use TypeScript as a build coordinator to enforce a project dependency tree.

primitive

An immutable data type built into JavaScript that is not an object. They are: null, undefined, boolean, string, number, bigint, and symbol.

privacy, private field

A feature of JavaScript where class members whose names begin with # can only be accessed inside that same class.

readonly

A TypeScript type system feature where adding the readonly keyword in front of a class or object member indicates it can't be reassigned.

refactor

A change to code that keeps most or all of its behaviors the same. The TypeScript language service is able to perform some refactors on source code when asked, such as moving complex lines of code into a const variable.

return type

The type that must be returned by a function. If multiple return statements exist in the function with different types, it will be a union of all those possible types. If the function cannot possibly return, it will be never.

Rick Roll

An internet meme where users are tricked into listening to and/or watching a music video of Rick Astley's seminal classic "Never Gonna Give You Up." I have hidden several in this book.

See also *https://oreil.ly/rickroll*

script

Any source code file that is not a module.

See also module.

strict mode

A collection of compiler options that increase the amount of strictness and number of checks the TypeScript type checker performs. This can be enabled for tsc with the --strict flag and in TSConfiguration files with the "strict": true compilerOption.

strict null checking

A strict mode for TypeScript where null and undefined are no longer allowed to be provided to types that don't explicitly include them.

See also billion-dollar mistake

structurally typed

A type system where any value that happens to satisfy a type is allowed to be used as an instance of that type.

See also duck typed

subclass

A class that extends another class, referred to as a base class. Doing so copies members of the base class prototype to the child class prototype.

target

The TypeScript compiler option to specify how far back in syntax support JavaScript code needs to be transpiled, such as "es5 or "es2017". Although target defaults to "es3" for backward compatibility reasons, it's advisable to use as new JavaScript syntax as possible per your target platform(s), as supporting newer JavaScript features in older environments necessitates creating more JavaScript code.

Thenable

A JavaScript object with a `.then` method that takes in up to two callback functions and returns another Thenable. Most commonly implemented by the built-in `Promise` class, but user-defined classes and objects can work like a Thenable as well.

top type

A type that can represent any possible type in a system.

See also `any`, `unknown`

transpile

A term for compilation that turns source code from one human-readable programming language into another. TypeScript includes a compiler that turns *.ts*/.*tsx* TypeScript source code into *.js* files, which is sometimes referred to as transpilation.

See also compile

TSConfig

A JSON configuration file for TypeScript. Most commonly named *tsconfig.json* or in the pattern *tsconfig.*.json*. Editors such as VS Code will read from a *tsconfig.json* file in a directory to determine TypeScript language service configuration options.

tuple

An array of a fixed size where each element is given an explicit type.

For example, [`number`, `string | undefined`] is a tuple of size two where the first element is type `number` and the second element is type `string | undefined`.

type

An understanding of what members and capabilities a value has. These can be primitives such as `string`, literals such as `123`, or more complex shapes like functions and objects.

type annotation

An annotation after a name used to indicate its type. Consists of : and the name of a type.

type guard

A piece of runtime logic that can be understood in the type system to only allow some logic if a value is a particular type.

type narrowing

When TypeScript can deduce a more specific type for a value inside a block of code that is gated on a type guard.

type predicate

A function with a return type annotated to act as a type guard. Type predicate functions return a `boolean` value that indicates whether a value is a type.

type system

The set of rules for how a programming language understands what types the constructs in a program may have.

undefined

One of the two primitive types in JavaScript that represents a lack of value. `null` represents an intentional lack of value, while `undefined` represents a more general lack of value.

See also `null`.

union

A type describing a value that can be two or more possible types. Represented by the | pipe between each possible type.

unknown

The TypeScript concept representing the top type. unknown does not allow arbitrary member access without type narrowing.

See also any, top type

visibility

Specifying whether a class member is visible to code outside the class. Indicated before the member's declaration with the public, protected, and private keywords. Visibility and its keywords predate JavaScript's true # member privacy and exist only in the TypeScript type system.

See also privacy.

void

A type indicating the lack of returned value from a function, represented by the void keyword in TypeScript. Functions are thought of as returning void if they have no return statements that return a value.

Index

autocompletion when writing code, 8-9, 186-187

automatic numeric values with enums, 241-242

B

Babel, 10, 207, 249
bigint primitive, 17
billion-dollar mistake, 36-37
bivariant function parameters, 216
boolean primitive, 17, 34
bottom types, 56
build mode (tsc command), 229-230
built-in declarations
    DOM types, 172-173
    library files, 170-172
    purpose of, 170

C

call signatures in interfaces, 92
checkJs compiler option, 223-224
class generics for arrays, 76
classes
    abstract
        described, 119-120
        finding implementations of, 185-186
    constructors
        overriding, 116
        parameters, 104
    extending, 114
        assignability, 114-116
        constructor overrides, 116
        method overrides, 117
        property overrides, 118
    generics for
        declaring, 147-148
        explicit types, 148-149
        extending, 149-150
        implementing interfaces, 150
        method generics, 151
        static class generics, 152
    interfaces and, 111-114
    member visibility, 120-122
    methods of, 103-104
    parameter properties, 236-238
    properties
        declaring, 104-105
        disabling initialization checking, 107
        as functions, 105-106
        initialization checking, 106-107

optional, 108
read-only, 108-109
strictPropertyInitialization compiler option, 217
as types, 109-111
code actions when writing code
    purpose of, 188-189
    quick fixes, 191
    refactoring with, 191
    renaming with, 189
code navigation
    implementations, finding, 185-186
    references, finding, 184-185
    type definitions, finding, 183-184
code style in TypeScript, 12
code writing
    autocompletion, 186-187
    code actions
        purpose of, 188-189
        quick fixes, 191
        refactoring with, 191
        renaming with, 189
    import updates, 187-188
combining type aliases, 40
CommonJS interoperability, 220-221
compilers
    compiling TypeScript, 10
    definition of, 6
    error handling, 11, 191-196
composite compiler option, 228
conditional checks, narrowing with, 32
conditional types
    distributivity, 261
    generic, 260-261
    inferred, 262
    mapped types and, 263
    never type and, 264
    purpose of, 259
configuration bases (TSConfig), 227
configuration options
    emitting JavaScript, 207
        declaration compiler option, 209
        emitDeclarationOnly compiler option, 210
        noEmit compiler option, 212
        outDir compiler option, 207-208
        source maps, 210-211
        target compiler option, 208-213
    file extensions

in TypeScript, 8
DOM declarations, 172-173
double type assertions, 137
duck typing, 46
dynamically typed languages, 4

E

ECMAScript
    module import/export, 218-220
    new versions, 3
ECMAScript Modules (ESM), 25, 248
editor features (TypeScript), 12
Eich, Brendan, 3
ellipsis (. . .), spread operator, 64
    for arrays, 79
    tuples as rest parameters, 82
emitDeclarationOnly compiler option, 210
emitting JavaScript, 207
    declaration compiler option, 209
    emitDeclarationOnly compiler option, 210
    noEmit compiler option, 212
    outDir compiler option, 207-208
    source maps, 210-211
    target compiler option, 208-213
enums
    automatic numeric values, 241-242
    const enums, 243-244
    purpose of, 239-241
    string values, 242-243
error handling
    with IDEs, 191-192
        Problems tab, 193
        running terminal compiler, 194
        type information, 194-196
    with type assertions, 133
    useUnknownInCatchVariables compiler
        option, 217-218
errors
    assignability errors, 22
        for function types, 68
        for intersection types, 56
    syntax errors, 20
    type errors, 21
ESM (ECMAScript Modules), 25, 248
esModuleInterop compiler option, 221
evolving any type, 22, 77
excess property checking in structural typing,
    47-48
exclamation point (!)

disabling initialization checking, 107
non-null type assertions, 134
exclude property, 204
experimentalDecorators compiler option,
    238-239
explicit return types, 66
explicit tuple types, 83
explicit type annotations, 167
explicit type arguments
    for generic classes, 148-149
    for generic functions, 143-144
explicit unions of objects, 52-53
exporting
    namespaces and, 245-247
    type-only imports and exports, 249-250
    via modules, 25-27
        configuration options for, 218-222
exposing package types, 176
extending
    classes, 114
        assignability, 114-116
        constructor overrides, 116
        method overrides, 117
        property overrides, 118
    generic classes, 149-150
    interfaces
        multiple interfaces, 99
        overridden properties of, 98
        purpose of, 97-98
extends compiler option, 225-226

F

falsiness, 37
file extensions
    JSON files, 206
    JSX syntax, 204-206
file inclusions, 203-204
finding
    implementations in code, 185-186
    references in code, 184-185
    type definitions in code, 183-184
fixed-size arrays (see tuples)
freedom
    in JavaScript, 4
    in TypeScript, 7
functions
    async, Promises and, 158
    of classes, properties as, 105-106
    generics for

inferred tuples, 83
inferred types, 262
inferred unions of objects, 51
--init command (tsc command), 202
initial values, lacking, 38
initialization checking of class properties,
    106-107
installing TypeScript, 10
Integrated Development Environments (see
    IDEs)
interface keyword, 45
interfaces
    call signatures, 92
    classes and, 111-114
    extensions
        of multiple interfaces, 99
        overridden properties of, 98
        purpose of, 97-98
    finding implementations of, 185-186
    functions in, declaring, 91-92
    generics for, 145-147, 150
    index signatures
        numeric, 95
        properties and, 94-95
        purpose of, 93-94
    merging, 99-101, 168
    nested, 96
    properties
        optional, 89
        read-only, 90-91
    type aliases vs., 87-88
intersection types
    dangers of, 55-57
    described, 54
    never type and, 263
intrinsic string types, 267
isolatedModules compiler option, 221

J

JavaScript
    compiling TypeScript into, 10
    configuration options for, 222
        allowJs compiler option, 222
        checkJs compiler option, 223-224
        JSDoc support, 224-225
    emitting, 207
        declaration compiler option, 209
        emitDeclarationOnly compiler option,
            210

noEmit compiler option, 212
        outDir compiler option, 207-208
        source maps, 210-211
        target compiler option, 208-213
    history of, 3
    limitations of, 4-5
    primitives, 17
    relationship with TypeScript, 13
    speed compared to TypeScript, 13
    syntax extensions
        class parameter properties, 236-238
        decorators, 238-239
        enums, 239-244
        limitations of, 235
        namespaces, 244-249
        type-only imports and exports, 249-250
    type aliases and, 39
    type annotations, 13
    vanilla, 4
joining arrays with spread operator, 79
JSDoc, 4, 224-225
JSON files, 206
jsx compiler option, 205
JSX syntax, 204-206

K

Kernighan, Brian, 270
keyboard shortcuts
    in IDEs, 181-182
    opening code actions menu, 189
keyof type operator
    constrained type parameters, 156
    described, 129-130
    mapped types, 254-255
keyof typeof type operator, 131

L

language services, definition of, 6
lib compiler option, 212, 213
library declaration files, 170-172
literals
    assignability, 35
    described, 33-35
    as literals, 137

M

mapped types
    changing access control modifiers, 256-257

About the Author

Josh Goldberg is a frontend developer from New York with a passion for open source, static analysis, and the web. He is a full-time open source maintainer who contributes regularly to TypeScript and open source projects in its ecosystem, such as typescript-eslint and TypeStat. His past work includes spearheading Codecademy's usage of TypeScript, helping create its Learn TypeScript course, and architecting rich client applications at Microsoft. His projects range from static analysis to meta-languages to re-creating retro games in the browser. Also cats.

Colophon

The animal on the cover of *Learning TypeScript* is a sun conure (*Aratinga solstitialis*), a colorful parrot native to northeastern South America.

Sun conures, also known as sun parakeets, are mostly yellow with green wing tips and an orange face and chest. They are olive green at birth, with bright colors developing gradually over time in both males and females. They are monogamous, and females lay three to four eggs in a clutch with 23 to 27 days of incubation. Their typical diet is fruits, flowers, seeds, nuts, and insects.

Sun conures are popular as pets because of their beautiful plumage and endearing personalities. They are curious birds but can also be quite loud.

Many of the animals on O'Reilly covers are endangered; all of them are important to the world.

The cover illustration is by Karen Montgomery, based on an antique line engraving from George Shaw's *Zoology*. The cover fonts are Gilroy Semibold and Guardian Sans. The text font is Adobe Minion Pro; the heading font is Adobe Myriad Condensed; and the code font is Dalton Maag's Ubuntu Mono.

9 781098 110338